*The*
# NEW ENGLAND
# GRIMPENDIUM

# *The*
# NEW ENGLAND
# GRIMPENDIUM

*A Guide to Macabre and Ghastly Sites*

## J. W. OCKER

THE COUNTRYMAN PRESS
WOODSTOCK, VERMONT

The New England Grimpendium
978-0-88150-919-9
CIP data are available.

Interior photographs by Lindsey Ocker or the author unless otherwise specified
Book design and composition by Eugenie S. Delaney
Cover concept and illustration by Brian Weaver

Published by The Countryman Press, P.O. Box 748, Woodstock, VT 05091
Distributed by W. W. Norton & Company, Inc., 500 Fifth Avenue, New York, NY 10110

To my wife, Lindsey, who is at my side through just about all of my treks, even, as was the case with this book, when pregnant.

And to my daughter, Esme Noelle, who I hope will one day marvel at the macabre places she visited in utero.

# contents

# INTRODUCTION

I GUESS THIS IS THE PART OF THE BOOK where I analyze and defend my (and, I assume, your) interest in the macabre, the grisly, the horrific, the dreadful, and all those other things not intended for polite dinner conversation. Truth is, the fact of death is a fact of life, and it's no weirder to be fascinated with it than with the physical and intellectual feats of humankind or with the natural world around us. I mean, sure, there are nuances, factors, and contexts that make this topic a lot more of a complex one, but, honestly, "death happens" is probably as far as you need to go for a book about visiting stuff.

Of course, this book isn't just about the grim. It's also about New England, those six northeastern states that continue to share a common identity despite there being no reason to anymore. In the rough rectangle comprising the continental United States, New England is surely its darkest corner. Maybe it's because of its age; maybe it's because its landscape dies more gloriously in autumn than in many places and then is buried deeper and more somberly in its winter than many other places. Maybe it's because so many of our classic horror authors were born here, making one surmise that whatever interior darkness they were able to express with their unique talents might be present in most New Englanders.

Okay, that last might be stretching it a bit. More than likely, New England has no more ghastliness than do any other random six states lumped together. Still, man, that doesn't mean that's not a whole lot of darkness.

Now, there's one thing I've got to establish before you turn another page. This book—this grimpendium—is not one of those registers of haunted places that are so popular these days, nor is it a collection of vague folklore. Sure, it does contain both haunted places and folklore, but this book is about actual things you can see and actual places you can visit.

This book is a travelogue, yes, a spooky and at times gruesome travelogue, but a travelogue nonetheless, and it features somewhere in the neighborhood of 200 macabre sites, attractions, and artifacts that can be seen throughout New England. The subject of each chapter in this book is either a tangible, visitable thing or is connected to at least one tangible, visitable thing—for instance, a monument, a building, a museum artifact, and much, much stranger. I know, because I have visited all of them. And I have the carsick odometer to prove it.

If New England is the spooky attic at the top of the country, then you're about to read the account of a man who has rifled through that attic as if it were the afternoon before Halloween and he hasn't found a costume yet. While compiling it I've gotten to know a fascinating side of New England . . . even if I can't use a lot of it for polite dinner conversation.

For the purposes of this book, I've divided every bit of eeriness and morbidity I found into five sections. "Horror Legends and Personalities" traces the traces left in New England by the many artists, writers, musicians, actors, and uncategorizables who have made a name for themselves in the macabre. "Infamous Crimes, Killers, and Tragedies" details the many ways New Englanders have memorialized people, events, and atrocities that it would be easier on their peace of mind to forget. "Horror Movie Filming Locales" involves all the pieces of New England real estate that the horror film genre has staked a claim to with its celluloid flags. "Notable Cemeteries, Gravestones, and Other Memento Mori" is about, well, notable cemeteries, gravestones, and other memento mori. Finally, "Classic Monsters" delves into all the different creatures we've invented to scare ourselves with because Nature herself apparently didn't provide enough ways to frighten us.

In the end, the macabre yields an irresistible intrigue to most of us, whether that intrigue manifests itself as an obsession with the luridness of the nightly news, a hunger for horror novels, or a simple quick rubberneck at an auto accident.

Whether it should or not, that intrigue still just makes sense to me. After all, the human skull is one of the more compelling shapes ever created, the graveyard is one of the weirdest ideas the human race has ever had, fear of monsters is more universal than appreciation of Shakespeare, and death is something we will one day all have in common. It's a dark world, New England is no exception, and it could use your headlights to light it up a little on your own New England road trips.

Like death itself, getting there is a lot of the adventure.

J. W. Ocker
Nashua, NH

# Horror Legends and Personalities

*S*OME MEN AND WOMEN make their mark in life through death, earning fame from the funereal. These horror legends and personalities include writers, artists, actors, directors, musicians, and other public figures of less categorizable pursuit. These artists have toiled in the mines of the macabre and have unearthed blood and bone, death and dread, horror and terror . . . both to figure out the blacker parts of our existence, and—as every child who has ever jumped out of a closet or thrown a spider to scare a sibling knows—because it's fun to do. Some of those mentioned in this section became masters of the morbid, elevating the craft of the darker genres. Others only dallied with the macabre, although in such ways as to catch the imagination of the public, who now forever associate those artists with the grim and unearthly.

Tempting though it be for me to broadly claim that this area of the country uniquely breeds and draws this type of artist, the fact is that New England certainly boasts some of the most famous practitioners of the ghastly, including Edgar Allan Poe, Claude Rains, Edith Wharton, Henry James, and many others, all of whom are memorialized within its borders. These legends and personalities have more than the dark arts in common. They have also made their mark in some way in New England: They were born here, lived here, were buried here, sojourned here, erected works here, or were honored here . . . each leaving behind imprints on the often frozen New

England soil. Some of these imprints have been memorialized with plaques and gravestones, markers and museums. Other imprints take a bit more digging to discover.

Some of the sites in this section are worthy of pilgrimage. Others might merit a side trip if you happen to find yourself in the neighborhood. A few are probably only worth reading about. But each allows those of us who appreciate the macabre the chance to share a physical connection with the artists whose works have intercepted, enriched, and terrified our lives . . . and made the horror genre what it is today.

# Joan Bennett
## OLD LYME, CT

ACTRESS JOAN BENNETT really appears at only two points in the horror genre continuum. But they are two very important points.

Bennett was born in 1910 in New Jersey into a family of actors, and her career spans from silent film all the way through to television movies, with somewhere around 80 feature films on her resumé. Throughout that long career, she worked with many of the legends of the business, including such directors as Fritz Lang and James Whale and such actors as Humphrey Bogart and Katharine Hepburn.

Her horror credits occurred later in her life. In 1966 she began playing Elizabeth Collins Stoddard, the reclusive matriarch of the Collins family in the darkly supernatural soap opera *Dark Shadows.* During the course of the series, she played other roles besides Elizabeth due to plotline conceits that involved time travel, parallel universes, long genealogies, and immortal creatures. She's supposedly one of the few cast members to remain in the soap opera from its premiere all the way to its end in 1971. I'd substantiate that, but that's, like, 1,225 episodes to get through. At the very least, she did appear on the first and last episodes of the series, as well as the first Dark Shadows movie in 1970, entitled *House of Dark Shadows.*

The series subjected daytime television to all manner of monsters romancing gothically about, including ghosts, werewolves, vampires, and witches, but since the exterior for the Collinwood Mansion where she lives was filmed in New England, I dedicate a whole entry to that show on page 104. Besides, her other relevant role is very much worth getting to.

For, while she's notable for trading melodrama with Barnabas Collins for five years, Joan Bennett also cackled under the direction of Italian horror movie director Dario Argento in the cinematic masterwork of imagery and music that is the 1977 film *Suspiria*.

*Suspiria* tells the story of an American student who is accepted into a posh ballet school in Germany where the staff is more interested in darker shades of art than dance. It's a movie that lacks an energetic plotline, well-rounded character development, engaging dialogue, and original subject matter, but makes you realize how overprioritized those things can be in a horror movie.

In the film, Joan Bennett plays the character of Madame Blanc, the vice directress of the school and the head of the coven it hides. She runs the school for the mysterious and supposedly absent directress, and is pretty creepy even without the underlying witchery of her character.

Throughout this latter phase of her career, she also performed in a couple minor spooky made-for-television films, namely *The Eyes of Charles Sand* in 1972, about a man who has visions of the dead, and *The House Possessed* in 1981 about, well, a house that is possessed.

Bennett died at the age of 80 in 1990 and was buried in a family plot in New England. Her grave can be found in Pleasant View Cemetery, right off Salem Road in Old Lyme, Connecticut. While small, the cemetery is set on a hill and commands a rather majestic view of the area, and the family stone is dramatically tall and shaped like cathedral window. As a result, it stands out from the surrounding tombstones and is easy to find.

I'm not sure for which of her many roles Bennett would want to be remembered, or whether Elizabeth Collins Stoddard and Madame Blanc rank anywhere near her favorites. I'd assume she would have at least soft spots for them, as she played the former for so long and was nominated for awards for both portrayals; but when it comes down to it, the dead don't get favorites (although they do get soft spots). It's up to the living to choose favorites, and thanks to the ardent devotion of horror aficionados, those two roles by themselves will ensure that Bennett will long be remembered.

# Joseph Payne Brennan
## NEW HAVEN, CT

THE HORROR LITERATURE GENRE needs obscure writers. One of the rare, unique pleasures of a macabre story is that it can seem to delve into the forbidden, the esoteric, and the arcane. At its best it can offer the illusion that what you hold in your hands was not meant to be read . . . despite its copyright and mass market publishing imprint. To get that feeling you often have to not be able to trust the author, and if that author is a stranger, well, you know the rest of that public service announcement.

So when you come across that unfamiliar name hidden under piles of mainstream authors in a shadowy corner of a used bookstore, the illusion that you might have just stumbled across something that was actually not meant to see the light of day is thrilling with its potential for undreamt of horrors.

Sometimes that unfamiliar name is Joseph Payne Brennan.

Brennan was born in Bridgeport, Connecticut, in 1918, but spent pretty much his entire life in the nearby city of New Haven. He penned a large amount of horror short stories, as well as poetry. Most famously, his work appeared in such magazines as *Weird Tales* and *Macabre,* the latter of which Brennan, himself, started and edited.

Unfortunately, if you find one of his works in that aforementioned shadowy corner, you won't discover someone probing ideas unfit for the human race. Instead, Brennan dealt in straightforward monsters and the unknown, in plain language and compressed length. That's okay. The horror genre needs that, too.

However, the one item that goes at the top of his resumé, obituary, and

certificate of appreciation is that he created the Blob, more or less. In his 1953 novelette *The Slime,* an ancient black, viscous "hood of horror" is cataclysmically thrown from its sea-bottom home to adapt and absorb the new prey that it finds running around on two legs in terror. Since then, the Blob has become a classic monster that has been ripped off by, well, everybody, but most notably the 1958 movie that officially named the creature in a way that stuck.

Although *The Blob* did wonders for Steve McQueen's career, horror writing remained only a side gig for Brennan. His main source of income was through his job as a librarian—at Yale University Library, no less, so he had enviable business cards. He started working there in 1941, left for the army and World War II, and then returned to Yale in 1946.

The library is an amazing place to visit, and you obviously don't need the excuse of its having employed an obscure horror writer to go there. The Yale University Library system is comprised of some 20 different libraries at various locations on the site of the university in New Haven. The central and largest building is the 80-year-old Sterling Memorial Library, located at 120 High Street, which holds around 4 million volumes and is absolutely cathedral-like.

Brennan died in 1990, and, currently, his fame is at a bit of a teeter point, where fashionably obscure slips into tragically lost. It's hard to get hold of his works without shelling out close to rare books–type money, and there's not a lot of information easily available about him as an author. At least the Blob will live forever. I'd consider that a legacy worth bragging about in the afterlife.

# Aleister Crowley
## HEBRON, NH

"THE DARK ARTS are no way to get ahead in life, Boy." I don't really know anything about Aleister Crowley's father, but that's what I imagine him saying to the young Alick. I also imagine the senior Crowley as an overalls-clad, straw-chewing Midwestern farmer, although Aleister's parents were actually rich brewery owners in Warwickshire, England.

Still, Crowley somehow managed to make an international name for himself in occultism. Of course, that name was the "Wickedest Man in the World," but it suited him just fine.

Born in 1875, Crowley took advantage of his silver spoon and spent his time mingling among the ranks of secret societies, traveling abroad to learn and practice various types of "magick," alarming as many people as he could, and generally doing all kinds of silly things that somebody who is born wealthy and bored and has a predisposition toward attention-mongering, egoism, and contrarianism will do.

He also wrote a lot of books of both the fiction and nonfiction varieties, although the latter were often about his experiences in diabolism, so categorize those wherever you think they should go. His works include *Diary of a Drug Fiend, The Magick of Thelema,* and *The Book of the Law,* in which among all sorts of gobbledegookery he articulated the succinct maxim, "Do What Thou Wilt."

A lot of the things Crowley advocated or performed, or at least proclaimed he performed, were apparently pretty shocking for his time, enough in fact that he got kicked out of Italy for some of his carryings-on at the Abbey of Thelema in Sicily. It often involved copious amounts of drugs and sexual experimentation, to such an extreme degree that he probably would have fit right in here in 2010.

Anyway, that's the sex and drugs part. Now the rock 'n' roll.

Somehow, Crowley's influence permeated beyond the ranks of the dark-minded to intrigue many of the musicians in the genre we now know as classic rock.

For instance, the legendary Jimmy Page of the legendary Led Zeppelin maintains a collection of Crowley memorabilia and had such an interest in the infamous occultist that he bought the Boleskine House, Crowley's former residence on Loch Ness, and featured the location in the Led Zeppelin film, *The Song Remains the Same.* David Bowie namedropped Crowley in his song "Quicksand." The Beatles included him on the multifaced cover of the *Sergeant Pepper* album. The Doors posed with a bust of him on the back cover of their album *Doors 13.* Not surprisingly, the Rolling Stones were supposed to have an interest in his work, as well; and then there's Ozzy Osbourne's song "Mr. Crowley." It's symbolic, of course.

The exact reason for this peculiar brand of interest isn't quite clear, but I think it has to do with rock 'n' roll and Crowley's shared appetite for sex, drugs, attention-mongering, egoism, and contrarianism (or "rebelliousness" in the parlance of the times). Good old classic rock.

I know it has taken me a long time to get here, but Crowley's connection to New England involves a small cottage in the barely larger town of Hebron, New Hampshire, on the tip of Newfound Lake. Between 1913 and 1918, the house was owned by a medium named Evangeline Adams who had coauthored a couple of books on astrology with Crowley and been pretty famous in her day, as far as astrologers go.

In 1916, Crowley stayed at that house for four months as part of his infamous "magickal retirement," in which he did all sorts of secret and arcane things the likes of which the current property owners are probably better off for not knowing.

The original 200-year-old house is still there, right beside a church at 14 Church Road, which isn't really a road but a stretch of ground off North Shore Road right in the middle of Hebron. There are two white buildings on the property: the main house, and a second smaller one that Adams actually had built for use as a study.

It's currently a private residence, and although I didn't ask, I'm sure the people that live there could care less about Crowley or anybody that would be interested in him. Some folks are just born smart.

# Bette Davis

LOWELL, MA, AND SUGAR HILL, NH

BETTE DAVIS STARTED HER MOVIE CAREER in the 1930s and became a film legend over the course of more than 100 films. However, it wasn't until 1960s that she became a horror film icon . . . and she did it in three movies or less.

It all started in 1962 with *What Ever Happened to Baby Jane?* In that movie, Davis portrays an ex-child star with mental issues, haunted by the past tragedy of her sister, played by Joan Crawford, who was crippled in a car wreck.

The film earned her an Academy Award nomination and was such a success that she followed it up two years later with *Hush . . . Hush, Sweet Charlotte,* in which she portrays an aging Southern belle with mental issues, haunted by the past tragedy of her lover's being hacked to death with a hatchet.

Finally, in 1965, *The Nanny* was released, which is the lesser known of the three, although that's probably more due to the lack of title creativity than the quality of the movie. In it, she portrays a nanny with mental issues, haunted by the past tragedy of a child's drowning while under her care.

I did silly things with those synopses, but the truth is that each movie has its own distinctive elements that recommend it . . . above them all, is Bette Davis herself. Playing the titular role in each of those films, she's able to achieve a unique brand of creepiness in her character depictions that pretty much elevates each film artistically higher than they might be otherwise.

Later on in her career, she flirted with the genre in such films as *Burnt Offerings* (1976) and such made-for-TV fare as *Scream, Pretty Peggy* (1973) and *Dark Secret of Harvest Home* (1978). She even finished off her career with a turn as a witch in her last film, *Wicked Stepmother* (1989), but it was her 1960s trilogy of gothic horror films that have had the most success at, well, creeping us out.

But all that was happening in Hollywood. Her connection to New England is that she was born there . . . in the not-so-picturesque town of Lowell, Massachusetts, in fact, on April 5, 1908. Of course, she only spent her infant years in Massachusetts, but that's more than any other universally acclaimed screen diva has, and somebody in Lowell decided that it needed to be memorialized.

These days, the house where she spent the first writhing, crying moments of her existence is still a private residence . . . two of them, actually. It's large, pink, two-family Victorian affair at 22 Chester Street, right across from a funeral home . . . and it's officially plaqued. However, instead of the usual humble historical plaque tactfully inset by the front door, the Bette Davis house has a large one stating that she lived there, brazenly attached to the exterior between the first and second floors, making it look as if the house has a brand label. Considering who it's memorializing, such a boldness seems fitting.

This isn't the only Bette Davis–related memorial in New England. On a random boulder near Coppermine Brook in Sugar Hill, New Hampshire, off the trail to Bridal Veil Falls, is an obscure plaque that reads:

*In Memoriam*

*to*

*Arthur Farnsworth*

*"The Keeper of Stray Ladies"*

*Pecketts 1939*

*Presented by a Grateful One*

Arthur Farnsworth was Bette Davis's second husband, and she met him close to that spot in 1939, when he helped her find her way when she wandered off the path in those woods. She owned and spent time at a property in

the Sugar Hill area called Butternut Farm, and Farnsworth worked at a nearby inn. They were married for less than three years, then he died after a blow to the head that was ruled an accident. Bette Davis had the plaque installed after his death.

Anyway, I suppose you could chalk up Davis's success as a horror actress to the notion of old women automatically having that special brand of creepiness that she showcased in those particular movies. And while that's true in a sense, it should be remembered that she didn't need the usual Hollywood beauty to compel us in her younger days of acting, so she probably didn't need mere age to unnerve us in her elder years. Bette Davis just knew how to disturb . . . and that would be the title of her biography if it were written by me.

# Charles Dickens
## BOSTON, MA

YOU KNOW THAT warm feeling you have when you get to the end of Charles Dickens's *A Christmas Carol*? It's heated by the fires of damnation, man.

When it comes to Christmas, Dickens pretty much tops every tree, being one of the stronger influences on how we view Christmas in the ideal. His top hat was stuffed with pine needles and holly branches, his pen leaked candy cane and gingerbread ink. In his sizeable body of written work on the subject, he was able to depict the holiday in ways that made the tinsel grow a bit brighter, the magic seem a little deeper, and the peace on earth and good will to men seem a bit less cheesy than usual.

The funny thing is, his most popular Christmas story, indeed probably the most popular Christmas story of all time . . . is a ghost story, and a rather horrific one, at that.

Despite its gentle name, *A Christmas Carol* is a story of terror and dread, in which the skies are filled with the chained souls of the damned; where spirits whisk a wretched, miserable man away in the darkness of night to awaken painful memories; and where a cowled, black specter introduces that same wretched, miserable man to his own corpse and the pitiful grave in a dismal graveyard "choked up with too much burying" where it will eventually lie.

It's exactly the kind of story you'd like to be told out loud, actually, and Charles Dickens did exactly that. He regularly performed public readings of his works in various locations across Europe and America, and *A Christmas Carol* was one of his most popular readings. The first time he read it in public in the United States occurred on December 2, 1867, at the Tremont Temple in Boston.

Originally called the Tremont Theatre when it opened in 1827, the building was bought in 1843 (the same year as Dickens's *A Christmas Carol* was published) by a Baptist group, renamed the Tremont Temple, and used for religious observances. However, over its history as a church, it was still utilized for various public events such as plays, movies, exhibits, and speeches. At least, between fires.

You see, the fires of damnation do a lot more than just fuel stories. In 1852, the Tremont Temple burned down and had to be rebuilt. It happened again in 1879, a little over a decade after Dickens's reading, and then again in 1893. As a sad result, you can't go in and see the podium behind which Dickens read such sentences as, "Darkness is cheap, and Scrooge liked it" or "There's more of gravy than of grave about you," nor can you sit in the seats of the lucky masses who got to hear them.

The current version of the Tremont Temple was built in 1896, and stands, no, looms in the same spot as the original(s) on 88 Tremont Street, right on the Freedom Trail. It's a massive, golden stone edifice that, like its predecessors, seats a couple thousand and is squeezed between other titanic edifices like some satirist's version of a strip mall. It is still actively used as a church.

Also of note, just around the corner from Tremont Temple, at 60 School Street, is the famous many-times-over Omni Parker House, where Charles Dickens conducted his first private reading of *A Christmas Carol* in the United

States, just before his public reading, to some the legendary literati of the day who frequented the hotel and club.

Incidentally, *A Christmas Carol* wasn't Dickens's only spook story. He wrote quite a few, actually. More interesting, it wasn't even his only *Christmas* spook story. He wrote a whole series of them, including "The Story of the Goblins who Stole a Sexton," "The Haunted Man and the Ghost's Bargain," and "The Chimes," each of which involves somebody's being taught a lesson by some brand of unearthly creatures around Yuletide. Apparently, to Dickens, Christmas was a time of cheer, a time of being terrified, and a time of learning lessons.

Our own lesson for this, I think, is one we relearn every year . . . you have to go through Halloween to get to Christmas.

# Myrna Fahey
## BANGOR, ME

SOMETIMES IT'S HARD TO BE THE FEMALE LEAD in a horror movie. Often, you can be a victim, a heroine, or both, but chances are you'll still be out-shined by the main fiend of the picture. And that's especially true when you're up against a horror movie legend. Myrna Fahey gave it a good go, though.

Fahey was mostly a television actress, starring in a whole *TV Guide* worth of programs, including *Boris Karloff's Thriller, Batman, Bonanza,* and *Perry Mason.* But the one big movie she starred in has become a horror classic and found her sharing a set with the inimitable Vincent Price.

The 1960 film *House of Usher* (or, depending on which print you saw, the more source-material-accurate title *Fall of the House of Usher*) was the first of the famous Edgar Allan Poe story adaptations directed by the legendary Roger Corman and starring the legendary Vincent Price. It was adapted for the screen by the legendary Richard Matheson. In Hollywood, everybody's a legend.

In it, Fahey plays Madeline Usher, the sister of Roderick Usher, portrayed by a blond-haired, elegantly ominous Price. They are the last scions of a decaying family and bear their parts of a hereditary morbid curse of mad-ness and sickness, all within the fetid walls of a crumbling ancestral castle out in the middle of a dank tarn. As Price paints it, they are like "two pale drops of fire, guttering in the vast, consuming darkness." However, when a man who claims to be Madeline's fiancé shows up, and with him the promise of a continued Usher line, Roderick and the House of Usher have a problem with that.

In the end, although pretty much the only space you want to look at on the screen is the bit occupied by Price, Fahey did get to out-mad Mad Vincent, returning from being buried alive to help end the Usher line moments before the falling house does. One image of a close-up of her mad, screaming face; her (Poe's) raven black hair streaming; her purple, sunken eyes backlit by lightning; and her upraised hands streaming blood from clawing at her coffin should've been the entire marketing campaign.

Fahey was born in Carmel, Maine, in 1933, but lived most of her life in California. She died in 1973 from cancer at the young age of 40. She's buried in the Fahey family plot at Mount Pleasant Catholic Cemetery at 449 Ohio Street in Bangor, Maine.

Her grave can be found about halfway into the cemetery, along a tree lined path that parallels Ohio Street. The main Fahey family headstone is the usual plain gray stone, and her individual marker is a nearby small stone plaque inset flush with the ground. It simply states her name and years of existence.

Even with an acting career mainly confined to ancient television sets, if your one major movie features the talents of such genre names as Poe, Price, Corman, and Matheson, that's kind of something. Strangers will visit your grave for that. Or at least this one did.

# Edward Gorey
## Yarmouth Port, MA

IN ONE OF HIS MOST FAMOUS WORKS, artist, storyteller, and illustrator Edward Gorey killed 26 children in 26 different ways . . . and he is highly beloved for it.

Gorey worked mostly in pen and ink, drawing highly textured images of a world populated with what are usually described as British Edwardian- or Victorian-era characters, along with strange creatures and highly vulnerable children. It's a description that falls far short of encapsulating his world, which, regardless of how many similes you can come up with, remains uniquely Gorey's own. Wearing a stoic expression and bearing a stiff carriage, each character seems to be hiding a secret, perhaps sinister life, and each concise bit of accompanying text seems to be an understatement for some grand irony or horror of existence.

The tone of his works somehow simultaneously and successfully meshes the morbid and the light-hearted. It really shouldn't work, but Gorey gets away with it. Actually Gorey gets away with a lot. In fact,

you won't find the review of his work that doesn't include both the descriptors *macabre* and *whimsy* in laudatory ways, including this one.

Gorey's images are simple in content yet seem painstakingly rendered to the point where you don't want to turn the page, and his restrained and polished use of words supports the effect. For instance, when he draws a picture with a caption like, "That year Mona Gritch was born to a pair of drunkards," you almost don't need the rest of the story. That one page is interesting enough to frame and glance at every day when you walk down your hall. But then you'd miss out on the delightfully scarring experience of *The Loathsome Couple,* which follows a pair of lovers whose life's work is to murder children.

Gorey wrote over 100 sparsely worded but densely drawn books, and he also illustrated the works of many others, including John Updike, T. S. Eliot, H. G. Wells, Bram Stoker, and Charles Dickens.

Highlights of his career include the aforementioned book *The Gashlycrumb Tinies,* which illustrates the alphabet in inventive and violent ways, and the 1977 Broadway version of *Dracula,* for which he designed the stage and costumes, winning a Tony in the process. The effort that brought him the most mainstream attention, though, was his work on the opening credits and set of the popular PBS show *Mystery!*

Edward Gorey was born in Chicago and educated at Harvard in Massachusetts. After stints in a variety of places, he ended up in New York for a few decades where, among other things, he worked as an illustrator for the publishing house Doubleday. The last 15 years or so of his life he lived on Cape Cod in Massachusetts, where he died in April 2000 at the age of 75. His home there, which he called Elephant House for various reasons of his own fancy, is now a museum dedicated to his work and life.

Located at 8 Strawberry Lane in Yarmouth Port, the Edward Gorey House is a humble enough home in a surprisingly residential neighborhood. Because it has only been a decade since Gorey's death, visitors are treated to an intimacy with the artist that one can't get at other similar museums. When you walk through the kitchen where he cooked his meals (and sorted his rock collection), it seems very much as if he'll be coming downstairs at any minute to continue doing so. This intimacy is highlighted further when you learn that the museum staff includes friends and relatives of Gorey's. In fact, on our visit, his cousin Skee Morton even gave us the tour. Skee is featured in one of Gorey's works, *The Deranged Cousins,* which is the story of three cousins who, well, die. Skee told us that she remembered the events of the memorialized day slightly differently.

Only the downstairs is open to the public, but it's packed with interest. Pictures of Gorey reveal a bald, bearded, bejeweled man often bracketed by the pet cats that regularly showed up in his art and stories. A raccoon fur coat that Gorey often wore and often drew himself wearing is on display. Scattered about the house are also cardboard set pieces from the PBS television show *Mystery,* exhibits on his work for *Dracula,* and various other artifacts from both his personal and professional lives.

*The Gashlycrumb Tinies* is memorialized at the museum by a small graveyard erected underneath a sprawling magnolia tree that grows beside the house. In addition, various implements are placed here and there referencing the story, including a bottle of lye for James who took it by mistake, and a pair of diminutive legs sticking out from under a rug for George who was smothered by one. The museum hands out scavenger hunt sheets for visitors to keep track of how many *Gashlycrumb* allusions they can find.

All in all, there are actually a lot of surprises at the Gorey House and about Gorey himself, including collections of plush creatures he himself sewed and various random items he collected, such as strange bits of metal, curtain rod ends, tassels, and other yard sale detritus.

However, prominently nestled among all the life traces of Gorey is a genuine human skull that was given to him as a gift . . . and which he adorned with a pair of antique-looking spectacles perched on the crumbling bridge where once protruded a nose.

It's Gorey in a single image.

# Margaret Hamilton
## SALISBURY, CT

THERE ARE LEGENDS OF WITCHES throughout New England and, as a consequence, this book. But there is only one legendary witch in American popular culture, and it would be a shame if we weren't able to at least mention her somewhere in these pages. I'm writing, of course, about the evil grandmother of them all, the Wicked Witch of the West from the 1939 film *The Wizard of Oz*. Fortunately, we can do more than just mention her, we can dedicate a whole entry to her.

You see, the Wicked Witch was seared into the soft gray matter inside our tiny child skulls by actress Margaret Hamilton, who lived out the last few months of her life in New England.

But you'll get no "Hail, Dorothy" here. Hamilton vividly brought to Technicolor black-and-green life one of the most enduring villains of all cinema, an even more spectacular feat when one realizes that evil is rarely played well. It's often confused with cleverness or mere monstrosity. Hamilton nailed evil in all its bitterness and wretchedness in her portrayal of the Wicked Witch. After all, few people could out-terrorize a tornado.

Whether on bicycle or broomstick, her Wicked Witch was vile and nefarious, and every one of her cackles, squints, spider-fingered gestures, and venom-spittled words proclaimed it. She looked as if she was being eaten from the inside out, somehow managing to make her characters stand out in a movie filled with wonders.

Of course, the Wicked Witch role wasn't the only genre credit on her resume. She also had parts in Universal's *The Invisible Woman* (1940), William Castle's *13 Ghosts* (1960), the television movie *Ghostbreakers* (1967), and the Kolchak film *The Night Strangler* (1973). Heck, she was even a member of the

*Addams Family,* playing Morticia's mother Granny Hester Frump in a few of the episodes of that television show. While she had relatively minor roles in all those films and TV programs, she could have played nine out of the 10 top female roles in all cinema and she still would have been known as the Wicked Witch of the West. Some things you just can't top, even with a cherry.

Hamilton was born in Ohio, and went to school at Wheelock College in Boston, Massachusetts, to become a teacher. Then, in one of those great plot twists that life is known for, she became an actress and ended up terrifying children instead of educating them. Of course, terror is an education far undervalued these days.

After living in a few different states across the country, Hamilton eventually settled at a retirement community in Salisbury, Connecticut, where she passed away only a few months later on May 16, 1985, at the age of 82. Her ashes were scattered in New York.

The nursing home is called Noble Horizons, and it's still doing its graceful exit thing 25 years later. The address is 17 Cobble Road. Watch out for any lingering flying monkeys.

# Nathaniel Hawthorne
## Salem, Boston, and Concord, MA

I F THE BEWITCHERY OF THE LATE 1600S had never happened, Salem would still have a claim to fame, even if it couldn't market it to the point of absurdity as it currently does with witches. About 100 years after the fervor of those infamous trials, Salem became the birthplace of Nathaniel Hawthorne, one of the original innovators of American fiction who helped define an authentic, unique American style that we now have pretty much no use for because it's hard to read.

In fact, Nathaniel Hawthorne was the great-great-grandson of John Hathorne, who has been called the "Hanging Judge of Salem" for his role in the witch trials. Some even say that this family connection repulsed Hawthorne enough that he added the *w* to his surname to distance himself from the lineage. Also because it's a cooler name.

Although Hawthorne might not be too proud of certain branches of his

family tree, Salem is certainly proud of Hawthorne, naming various locations after him, erecting a prominent statue to him, and preserving some of the locations from his life. For instance, the original House of the Seven Gables.

Hawthorne's 1851 *The House of the Seven Gables* is the story of an empty peanut butter jar of a family, the titular house serving as the stage for and symbol of generations of that family's burden of guilt. Hawthorne based *Seven Gables* on an actual house in Salem, and it still exists. The house was originally located on Washington Street, but the folks at Salem moved the entire building to a more tourist-accessible location a few blocks away, in the town center.

Also called the Turner-Ingersoll Mansion by pretty much nobody, Seven Gables is located right on the water of Salem Harbor at the intersection of Derby and Turner Streets. The house is large, and with its many pointed gables (seven, I assume, unless Hawthorne forgot to fact-check his own title), multiple chimneys, and dark, foreboding exterior, seems like the perfect place for trick-or-treating at.

For a fee you can enter the house as part of a tour group and see displays on Hawthorne's life, work, and historic Salem in general. I'm not much one for tours, but by taking this one I was able to check off "use a secret passageway" from my lifetime to-do list.

As part of the tour, you can also see the small house of Hawthorne's birth, because they also moved it from its original location on Union Street to right behind the House of the Seven Gables. I guess Salem loves to move houses. I also guess that moving houses is a lot easier than I think it is.

After you house it, you can statue it. A few blocks away on Hawthorne Boulevard towers a large statue of Nathaniel Hawthorne, himself, seated in a chair and looking all billowy and dramatic above you with his cloak and fierce mustache.

If that doesn't sate your interest in all things Hawthorne, there are quite a few other locations in Salem that you can visit relevant to Hawthorne's life, including the Salem Common House on Derby Street, where he worked for a few years, and a couple of houses where he lived at different points in his life. You're probably just there for the witches, though. I don't blame you.

However, Salem isn't the only city in Massachusetts with important ties to Hawthorne's life. In Boston, you just have to follow the Freedom Trail to see some of that city's Hawthorne-related sites. For example, he frequented the ridiculously historic Omni Parker House on 60 School Street—the oldest continually running hotel in America and one that has hosted a steady stream of literary lights throughout the years. Hawthorne was a member of the fabled

Saturday Club there, where he and other literati such as Ralph Waldo Emerson, John Greenleaf Whittier, and Henry Wadsworth Longfellow would get together monthly and be super literate together.

Farther down the trail is the former site of the Old Corner Bookstore, at the intersection of Washington and School streets. The Old Corner Bookstore was, among many other things since its construction in 1711, the headquarters of Ticknor and Fields, one of the most important American publishers of its day, producing some of colonial America's most famous works, including Hawthorne's *The Scarlet Letter*.

Speaking of *The Scarlet Letter*, it is said that the inspiration for protagonist Hester Prynne can be found buried in King's

Chapel Burying Ground, located at the corner of Tremont and School streets. Hawthorne mentions this graveyard in the final paragraph of the book, and in the cemetery can be found the gravestone of one Elizabeth Pain, close to the wall of King's Chapel itself on the right-hand side of the cemetery from the entrance. Many people claim to see a letter *A* in the shield engraved on her tombstone. I didn't see it, but belief makes people's lives worth living, I guess.

Hawthorne finished his life out in the town of Concord, where he lived first in the historic Old Manse, and then later in the Wayside, both homes that still stand in their historic splendor today, the former at 269 Monument Street and the latter at 455 Lexington Road. At the Old Manse, he penned *Mosses from an Old Manse,* a trove of Poe-lauded stories that features some of his darker forays, including "Rappaccini's Daughter," "The Birthmark," and "Young Goodman Brown."

Hawthorne is also buried in Concord, in the famous Author's Row in Sleepy Hollow Cemetery on Bedford Street. The neighboring graves that his ghost borrows sugar from belong to Henry David Thoreau, Ralph Waldo Emerson, and Louisa May Alcott.

As you can see, there's enough of Hawthorne in Massachusetts that you could trace his entire life without picking up a single biography of him. And it's not stalking if you trace a man's life after he's dead.

# P. T. Barnum
## BRIDGEPORT, CT

PHINEAS TAYLOR BARNUM WAS A HOAXER, a purveyor of frauds, a false advertiser, a flim-flam man, a master of exploitation, a money chaser, a huckster, a charlatan, a sensationalist, and a humbugger—and all to such a degree that, as you've already noticed, I had to dig up adjectives that have been out of popular use for half a century just to adequately describe him. However, despite all those pejoratives, he's also venerated as a legend. For good reason. Simply put, he was bigger than us. After all, you'd have to be big to bring the world to the world. And he and his exhibits pop up way too many times in this book to omit the man himself from it.

Barnum was born in Bethel, Connecticut, in 1810 and lived in nearby

Bridgeport for his latter four decades, during which time he served as its mayor, established some of its public works, and died there in 1891. Overall, however, his life was a phantasmagoria of unusual creatures, strange artifacts, foreign wonders, mechanical inventions, performers, and all the human medical aberrations you can eat.

Barnum's American Museum in New York housed hundreds of thousands of exotic animals, oddities, and acts of amazement over the course of its existence. If you were or owned an oddity in the second half of the 19th century, you reckoned with Barnum. Interestingly enough, the thing he's most known for, the circus, wasn't a venture he started until he was in his 60s. (Which, coincidentally, is also my retirement plan.)

And he's remembered for all this in Bridgeport with a museum, a statue, and a gravestone.

The Barnum Museum sticks out in Bridgeport like Connecticut doesn't in the history of statehood. Actually, the Barnum Museum would stick out anywhere . . . except for maybe in the capital city of some ancient Mediterranean empire or on the desert planet of Tatooine. The exterior of the building, which is located at 820 Main Street, is fantastic and makes me wish metal and plate glass had never been added to the palettes of architects.

The three-story, yellow and red, stone and terra-cotta building is adorned by sculptures of various culturally significant people and moments in U.S. history. It's also somehow simultaneously domed, gabled, and steepled, as if a cathedral and a mosque mated and this is the heresy they spawned. Barnum, himself, designed it as an institute for science and history. It wasn't until years later that it became a museum dedicated to the man who financed it.

The first floor of the museum is a gift shop and admissions counter, with a few random displays, including an actual preserved elephant; but the highlight of this floor is the fabled Feejee Mermaid (actually a facsimile of the original, though still cool), that glorious apex of taxidermy art that combines monkey and fish in ways that make the Creator's jaw muscles tense. The story of the Feejee Mermaid and all its New England ilk is included elsewhere in this book.

The second floor is mostly a description of Bridgeport society during Barnum's time. Clothing, furniture, culture—boring stuff, actually. The third floor is the big reason you'd enter the building. Most of the entire floor is covered by a miniature circus. And when I say miniature, I mean its thousands of individual components are tiny. All told, the model is gigantic. It covers, like, 1,000 square feet and makes you feel God- or Godzilla-like.

Another great find on the third floor resides in a room around the corner from the giant mini-circus: a mummy named Pa-Ib. He also has a whole entry dedicated to him elsewhere in this book, so I'll skip over him here. But you're starting to see why Barnum had to be included in this book, right?

Barnum's statue is located just down the road a bit from the museum in Seaside Park, which overlooks Long Island Sound. The park is a beautiful tract of land with sports fields, statues, benches, and, of course, a great view of the sound. The statue is surrounded by a locked wrought-iron gate and is set on a tall pedestal, while the statue depicts Barnum seated in a way that makes him look venerable and sedate, which are the only two adjectives that never spring to my mind when I think about him, or at least the caricature of him that I have in my mind.

Barnum is buried in Mountain Grove Cemetery, which is located at the intersection of Dewey and Mountain Grove streets, not far away from the museum and park. His grave stands out from the surrounding tombstones because his plot marker is as tall as a circus tent pole . . . which would be a more creative simile were the subject matter of this article otherwise.

Across the path from Barnum's grave is another tall marker . . . that of Charles Stratton, Barnum's famous midget friend-performer and a Bridgeport native whose stage name was General Tom Thumb. Atop the towering shaft of his grave marker is a life-size statue of his diminutive personage.

So when in Bridgeport, be sure to see Barnum's museum . . . and statue . . . and grave. Go one. Go all.

# Shirley Jackson
NORTH BENNINGTON, VT

IT MUST BE DIFFICULT to be a Vermont-based horror author. With the state's verdant scenery, state-mandated lack of billboards, and quaint little towns, it's a pretty place. Of course, every object of beauty casts a shadow, and there must have been something in those Vermont shadows that inspired Shirley Jackson to conjure the nightmares that now haunt our cultural dreamspace.

Born and raised in California and educated in New York, Jackson moved to North Bennington, Vermont, with her husband in 1940 while in her early twenties. They lived in that town for the rest of their lives, he teaching on the faculty of Bennington College and she keeping house, raising their four children . . . and writing stories unsettling enough to secure her a hallowed place in the halls of the macabre.

Two of her tales in particular have helped secured her fame. The first story, "The Lottery," has achieved a status level that belies the simplicity of the story itself. Published in 1948 in *The New Yorker,* the story centers on a seemingly ordinary New England village engaged in a mundanely enacted rite of coldhearted monstrosity.

She based the village on her own town of North Bennington, supposedly

on its Lincoln Square, a small bit of trapezoidal area formed by Sage, Prospect, Nash, and Main streets. Jackson and her family lived for a time nearby at 12 Prospect Street, and it was there that she wrote "The Lottery" after an errand run to the square.

Lincoln Square is not much more than an intersection and some stores, but if you look deep into those Vermont shadows and squint just enough pressure onto your eyeballs, you might be able to just make out a few ominous piles of rocks and a black wooden box. In my case, I also had to ignore the life-size painted fiberglass moose that stood there . . . part of a Bennington civic art project called Moosefest and a real mood-breaker when trying to research scary topics.

The other of Jackson's better-known works is her novel *The Haunting of Hill House.* Published in 1959, it's the story of a haunted house and—because far more than houses can be haunted, and by far more than ghosts—a haunted young woman named Eleanor, and the tragedy that occurs when those two hauntings collide.

It's one of the best haunted house stories ever published in a genre absolutely suburban with them. In fact, the story was so powerful that a 1963 Robert Wise movie adaptation of it has gone on to become one of the more compelling movies of its type.

The building rumored to be the inspiration for *The Haunting of Hill House* can be found on the campus of Bennington College, where Jackson's husband worked. It's called Jennings Hall and, even if it's not the inspiration, it's still an eerie-looking place.

Jennings Hall is an old, imposing, gray-stoned mansion covered in creepers and very much secluded from the rest of the campus in an idyllic/terrifying location on a hill. Its appearance and setting certainly seem to fit the description from the opening sentences of the book, "Hill House, not sane, stood by itself against its hills, holding darkness within; it had stood so for eighty years and might stand for eighty more."

When it's not inspiring classic horror stories, Jennings Hall is used by the music department, although I'm not sure how much I'd be into practicing the piano, violin, or any other instrument commonly used to score horror movies there at night. It definitely looks like whatever walks there, walks alone.

Bennington College is located at One College Drive in Bennington. To find Jennings Hall therein, you just have to follow the campus signs . . . if you dare.

And Shirley Jackson certainly dared . . . regularly. And in Vermont, no less. I mean, with its wide swathes of wilderness, lack of familiar markers, and insular, sparsely populated towns, Vermont's a terrifying place.

# Henry and William James
## CAMBRIDGE, MA

ONE WAS A FAMOUS WRITER whose most well-known work is a ghost story. The other was a famous psychologist whose most well-known work was his investigations into mediums who channeled ghosts. Together, they were . . . well . . . brothers.

Henry James (1843–1916) is esteemed as an important literary figure for the nature and style of his works, but he's a popular read for his ghost stories. Although you would never know it from their titles, "The Friends of the Friends," "Sir Edmund Orme," "The Jolly Corner," and "The Private Life" are all examples of his work in that genre. However, Henry James will always be remembered above all for his masterwork of the spectral, *The Turn of the Screw.*

*The Turn of the Screw* is a beautifully ambiguous, compelling, and densely written story of a live-in governess and the possible corruption of her two child wards by ghosts. Or it's a beautifully ambiguous, compelling, and densely written story of a sick live-in governess and her sicker delusions of corrupted children. Either view can be easily backed by the laziest of debaters. Both are spooky as all get-out.

Henry's just barely older brother William (1842–1910) also had an interest in the ghostly, although his pursuit of it took a different tack. First and foremost, William was a medically trained psychologist and Harvard professor who wrote many influential and highly lauded works in that field, as well as in philosophy.

However, he also spent many years of his life investigating the proclaimed medium and New England–born Leonora Piper, who had become famous worldwide for her apparent ability to channel spirits, conduct séances, and

conjure all sorts of delightfully Victorian ghastliness. Now, William James wasn't necessarily a believer in the paranormal, but he did believe that scientists should at least legitimately test claims, just in case. His accounts of her séances are pretty wild, even "disgusting," as he called them, but he did find himself somewhat compelled against his Harvard-trained judgment by the idea of spiritualism.

Henry, William, and the rest of the James Gang are all buried in the same plot in Cambridge Cemetery in Cambridge, Massachusetts, a rather boring, modern-looking cemetery on Coolidge Avenue, right across the street from the more pleasant Mount Auburn Cemetery.

The plot can be found on Prospect Avenue and is comprised of a row of six headstones in front of a short, oblong, red brick wall with the name "James" inscribed in a stone centerpiece at the apex. The stones of William and James are the second and fourth, respectively, from left to right, and each inscription offers a poetic summary of its permanent resident's accomplishments. The cemetery is sizable and has a lot of rows, so I'd advise printing out a copy of the map from the cemetery Web site or consulting the map hanging on the outside wall of the cemetery office. Or you could do shoddy research and stumble across it like myself.

These days, there are way too many ghost-mongers and kooks into spooks. Few are qualified to address the paranormal with any sort of rigor or dignity, and instead resort to melodrama and techno-gibberish. The James brothers, the scientist and the novelist, were successful in simultaneously earning a lofty reputation in their respective hallowed field while still harboring a public fascination with the ghastly. That's a life lesson. Always balance out your crazy.

# Stephen King
### BANGOR, ME

YOU DON'T LEARN ABOUT STEPHEN KING in literature class. You learn about him at the bookstore. Each inevitably devotes three shelves' worth of its horror section to this prolific author, and every single book he has released over the past few decades has been a pop culture event.

Although the power of his brand is irrefutable, a lot of debate continues on King's worth as an actual writer. Either way, he's still an icon of modern horror. And New England.

King has spent most of his life in the basically Canadian state of Maine and has set just about every one of his stories there and in the surrounding environs of the northeast United States. Despite his stratospheric fame and wealth, he actually still lives in Maine. His house is located just outside downtown Bangor, at 47 West Broadway. The surrounding neighborhood is more inviting than I would have thought the residence of a world-famous millionaire would be. But then again, I never would have thought to look for a world-famous millionaire in Bangor, in the first place.

The houses on West Broadway are all large and expensive-looking, but they're close to the street, which is wide, open, and ungated, and a public sidewalk does what public sidewalks do directly in front of them. The area is highly accessible, and you can go there without feeling like the neighborhood watch is burning sideways 8s into your back with binoculars. Stephen King's house is red with white trim, old enough to look historic, and absolutely (dark) towers over a person. It's also in complete full view and not at all hidden behind the small gate that envelops the place.

Speaking of which, Robert Frost, another New Englander, once wrote something about cool fences making cool neighbors, so based on just that, King must be a hit at the neighborhood yard sales. His fence is a big reason why the appearance of the house is so notable. Spiders, bat-winged creatures, and a three-headed reptile all decorate the black wrought-iron in subtle ways. And by subtle, I mean not annoying. It's exactly something you'd hope a nice guy steeped in horror stories would do to his house: acknowledge who he is without megaphoning it.

King wasn't home the first time I went to check out his house. I know this for a couple of reasons. First, while I was sitting across the street in my car with its obvious out-of-state plates, trying to screw up the courage to be mistaken for a Stephen King fan, a tour bus arrived, out of which jumped about five camera-handed people in raincoats (because it was raining), which definitely put me in perspective and made it even harder to get out of the car. I've heard somewhere that the tour bus is only allowed to stop by when King's not home. Second, that night was the first game of the 2007 MLB American League Championship Series between the Boston Red Sox and the Cleveland Indians. It was in Boston, and apparently King is supposed to be like *Rain Man* about attending Red Sox games.

Then I went by his house again a couple of years after my first visit, and although this time I had no way of knowing if he was inside pecking away at a new story or not, the cavalcade of people and cameras appeared undiminished. And for good reason. In the end, regardless of what a person might think of King's work or taste in baseball teams, it's impossible to not be impressed by his house.

# H. P. Lovecraft
## Providence, RI

HOWARD PHILLIPS LOVECRAFT WAS PROVIDENCE. It says so in small block letters on his gravestone, and that makes it, well, set in stone, I guess. But even if it weren't funereally engraved, the fact that H. P. Lovecraft had an affinity to the point of self-identity with his home city is implied in just about every personal letter and short story that he ever wrote. Judging by the content of those letters, he was enthralled by the place. Judging by the content of those stories, he was terrified by the world outside it. You see, besides being Providence, H. P. Lovecraft was also a horror fiction writer. He wasn't really recognized for his work during his short, impoverished life (1890–1937), but since his death, he's grown in stature to become, for many, second only to Edgar Allan Poe in that arena.

I can see why a person would become enthralled with Providence, Rhode Island. It's many of the most pleasant adjectives of a city without being most of the more negative ones. Providence's biggest flaw, though, is that it doesn't quite recognize its own master yet. Not a single statue, bust, museum, or "Lovecraft lived here" medallion marks this native son's place in local history.

This omission is particularly glaring when it is realized that Lovecraft lived in Providence his entire life, minus a brief, unhappy stint in New York. He's been called a homebody and a hermit, but that's not quite true. Sure, most of his friends were pen pals. Sure, he lived much of his life with his mother and then his elderly aunts. Sure, his short-lived marriage was only barely one. Sure, he never really figured out how to make a living. But that just means his life was a bit sedate. Like most of ours, honestly. Except that we have television and the Internet to help us pretend otherwise. Lovecraft had only swollen black nightmares of colossal creatures impinging upon the weak fabric of this dimension. Nevertheless, despite the seemingly bland texture of

his waking life, Lovecraft appeared to wring plenty of wonder and joy out of his life in Providence.

But he's not famous for his close-held joys. He's famous for his tentacled terrors.

What makes Lovecraft's work valuable and unique is the fact that it is predominantly philosophical. It's not ax-wielding psychopaths and possessed kitchen appliances. Lovecraft's concept of horror can be engulfing to the point of despair if you let it do its work. His horrors are not the edge-of-your-seat type; they are the edge-of-a-profound-abyss type. In Lovecraft's conception of the universe, myopia is the only thing that keeps us sane.

If you want to do a full tour of Lovecraft's Providence, you have to go, well, everywhere, from the spot where his first residence and birthplace once stood to the hospital where both his mother and father died insane to the funeral home that held his services to the library and neighborhoods that he frequented to all the places he incorporated into his stories. Like the gravestone says, Lovecraft was Providence. However, three highlights belong on any Lovecraft itinerary.

The first is, of course, his grave, which is located in Swan Point Cemetery, a large, well kept, parklike rot garden on the outskirts of the city along the banks of the Seekonk River. The street address is 585 Blackstone Boulevard. His grave is located right at the intersection of Pond Avenue and Avenue B (which turns into Hemlock Avenue at some point) in the cemetery. His marker is boring, small, and hidden by the tall obelisk that denotes the Philips plot. The only real noticeable part of his gravestone is the inscription that I mentioned earlier, so I already stole my own thunder as far as that goes.

The second location is Lovecraft's final place of residence. It was also the house upon which he based the home of his character Robert Blake in his story "The Haunter of the Dark." The house was originally located at 66 College Street, a spot that has since been overtaken by the expanding Brown University. I'd like to hope that Providence relocated the house out of respect for the author who finished his life there, but the fact that the only plaque on the house reads SAMUEL B. MUMFORD HOUSE tells me otherwise. Either way, the house now resides at 65 Prospect Street, close to Prospect Park, a small square that Lovecraft visited frequently, which magnificently overlooks the city and features a giant statue of the founder of the state with his remains interred therein.

It was in this house that Lovecraft also wrote his autobiography, *Some Notes on a Nonentity* (pretty much the best title of any autobiography in the history of the genre), in which he mentioned the house and the "haunting vista" that could be seen from there (but which can't be anymore because they moved the house). *Notes* is only a pamphlet, but I'm pretty sure if most people were honest about the value of their own personal experience and insights, their autobiography would be as short. (Mine's a sentence long, and I'll spend my whole life editing it to a gleaming sharpness capable one day of piercing flesh.)

The final place to visit is a small, humble memorial in front of the John Hay Library at Brown University, where the largest collection of original Lovecraft manuscripts is kept. The memorial is a 2-foot-tall, 4-foot-wide stone slab with a small black plaque that quotes one of Lovecraft's poems, the date of its dedication (August 1990, 100 years after Lovecraft's birth), and the relevant parties involved in the dedication. Of course, this little tribute was in no way erected through the initiative of the city of Providence itself, but by a group of ardent Lovecraft fans. The plaque does claim to be dedicated by the city of Providence, but to me that means little. I'm sure that as long as somebody else raised the money for it and planned it and the monument didn't draw too much attention to itself (it doesn't), the city would rubber-stamp anything.

One day Lovecraft will get his full due in the city of Providence. Let's just hope it doesn't take an apocalypse of ancient elder gods to bring it about.

# Tomb of the Mather Family
### BOSTON, MA

FOR REASONS OF HISTORICAL ACCURACY, I don't want to rewrite powerful American colonial father-and-son figures Increase and Cotton Mather as paranormal investigators. But for kicks, I kind of do. The thing is, it wouldn't be too hard.

Increase Mather lived from 1639 to 1723 and was a Puritan minister at the original Old North Church in Boston, as well as a president of Harvard College. Cotton, his son, who lived from 1663 to 1728, followed in his father's footsteps and served at the same church in the role of assistant pastor, taking over for Increase when he died.

Meanwhile, these two men, who were both huge forces in colonial America due to their positions and connections in this new society, wrote influential works on the spectral world based on their experiences and research.

In 1684, Increase published *Remarkable Providences, An Essay for the Recording of Illustrious Providences. Providence* was basically the religiously correct term back then for a supernatural event. In that work, Increase listed various New England occurrences that apparently involved witchcraft, demonic activity, and other strange phenomena, including an account of Lithobolia, the stone-throwing devil of New Castle, New Hampshire. While not exactly *Tobin's Spirit Guide,* the work was popular in its day and remains an interesting account of the type of stories passed around during that time.

Cotton Mather's works garnered as much, if not more, attention than the writings of his father, and Cotton authored multiple works on the supernatural. One example of these was published in 1689 as *Memorable Providences, Relating to Witchcraft and Possessions.* In it, Mather recounted his firsthand experience with demonic activity, which involved the oppression of a family in Boston.

Other of his writings involved the Salem witch trials of 1692. In fact, both he and his father supported and defended the witch trials in their writings, which turned into a defining black-eye moment of their careers. Most famous of these writings is Cotton's *Wonders of the Invisible World,* published a year after the trials, which was basically a defense of the trials and an exposition on witches in general.

At one point, Cotton even came in person to witness one of the hangings. The story is recounted that the gallows-mounted victim perfectly recited the Lord's Prayer, something a witch was not supposed to be able to do. This evidence caused the attendees to call for the victim's release, until Cotton successfully exhorted the crowd to carry out the hanging regardless.

Of course, the Mathers couched these investigations, research, and publications as studies into defeating evil in God's service, but these works on the paranormal helped to further validate the supernatural in a Puritan society that was already steeped in that type of belief.

As you can see, it's easy to imagine In'crease and Cotton running around in powdered wigs, with quills and parchment, chasing down a few television seasons' worth of ghouls. The truth is, these works were just a few entries in a giant oeuvre produced between the two men. Cotton alone penned around 400 works on topics as far-ranging as history, philosophy, religion, biography, and science.

Still, that hasn't stopped H. P. Lovecraft from citing their supernatural works in stories where his Necronomicon needed some supporting documentation.

Increase and Cotton died five years apart and were both interred in their family tomb in Boston. It can be found in Copp's Hill Burying Ground on Hull Street, right on the Freedom Trail. The Mather tomb is marked by a low, brick, tablelike structure in the corner of the cemetery close to the Charter Street entrance.

In the past few decades of television culture, we've had stories of newspaper journalists, FBI agents, and plumbers who investigate the paranormal. Why not a team of Puritan ministers?

# Statue of Elizabeth Montgomery
## SALEM, MA

A T THE END of the Essex Street Pedestrian Mall in Salem, Massachusetts, is the bronze statue of a witch. That's probably no big surprise to anyone. However, in this particular case, the witch is a member of none of the three species known to inhabit those parts, Wiccan, Puritan, and Hallow'an. This witch is Elizabeth Montgomery.

Or Samantha Stephens, depending on which side you prefer to err when blurring your reality and fantasy.

The statue was sponsored by cable channel TV Land as part of its ongoing quest to make old television shows more permanent than they should be (a slew of similar bronze television character statues hold down earth in various places across the country). In Salem, the statue commemorates the '60s-era sitcom *Bewitched,* the episodic story of a nose-twitching witch named Samantha who tries to live a normal married life with her nonwarlock husband, except that somehow she can never avoid using her spells and supernatural powers. The studio pitch just wrote itself, I'm sure.

Samantha was played by Elizabeth Montgomery, of, well, *Bewitched* fame, and that, naturally, is who TV Land chose to cast in bronze. Unveiled in 2005, the 6-foot-tall statue depicts a dress-clad Samantha/Elizabeth astride a broom, flying in front of a crescent moon.

Unfortunately, although I like the idea of it, the statue was a bit disappointing to me. First, they probably should have immortalized her in a witch's outfit, just for style reasons, much like the opening animated credits of the show. Second, due to the shape and substance of the statue, it looks kind of like a giant weathervane, and once you think of it as that, you can never unthink of it as that. Third, the likeness for the attractive Montgomery is slightly off. Unless the sculptor is careful, toothy smiles in metal always seem to come off as bared teeth, and the disconcerting look on Samantha's face is Exhibit A in that argument.

If you can believe it, a few of Salem's residents did raise a tiny bit of a ruckus when they found out about the plans for the statue. Something about taking offense at such a blatant exploitation of the serious history of the town. Then everybody took a fresh look around them and quieted down.

However, the statue is more relevant than just the mere fact that it portrays a witch in a town overrun by them. In 1970, *Bewitched* actually filmed a series of episodes on location there after a fire shut down its Hollywood set. The episodes have come to be known as the Salem Saga and featured many of the landmarks of the city. The arrangement ended up being a great tourist boon for the city, so in many ways, the statue is just a case of a witch's coming home to roost.

# José Clemente Orozco
## HANOVER, NH

THE WALLS OF DARTMOUTH'S LIBRARY are painted in shades of apocalypse, death, and monsters . . . all things conducive to a good study experience in the Ivy League.

The mural is called *The Epic of American Civilization*, and it wraps around the interior walls of both wings of the large reserve corridor in the Baker Library at 250-year-old Dartmouth College in Hanover, New Hampshire.

It was created by José Clemente Orozco, a Mexican-born artist whose life spanned the first half of the 20th century. He was a master of the form and

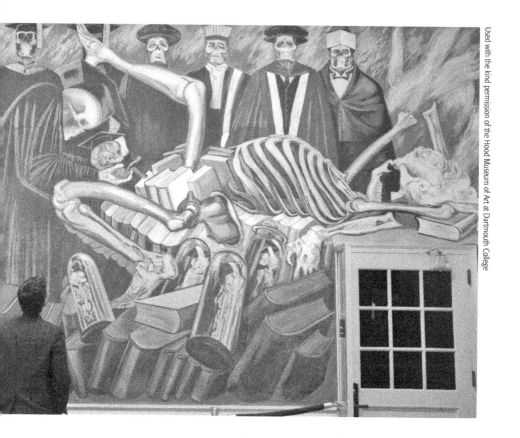

could paint thrilling and engaging expanses with one hand tied behind his back. The one that he lost in a childhood fireworks accident, actually.

Started in 1932, it took Orozco two years to finish this sprawling work, which is made up of 24 individual panels painted directly onto the wet plaster of the walls. All told, it covers a surface area of approximately 3,200 square feet.

As is evident by its title, *The Epic of American Civilization* depicts the history of America. Well, one of the histories of America, at least. There are no puffy-sleeved explorers, no powdered-wigged founding fathers, no buckskin-clad pioneers . . . none of the tropes of U.S. history books. Orozco's history dedicates half of its size to the rise and fall of the Aztec Empire, spends a few brief square feet on the influence of Spanish and European culture on North America, and then ends with a meditation on the promises and perils (mostly perils) of modern industrialized society.

However, instead of literal historic events, the narrative of the mural is told primarily through metaphor. It includes such images as human sacrifice, serpent-faced and fire-wreathed pagan gods, sinister-looking machines, Christ with an ax, Quetzalcoatl on a raft of snakes, prophecy-fulfilling knights in faceless armor, and vultures on carrion heaps of chains and weapons, as well as other forbidding scenes (Christ with an ax is a forbidding scene to everybody else, too, right?).

My personal favorite panel is "Gods of the Modern World." In it, a skeleton in academic garb delivers a similarly biretta-headed skeleton fetus from a pregnant skeleton awash in books and glass specimen jars filled with other skeletal embryos, while more collegiate-like robed skeletons look on in . . . well, whatever facial expression skulls are capable of, I guess. What can I say? I like skeletons.

Also, and you might have already inferred this, but every single one of the panels is somehow terrifying, regardless of its subject matter, whether it be something as simple as a Puritan village full of schoolchildren (of the damned) or the steel I-beam ribs of an under-construction tower (of terror).

The mural is open to the public during the library's regular operating hours, and the reserve corridor whose lowly walls Orozco immortalized is located in the basement of the library.

*The Epic of American Civilization* is one of the more welcoming macabre destinations I've ever visited. A sign actually encourages photographs, and a beautifully printed and illustrated brochure more worthy of a bookshelf than a scrapbook is available for free. The brochure goes into detail about the history and meaning of this bold, immersive mural, which is way worth standing in front of with your chin in your hand . . . or cowering beneath with your hands thrown in front of your face.

# Bobby "Boris" Pickett
### SOMERVILLE, MA

IF IT WEREN'T FOR "MONSTER MASH," Halloween would be an aurally impoverished holiday. And if it weren't for the spot in Somerville, Massachusetts, where an unremarkable supermarket now stands, there might not be any "Monster Mash."

Fifty years ago, that area was the location of a movie house known as the Capitol Theatre. The assistant manager was a man named Charles Pickett, and he would allow his son Bobby to watch movies there all the time; even letting him start the projectors. It was in that theater that Bobby was introduced to the horror movies that would influence him to record a song that would become a Halloween tradition from then on.

Bobby Pickett was an entertainer from early on in his career, including stints as a singer, comedian, impersonator, and actor. As people began finding out about and enjoying his dead-on Boris Karloff impersonation, he started working it into his acts.

Eventually, in 1962, when he was in his early 20s, he and his friend Leonard Capizzi sat down for a mere half hour of their lives and came up with the novelty song "Monster Mash." It became a graveyard smash.

The Capitol Theatre opened on Broadway Street in 1927. It was enormous, with 1,732 seats, and immediately wowed an audience not yet jaded by home theater systems, computer animation, and marketing for the tween consumer demographic. However, times were tough and it, like Somerville's many other historic theaters, eventually closed down. Almost 40 years after it opened, the Capitol was demolished, with nothing but an infamous gang hit on its premises to give it a sendoff. As is the fate of too many things, its current undeserved karmic incarnation is a supermarket, an abandoned one in this instance, its brick-walled, street-facing side once having been the grand entrance to the theater. Fortunately, the Capitol had already validated its existence on Earth.

Despite the fact that it caught on in a flash, it's hard to call Bobby "Boris" Pickett and his "Monster Mash" a one-hit wonder. I mean, by every definition he and it really should be called exactly that and then forgotten about. Problem is, 50 years and half a dozen recording media later, the song is still being sincerely (as opposed to ironically) enjoyed every year at Halloween. I mean, nobody calls Francis Scott Key a one-hit wonder for his own hit of the land.

Pickett died in 2007, still awash in the fame (and royalties) of "Monster Mash," still loving it and still performing it. And the saddest thing about the Capitol Theatre's not being here anymore is that there's no lobby in which to put a plaque in honor of him.

And that's what happened to your Transylvania Twist.

# Edgar Allan Poe

BOSTON AND WESTFORD, MA; PROVIDENCE, RI

IT SEEMS AS IF EVERY CITY across whose cobblestones Edgar Allan Poe drunkenly scraped a foot or upon whose tables he brilliantly slung black ink into blacker text has memorialized the honor. Richmond, Virginia; the Bronx, New York; Philadelphia, Pennsylvania; and, of course, his final resting place of Baltimore, Maryland, are just a few of the cities that have shrines to Poe. Even London tacked up a plaque to proclaim its connection to this master of words, visionary of the macabre, and inventor of literary genres.

So you'd think that with all the places clamoring for Poe relevance, the city of his birth wouldn't stop short of having a whole amusement park dedicated to him.

However, not only does that city not have a single Poe museum or statue, it tore down his birth home and obliterated the existence of the entire street on which he was born on January 19, 1809. Way to go, Boston.

To be fair, Poe made it hard for Boston to love him. His hatred for the city and its literary scene in general was no secret. And hilarious. When one of the greatest writers of the English language vents his phenomenally articulate fury on the writers you are proud to extol as your own, it stings a little. He vehemently felt that the Transcendentalist writers the Boston area is famous for were overblown by a few tornados worth of hot air.

He accumulated some private baggage with the city as well, as his time there over the course of his life included a badly received lecture, a U.S. army enlistment, a suicide attempt, and a poor reception for the work he published there. Still, if you're ever in an argument with a member of the New England literati, it's fun to throw at them what one of the greatest writers in the history of the language thinks of their literary tradition.

Nevertheless, in 1989 a forward-thinking but obscure group called the

Edgar Allan Poe Memorial Committee did affix a plaque dedicated to him on the side of a building in the general area of his birthplace, which is near the theater district. It's currently on the side of a burrito joint at the southeast corner of the Boston Common at the intersections of Tremont and Boylston streets. It shows a relief of his face in the somber expression that every picture depicts him with, mentions the no-longer-extant Carver Street on which the poet was born, and then lists every Boston connection he has, including his parents' stint at the Boston Theatre, the Boston locations where his first book and last story were published, and his enlistment in the army at Fort Independence in Boston Harbor, before grudgingly admitting that he died in Baltimore.

However, in 2009, the 200th anniversary of his birth, Boston started coming around a little. Due to some lobbying on the part of local Poe appreciators, the city renamed the small area in which the plaque can found "Edgar Allan Poe Square," per an easily missed sign on a post designating it as such.

It should also be mentioned, but only because of the extreme lack of other Poe memorials in Boston, that nearby on 15 Fayette Street, somebody installed a teacup-saucer-size bronze medallion with another of Poe's sad-faced reliefs on a red-brick, black-shuttered building that a handmade list of residents has named "Poe Condominium."

Elsewhere in Massachusetts, residents are a bit more fond of their Poe connection, or even the vague possibility of one. In the town of Lowell, which Poe did probably visit, people are happy to spread around the rumor (truth be irrelevant) that Poe stayed at a still-standing pub called the Worthen House, at 141 Worthen Street. It didn't actually become a pub until after his death, but the pub does feature on its signage the image of a raven perched on a glass of beer.

However, in the town of Westford, the truth is a bit more set in stone. In a copse of trees off to the side of the front lawn of a two-story white house at 11 Graniteville Road, a headstonelike marker with a black raven incised quietly proclaims a rather interesting little item. The Raven was a bit worse for wear when I visited, but text on the marker clearly reads,

*Edgar Allan Poe*
*Was Here*
*1848–1849*
*Reading Poems—Exploring the Town*
*Nurturing His Friendship With*
*Nancy Heywood Richmond*
*("Annie")*

That last bit's important because you track Poe's love interests by the poems he wrote to them. As to the veracity of the claim, I've never been one much to argue with a stone marker.

Massachusetts isn't the only state in New England with claims to Poe. Another of the poet's verse-immortalized paramours, Sarah Helen Whitman, was courted by Poe in the town of Providence, Rhode Island, where she lived. Most famously, the couple spent time in the Providence Athenaeum, a library at 251 Benefit Street. According to the Athenaeum's Web site, it was even the location of the dissolution of their engagement when Whitman found out Poe had taken up drinking again after promising her he'd stopped.

Still, the consolation prize that he got out of his relationship with her was "To Helen," one of his more famous poems. Whitman is buried in the North Burial Ground on Branch Avenue in Providence. It's a large cemetery, but the small stone block that is her headstone can be found in the Dahlia Path area beside a table-type tomb with a red-brick base common to the cemetery. Her house still stands, as well, at 88 Benefit Street.

From 12-year-old children whose literary teeth haven't even grown in to 80-year-old literary scholars whose reading teeth are falling out, Poe is one of the few artists to achieve near-universal acclaim. As a result, it's funny that New England, and especially Boston, which seems to memorialize every instance of its mentions in the history books, virtually ignores Poe, despite how pivotal the area was in his life. But that Raven never flitting, still is sitting, still is sitting . . .

# Claude Rains

MOULTONBOROUGH AND SANDWICH, NH

HE WAS NOMINATED FOR FOUR ACADEMY AWARDS; acted alongside the likes of Humphrey Bogart, Bette Davis, and Jimmy Stewart; and was directed by the powerful megaphones of Alfred Hitchcock, Frank Capra, and . . . um . . . Irwin Allen. Yet for some reason this London-born actor, who walked in the wardrobe-department-provided shoes of King Herod, Julius Caesar, and Napoleon Bonaparte, is moldering in a tiny cemetery in the middle of nowhere, New Hampshire.

His name? Claude Rains, and I had to see his headstone. Not because he *Casablanca*'d with Humphrey Bogart or *Notorious*'d with Cary Grant or *Lawrence of Arabia*'d with Peter O'Toole. I had to visit his grave because, as you and *The Rocky Horror Picture Show* both know, Claude Rains was the Invisible Man.

That's right. Bela is buried in California, Boris in England, and Lon Jr. was donated to science. But New Hampshire can claim the final resting place of its own Universal Studios monster, the Invisible Man from the 1933 film of the same name.

The Invisible Man doesn't get as much face time as some of the other Universal monsters, but that's because . . . eh, who am I kidding . . . I can't finish that pun. Still, he's not exactly a monster of the exterior sort . . . no decaying skin, no reptilian scales, no sharp fangs, no beastly hair. Just a human-shaped, monocaine-addled bit of nothing covered in bandages, goggles, and a Mr. Potato Head nose, which, I admit sounds silly, but anything does when described using an iconic Hasbro toy.

However, despite his lack of overt outward monstrosity, in some ways the Invisible Man is the most twisted, terrifying creature in the Universal cannon. He's fear of the unknown personified. He's the utmost in potential attainable human evil. He's a mass murderer who delights in all the most atrocious acts of human malevolence. Oh, and he cackles.

And as if playing the Invisible Man weren't enough, Rains further embellished his Universal monster cachet by also starring as Larry Talbot's father in the 1941 *The Wolf Man* and as the title role of the 1943 version of *The Phantom of the Opera*.

In 1967, at the age of 77, Rains died in the Granite State, and the proof of that is in a little front lawn of a graveyard called Red Hill Cemetery in Moultonborough, New Hampshire, a small town on the northern point of Lake Winnipesaukee. The cemetery is surrounded by a white picket fence and has only a handful of graves. It's bracketed on three sides by houses, so it looks like just an empty house lot.

The easiest way to get the graveyard is to use the address of the house across the street from Red Hill Cemetery: 289 Bean Road. I assume the cemetery itself has no address, as we all know the attitude of the dead toward grocery store circulars.

Rains is buried beside the last of his six wives, Rosemary, under a unique pair of matching 4-foot-tall bullet-shaped obsidian tombstones of Rains's own design.

Of course, as Rains was buried here, it makes sense he had a house close by. The house is located on Route 109 in nearby Sandwich, New Hampshire, at the intersection of Little Pond and Wentworth Hill roads. The number on the front of the L-shaped house is 357, and it's white with three columns, a red front door, black shutters, and outbuildings. All in all, it definitely fits the part of the country home of a rich actor from the first half of the century. Like most houses, it's a private residence, so if you want to go see it don't be jerky about it . . . like loitering too long in front of it for pictures and publishing the address in a book and stuff.

For me, it's a day worth writing about when I get to visit the grave and house of a horror cinema icon. It's pure buttered marshmallows, though, to find a brand-new reason to watch a classic movie . . .

. . . at the late-night, double-feature picture show.

# Home of Edith Wharton
## LENOX, MA

WHAT DOES THE HOUSE of a consummate author of ghost stories look like? Certainly you'd expect it to be somewhat on the creepy side. Dark stone, perhaps. Multiple pointed gables adorning an alarmingly slanted roof, maybe. A generous display of strange topiary and gargoyle accents, I guess. At the very least, you'd think it'd have a pair of creaky gates.

However, the home of Edith Wharton is anything but any of that.

Edith Wharton lived from 1862 to 1937, and for penning such tales as *The House of Mirth* and her Pulitzer Prize–winning *The Age of Innocence,* she has become one of the country's most celebrated authors. However, for those whose celebrations tend a bit to the macabre, she's also beloved for her ghost stories.

The ghost stories of Edith Wharton always tend to the eloquent, the refined, and the subtle, all of which hints at an obsidian blackness beneath the polite veneer of the society she portrays. Such classics as "The Eyes," "Pomegranate Seed," and "The Lady's Maid's Bell" all feature men and women pursued by something ghastly that seems to reflect more the ghastliness of life more than the afterlife.

Many of those elegant stories of dread were written at her home in Lenox, Massachusetts, which is located in the western part of the state. Wharton was born rich, married rich, and then became even richer off the popularity of her writing, so her be-it-ever-so-humble home is an enormous mansion. You can tell this without seeing it because it has its own name.

Called The Mount, Wharton's mansion was built in 1902 on more than

100 acres of land. It's a large, white, three-story, rectangular building with a black roof and shutters that is set on a hill overlooking an exquisitely landscaped garden and the surrounding woods and countryside. The Mount was actually designed by Wharton herself according to principles elucidated in her nonfiction work, *The Decoration of Houses*.

Wharton lived at The Mount for less than a decade, though, because of a divorce from her husband, Edward Wharton, after which she moved to France, where she spent the rest of her life and currently spends her death. In 1911, the Whartons sold the property, which went on to become a residence for others of the privileged class, a girls' dormitory, and the headquarters of the theater group Shakespeare & Company before being restored in the 1990s to The Mount as-it-was.

Located at 2 Plunkett Street, The Mount is now open to the public between the months of May and December. Despite its size, the layout of the mansion is pretty compact. The ground floor includes a forecourt and entrance hall, while the main floor houses a gallery, her husband's den, a drawing room, a dining room, and her library, which houses her original collection of books that until recently had been spending the past century in Europe.

Despite that impressive library, Wharton did most of her writing in bed, where she would throw the finished pages on the floor to be gathered and transcribed later. That bedroom is upstairs, which is pretty much made up of all bedrooms. Besides Wharton's, the house also showcases what it calls the Henry James Suite, after the noted author of *The Turn of the Screw* (and whose grave is covered elsewhere in this book). James was a friend of the Whartons, a fellow ghost story writer, and a regular visitor to The Mount.

When I visited, the rooms upstairs were pretty much empty of furniture, but the house uses the space for various exhibits on Wharton's life, as well as the French and American cultures in which she was immersed.

As is fitting, The Mount does make its obeisance to her ghost stories. The mansion conducts regular Friday Night Fright tours during its open season, which focus both on her ghost stories and the ghost stories of the actual property. While it should come as no surprise that a tourist attraction claims to be haunted, being over 100 years old gives it enough time to collect a few ghosts, I guess. Besides, if the house of an author of ghost stories isn't creepy, it should at least be haunted.

# Rob Zombie
## HAVERHILL, MA

ANY RANDOM HORROR FAN can change his last name to "Zombie," but if you can back it up with a macabre career that spans multiple media to the degree of international success that Rob Zombie has garnered, it could be argued that you've pretty much earned the name. Zombie has lived the genre more than most, creating popular works of horror-infused music, art, and movies. In fact, he is the only personality in this section of the book who is still alive, a testament to how much horrifying this New Englander has accomplished so far in his life.

Robert Bartleh Cummings was born in 1965, but he entered the public sphere in the 1990s under the name Rob Zombie with his techno metal group White Zombie, which was named after a 1932 Bela Lugosi flick. With its heavy guitars, satanic lyrics, horror movie references, and guttural screams, the music of White Zombie was everything that parents would call "racket" if they heard it emanating from the bedroom of their 16-year-old.

When Rob Zombie went solo in 1998, he was free to ramp up the horror movie tributes and dialogue samples to his dark heart's content. Everything from *The Munsters* to exploitation movies became his raw materials as he crafted them around driving beats and performed them in theatrical stage shows in which he would dress up in various monster costumes. Soon, after many paeans to the genre and quite a few music video director credits on his resumé, he was given the chance by a major studio to write and direct his own horror movie.

In 2003, amidst controversy over its subject matter, *House of 1000 Corpses* was released, an over-the-top carnivalesque freak show of sadism and serial killers. It was popular enough that he then followed up in 2005 with *The Devil's Rejects,* a borderline brilliant-but-unrecommendable-to-non-horror-fans sequel to *House of 1000 Corpses.* Since the success of that pair of movies, he's had no trouble procuring more movie projects from major studios, including the chance to regurgitate John Carpenter's 1978 touchstone *Halloween.*

In addition, in the midst of all that music and movie making, Zombie also found the time to contribute his monstrous style of art for album covers, animated movies, and comic books.

Far from being hellspawn, Zombie was born in the Boston suburb of

Haverhill, Massachusetts (pronounced in two syllables, "Havrill") and spent the first couple of decades of his life there before moving to New York.

And these days, Haverhill is proud of its demon son.

In 2007, the city decided to update the "Welcome to Haverhill" signs that it had posted at its major entry points. These signs now boast of its most famous residents, including TV host Tom Bergeron, colonial heroine Hannah Duston, professional baseball player Tony Pena . . . and Rob Zombie, giving every Haverhill kid the city-sanctioned rejoinder, "It's not racket . . . it's civic pride."

The Rob Zombie sign can be found on the section of Route 110 called Amesbury Road, in front of the water-treatment plant on Kenoza Lake. The large white sign sits close to the ground and bears the usual welcome in large letters, along with a range of colorful sigils representing various local community organizations. Underneath the welcome in small text almost invisible at car speeds is the simple declaratory sentence, "Rock/Movie Star Rob Zombie was born in Haverhill." The statement is a bit of a misnomer . . . Zombie's not a movie star, but I can understand having to sum up such a monster of many talents succinctly.

Although he's long left Haverhill for more famous grazing land, he has of late maintained a home in New England . . . just not in his home state. Zombie stays within commuting distance of New York and out of reach of the paparazzi in an old white manse in the historic district of Woodbury, Connecticut. Specifically, it's located at 63 Sycamore Road, and you can tell it's Zombie's by the large security gate. And the dark pall of hell gases that surround the place.

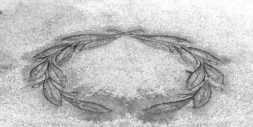

THIS PLOT OF GROUND
CONSECRATED BY THE
CITY OF HARTFORD AS
⊠ A RESTING PLACE ⊠
FOR THREE ADULTS AND
THREE CHILDREN WHO
LOST THEIR LIVES IN
THE CIRCUS FIRE
JULY 6 1944

THEIR IDENTITY
KNOWN BUT TO GOD

# Infamous Crimes,
# Killers, and Tragedies

*T*HIS SECTION IS A DARKER SHADE OF MACABRE than the rest of this book. A lot of people died in the making of it. Atrocity and tragedy need very little introduction, but I'll still attempt to make a go at it here. This section chronicles some of the more bizarre, violent, and captivating crimes and calamities that have scarred the New England soil and psyche. Many of the gruesome incidents in this section have been officially memorialized in different ways . . . sometimes by their survivors, sometimes by families of victims, sometimes by onlookers. Others have no physical marker or memoriam per se, but are unsettling enough that it will be a long time before history forgets . . . if it ever does. Either way, the stories told about these true events and actual people are often bandied about in dreadful detail on those nights when the darkness impinges too much on the windowpanes of our house or the glowing screen of our television to be ignored.

Some of these inclusions exist at a comfortable distance in time from us and can be treated lightly. (Or at least, I treat them lightly, regardless of whether I should or not.) Others are disturbingly recent and have about them not a single detail that can be joked about. Some inclusions are expected, such as the history lesson of the Boston Massacre and the tourist attraction that the Lizzie Borden ax murders have become. Others are more surprising in their connection to the region, including the Black Dahlia, Jack Kevorkian, and Ted Bundy.

Included in these pages is a book bound in the skin of a criminal and the home of quite possibly the most prolific serial killer in American history. There is fire and flood, massacre and murder, victim and violence. There is enough evil present in these pages to taint every positive belief you have about mankind. Not one New England state escapes unscathed herein. It's not the kind of section that you bid a reader enjoy, so I submit, for your interest, some of the blacker spots on the New England map.

# Lizzie Borden Bed and Breakfast
## FALL RIVER, MA

IT'S NOT EVERY DAY you get to spend the night at an infamous murder scene, and not just because it's impossible to spend any night during the day.

In 1892, the bodies of 70-year-old Andrew Borden and his wife 64-year-old Abby Borden were discovered in their Fall River, Massachusetts, home, each impolitely hacked to death with an ax. The main suspect of the double murder was Elizabeth "Lizzie" Borden, daughter of Andrew and stepdaughter of Abby. Lizzie was unmarried, 32, and lived at the house with her parents and older sister. She had every motive, a weak and inconsistent alibi, and tons of evidence against her. She was still somehow officially exonerated in court after a case that became an international sensation back when it was much harder to become an international sensation. Now, more than a century after the crime, Lizzie is still considered the murderess and the house has been turned into a bed-and-breakfast. Because of its inherent quaintness, of course.

The Lizzie Borden Bed and Breakfast offers eight different rooms, including Lizzie's own bedroom and the John Morse room, where Abby Borden fell prey to what medical textbooks describe as "hatchet repeatedly to the back of the head." I forget the Latin name for it.

Fall River is located an hour from Boston in that queer little hook part of Massachusetts that rudely shoulders Rhode Island away from the Atlantic Ocean. Lizzie's house is set in the middle of town at 92 Second Street. The house is forest green, well kept, and proffers a gift store in a separate shed-size building in the back.

My wife and I had managed to secure Lizzie's own bedroom for our stay. Normally when you get to a place where you're staying the night, you settle in, throw your underwear around, and call it home. An impending nightly tour for all the overnight guests prevented this, so we left the doors open and made sure our luggage was stacked unobtrusively and out of camera frame in the corner.

Our room was actually more of a suite. Because of the layout of the rooms on the second floor, the room of Lizzie's sister Emma opened only onto ours, so we had reserved both without realizing it. Our bathroom was across the hall, which we'd have to share with the couple in the John Morse room, and another door off our room led directly into Andrew Borden's room.

After visiting the John Morse room to see the stretch of carpet where Abby had been hewn, we wandered downstairs to the parlor where Andrew was given his own scalp massage. The original couch upon which he had been napping when he was killed wasn't there, of course, but they'd stuck in a close enough replica to help out the more macabre sectors of one's imagination. We grabbed some books on Lizzie from the shelves, took them up to

our room, and started reading about the murder . . . in the house where it was committed and the room where it was dreamed up.

Later that evening, we went down to the parlor for the tour. There were 10 guests in total that night, a perfect setup for a *Ten Little Indians* plot, and I think we were all acutely aware of that.

Our period-costumed tour guide led us through the house, offering ghost tales and historical tidbits, and performing a verbal reenactment of the deaths in situ, which really helped us make sense of the whole situation. And by situation, I mean, of course, the brutal hatchet murder of a sexagenarian and a septuagenarian by their naked spinster daughter.

We were also offered the opportunity for a séance, since merely treating the place like a tourist attraction and spending the night there wasn't quite enough to piss off any restless spirits who might be trapped in the ether. It cost an extra 10 bucks apiece, but that was fine. I've paid heftier long-distance rates. This was my first séance, but I learned a lot. Well, I learned that when you shove 10 people into a small room and then fill it with ghosts, it gets hot and stuffy fast. All in all, I was as unimpressed as I'd assumed I'd be, but, when it comes right down to it, I was involved in a séance at a house where two well-documented murders happened . . . I didn't care about the quality or my own beliefs on the matter, I just dug the fact of it.

Finally, the moment we'd been wondering how we'd react to came. Bedtime. The house was dark. All was quiet. We lay in bed, I in my kerchief and my wife in her cap. Honestly, the night wasn't spooky at all. The house was filled with sleeping people, the bed was comfortable, and there was no closet in the room for me to imagine Lizzie running out of with a hatchet above her head screaming, "Get out of my bed!" I probably could have freaked myself into a state of solid terror by just imagining Lizzie's lying there, staring at that same ceiling, dreaming dreams of violent bloodshed, but sleep came too fast. I didn't even have nightmares, despite the fact that every conversation of the day had involved violent murder in some way.

The next morning we awoke for the second half of bed-and-breakfast, feasting on what was supposed to be the exact same menu as the Bordens' last earthly breakfast in the dining room where the bodies underwent their autopsies.

Although the bed-and-breakfast is the central Lizzie attraction in Fall River, there are others. For instance, you can also visit her grave in Oak Grove

Cemetery, which is the final resting place of all the central players in the Borden fiasco, although I guess at some point in time "resting place" becomes an inaccurate term for a decomposing body.

In addition, there's Maplecroft, the house Lizzie bought with her inheritance after being cleared of the crime. Every cloud has a silver lining, even if you have to hack away the cloud to get to it. The house is a private residence and is located at 306 French Street, about a mile and a half from Lizzie's original house and half a mile from Oak Grove Cemetery.

Finally, a visit is probably in order to the Fall River Historical Society, which displays the ax head that was found on the scene, thought to be the actual murder weapon.

In the end, our Lizzie Borden Bed and Breakfast experience wasn't as creepy as you'd think and pretty much felt like what it technically was, a mere stay at a bed-and-breakfast. It actually took longer getting used to the idea of sharing a bathroom with strangers than to the fact that we were gallivanting around an ancient murder scene in our socks.

# Birthplace of H. H. Holmes
## GILMANTON, NH

SO WHAT MAKES A SERIAL KILLER? Apparently, Gilmanton, New Hampshire, does. It was 150 years ago in that small town 20 miles north of the state capitol of Concord that Herman Webster Mudgett—or H. H. Holmes as he styled himself—was born and spent his formative years . . . a phrase that takes on sinister meaning when used in reference to a future multiple murderer and the creator of Chicago's nefarious Murder Castle.

Holmes is generally acknowledged as America's first modern serial killer and was possibly also the country's most prolific, with final tallies varying widely and, chillingly, into the triple digits. He was an exact contemporary of Jack the Ripper, although he didn't have that guy's press agent, and his more appalling crimes were concentrated in the early 1890s in Chicago, Illinois. He was executed in 1896 at the age of 36 in Philadelphia, Pennsylvania, where his grave is still a badly healed and anonymous wound in the earth. But he was born in New Hampshire.

Located at 500 Province Road, the tall house is surprisingly prominent in the center of this improminent town whose only other claim to fame is that it was the home and is the final resting place of author Grace Metalious. She used Gilmanton and its surrounding area as the model for her best-selling novel *Peyton Place*, the semitrue and salacious story of a seemingly idyllic small town that harbors all manner of sordid scandal within its borders.

According to a shingle tacked to the outside wall of the Mudgett residence, the house was built in 1825, giving it genuine local historic worth beyond the macabre. Across the street sits a pair of similarly white-paneled and aged buildings. One of those buildings is Gilmanton Academy, where Holmes attended school before leaving the area for medical college and marriage. It now houses town offices and the local historical society museum. The other is Gilmanton Community Church, which still functions as a place of worship . . . probably better than most, in fact. Every church should have at hand such a definite reference point for the easy existence of evil.

When we visited the Mudgett House, the place looked empty and dejected, partially due to its peeling paint and scraggly lawn, partially due to the FOR SALE sign staked in front of it, but mostly due to its context.

It's impossible to look at a building connected to H. H. Holmes without thinking about his Murder Castle, where the most abhorrent of his deeds were committed. Horror author Shirley Jackson once wrote that some houses are born bad. The Murder Castle was rotten all the way to its blueprints. Officially built as a hotel to cash in on the crowds migrating to Chicago for the 1893 World's Fair, it was a three-story-tall, blocklong edifice at the corner of 63rd and Wallace streets. Holmes designed it, oversaw its construction, and financed it with funds drawn from various fraudulent schemes and the proceeds of a pharmacology business that he murdered into.

After his eventual capture, the castle was stormed and found to have a more grisly purpose. The hotel was a labyrinth of torture chambers, secret passageways, trapdoors, death rooms, body disposal apparatuses, gas chambers, and all manner of depraved constructions for use on the constant supply of diverse victims that only a hotel can offer. It was, in effect, one giant murder weapon.

An unknown arsonist burned down the Murder Castle shortly after Holmes was captured and hanged. A U.S. Post Office now stands there . . . haunted, if anything in this world is.

Back in Gilmanton, there's really not much more to say about this house or the man who grew up there, which is good, because I'm running out of modifiers for the perverse.

# Black Dahlia Memorial
## MEDFORD, MA

ELIZABETH SHORT WAS ONE of the most famous murder victims in the history of California, maybe even the country . . . but it was the state of Massachusetts that ended up erecting a memorial to her.

For whatever reasons that give humanity the dark clefts in its soul, it's rare that a murder victim gets more press than the murder villain. Even when the identity of the killer is completely unknown, like Jack the Ripper or the Zodiac Killer, we still find him a name so that it can live on in fascinating infamy while the victims molder anonymously in their graves.

The murderer of Elizabeth Short was never identified, but neither was he given a name, probably because a single murder is far below the threshold of attention we needed to spend time constructing a persona evil enough to interest us. We have, however, bestowed a nickname to the victim, even though we know her real name. Elizabeth Short is forever the Black Dahlia. Some suggest the nickname was drawn from her dark hair and preference for dark clothes, but nobody really knows why. What is known is that the simple

moniker has pretty much framed how history has remembered her, beautiful, enigmatic, dark, and short lived.

On January 15, 1947, 22-year-old Short was found dead in an empty lot in Los Angeles. She was naked, severed in half at the waist, with 3-inch gashes extending both corners of her mouth. Her lower body was arranged in a wide V, her upper body with her arms angled above her head in a rough Y, the initials of some unknowable atrocity. Her body was bloodless, as was the ground around it, indicating that she had been moved there from some other location.

The ensuing investigation became of national interest, with armies of investigators sorting through throngs of suspects, numerous leads, and scant evidence, all to no avail. Short was known for her playgirl tendencies, thrived on the attention of men, and spent many of her nights partying. It was probably through this lifestyle that she met the person who killed her. As uninteresting as that part of the story is, the grisly nature of the condition of her body at the time of its discovery made it worth a nation's worth of newspaper ink.

I could recount some of the many suspects and theories, but the end result of them all is the same. A young, mutilated girl whose death made her famous. Nobody knows what happened, why it did, or who did it.

Short was born in Hyde Park, Massachusetts, but was raised half an hour north in the town of Medford. She spent most of her short life there with her mother, in addition to stints out of state, in California with her estranged father and in Florida with family friends.

She's buried at Mountain View Cemetery in Oakland, California; however, for some reason (perhaps those dark clefts in the soul again), her childhood home of Medford wanted its connection to the tragedy remembered. Her actual home on Salem Street has been eradicated for a rotary, but just down the road the local historical society has erected a large rock with a plaque dedicated to Short.

The memorial was installed in 1993 and faces Salem Street at a point near the aforementioned rotary for Interstate 93. However, the easiest way to get to the trapezoidal stone is to take Fountain Street, which ends in a cul-de-sac directly behind the memorial. The simple plaque on the simple stone tells the Black Dahlia's story in three simple paragraphs, highlighting her connection to Medford.

We often memorialize tragedy to keep ourselves from forgetting its lessons and to attempt to equalize existence in some small way, as if victims' being remembered for longer than the rest of us somehow balances to some degree their living shorter. It's strange to memorialize someone merely for being a murder victim, though, especially when you have to sort through so many to get to that one. Regardless of why, the obscure marker sits in its obscure location, the length of the country away from where Elizabeth Short came to her violent and famous end.

# Spooner Well
### BROOKFIELD, MA

THIS IS THE STORY of a fetus hanged for murder. And as much as that might be my favorite opening sentence of anything I've ever written, the rest of this entry sleds rapidly downhill until finally crashing into a simple, unimpressive, tombstonelike monument.

In 1778 in the town of Brookfield, Massachusetts, back when the United States was in its terrible twos and more than a few people's loyalties were still on the rebound after breaking up with England, a woman named Bathsheba Spooner hired a trio of soldiers to kill her husband, Joshua Spooner.

Various motivations for the crime have been bandied about, none of which is particularly imaginative and all of which make me think that the job of criminal profiler is an overrated one. Ideas include Joshua's being abusive, Bathsheba's cheating with one of the aforementioned soldiers, a political disagreement between the two, her wanting more access to Joshua's sizeable estate, and so on. Plus I've always just assumed that every wife has multiple, less easily articulated reasons to kill her husband.

One night, the three men hired by Bathsheba beat Joshua to death and then dumped him down his own well. Two of these men were British soldiers awkwardly hanging around after their country had lost the Revolutionary War. The third was a Continental soldier who might've been romantically involved with Bathsheba.

Despite how elegantly contrived that plan seems to appear on paper, beat-and-dump is a surprisingly sloppy operation, and all the conspirators were soon caught. The trial took place in nearby Worchester, Massachusetts, and was, of course, a great time for all not involved, with the whole state apparently enrapt by the spectacle and the media touting it as "the most extraordinary crime ever perpetrated in New England." The region's topped it many times since then, of course, so yay it.

The conspirators were all hanged with the usual barbaric but mesmerizing fanfare, including Bathsheba, despite the fact that she claimed to be pregnant. After a premortem examination by midwives, she was deemed to be not with child; however, a postmortem reveled that she was, in fact, five months pregnant, so autopsist 1, midwives 0.

And that's the end of the story. No secret suspects, no late-breaking evidence, no twist ending . . . unless you include the bodies twisting on the end of a rope. Just three newly orphaned Spooner children, and the hangover and possible morning-after regret of a populace that had exulted too much in justice.

But apparently some murders need markers, and that's where this crime yields a visitable site. Somewhere along the line, somebody decided to mark the location of the actual murder scene, that round hole of a well where Joshua's square peg of a corpse was shoved. The Spooner Well marker is located on East Main Street, outside the center of the town of Brookfield. It's a few feet off the side of the road adjacent to an overgrown field. Across the street from it are a couple of houses whose front windows give the impression of ignoring the memento mori that is their neighbor. The marker is a simple, white, rectangular slab bearing the text: "Spooner Well—Joshua Spooner murdered and thrown down this well March 1, 1778, by three Revolutionary soldiers at the urging of his wife Bathsheba. All four were executed at Worcester, July 2, 1778." I searched around the marker a bit, but couldn't find a well or hole or anything like that. I assume it's either been covered up in the hundreds of years since its unholy use, or that I'm demonstrably bad at finding wells.

Joshua Spooner's actual grave can also be found in Brookfield, this time off West Main Street in Brookfield Cemetery, not too far from Spooner Well. The grave is located in the northwestern part of the cemetery, right up against the stone wall that separates the cemetery from the street. His epitaph also tells the tale of his murder. Nobody really knows the location of the graves of Bathsheba and her accomplices. Just the worst thing they ever did in their lives.

# Grave of the Boston Strangler
## PEABODY, MA

UNLESS YOU'RE A CRIMINAL INVESTIGATOR or a philosopher, there's no good reason to be fascinated by serial killers. But we all are. And that's because there are tons of bad reasons to be. However, of all the serial killers, there's even less reason, good or bad, to be fascinated by Albert DeSalvo, the Boston Strangler.

Unlike most serial killers, who have some part of their personal story that doesn't quite fit with our conception of reality, maybe a stable family life, a strange cunningness of mind, or perhaps even an unholy ability to do things to the human body that would make the most hardened man quail, Albert DeSalvo was just a wretched person who did wretched things and hailed from a wretched family. He was abused, taught the opposite of morality by a depraved father, and then, just like that recipe promises, turned out to be a repulsive creature. There's nothing really fascinating about him, no aspect to him that the study of which might yield clues into the evil that men do.

From 1962 to 1964, the Boston Strangler sexually assaulted and strangled around a dozen women who ranged in age from 19 to 85, many of them left with bows around their necks from the article of clothing that he used to strangle them.

Nine months after the last murder, DeSalvo was arrested for an unrelated series of sexual assaults he committed all over New England, which earned him the nickname of the Green Man for the green workpants he wore. While in jail for those assaults, he confessed to being the Boston Strangler. However, it was the Green Man assaults and not the Boston Strangler murders for which he was convicted and sentenced, as there was more evidence for the former than the latter.

In 1973, after six years of incarceration for his Green Man crimes, he was found stabbed to death in his jail cell. Sometimes the system works and brutality reaps more than mere justice.

Now, within the context of what I said a few paragraphs back, there is one thing in the overall story of the Boston Strangler that might be worth a little fascination. Although DeSalvo had a unique knowledge of some of the unpublicized aspects of the Boston Strangler crimes, there were a few major inconsistencies in his confessions. That, plus the absolute lack of physical evidence and eyewitness testimony, has caused some to believe that Albert DeSalvo was not the Boston Strangler.

For instance, some posit that due to the shifting methods in which the different victims were treated, as well as the wide variety of female victims, that multiple murderers were inaccurately lumped by the media under the Boston Strangler moniker. Others believe that the true Boston Strangler was actually DeSalvo's cell mate, George Nassar, who apparently fit the still-incomplete-at-that-time profile of a serial killer better than DeSalvo and could have fed him details of the crime in some kind of deal. DeSalvo, after all, had nothing to lose as he was already imprisoned for life for the Green Man crimes.

In 2001, family members of DeSalvo and the last Boston Strangler victim, Mary Sullivan, even went so far as to have the bodies of DeSalvo and Sullivan exhumed in an attempt to discover the truth. Not surprisingly, although more questions were unearthed, nothing conclusive was found either way.

What is surprising is that his family opted to have him buried in a labeled grave in the family plot in the first place. Besides completely undermining the idea of consecrated ground, such a memoriam is sure to draw unwanted attention. Like mine, I guess.

It's public information that the man history knows as the Boston Strangler is buried in Puritan Lawn Memorial Park at 185 Lake Street in Peabody, Massachusetts. However, the exact location of his grave has been closely held for years by both the DeSalvo family and the cemetery office. The graveyard itself also keeps the secret well. Indeed, it's mostly because of the nature of the cemetery that any type of concealment is at all possible.

First, Puritan Lawn is made up of 140 acres. That's a rather large area. Second, it has no tombstones. Instead, small bronze plaques are inset flush with the ground, making the discovery of a particular plaque near impossible without specific directions. In other words, every grave is pretty well hidden. If you ignored the cemetery gates and didn't look directly down to see what you were standing on, you'd think you were just in a field dotted with tree copses. As a result, it would take a lot of planning, time, and luck to find his grave unless you have inside information. Alternatively, you could just read the next paragraph.

DeSalvo's grave is located in the middle of an expanse delineated by the intersection of Cummings Way and Endicott Drive. To get there, take a left

onto Endicott from Cummings. The rows of graves in that section parallel Endicott, and DeSalvo's is located in the sixth from that street. We found it surprisingly quickly by matching up some nearby trees with a screenshot of the grave from a documentary on his crimes.

   Those directions should make it relatively easy for anybody else morbidly interested and up for an anticlimax, which is good. After all, whether Albert DeSalvo really is the Boston Strangler or not, his final mark upon this earth is certainly not worth exerting too much effort to find. Unless you're writing a book.

# Hartford Circus Fire Memorial
## HARTFORD, CT

TENTS ARE MEANT TO BE TEMPORARY STRUCTURES, but the one that was erected on July 6, 1944, in the large empty lot on Barbour Street in Hartford, Connecticut, has left permanent scars.

   On that summer day, the Ringling Bros. and Barnum & Bailey Circus was in town, which meant that it was a day filled with the promise of wonder and lasting childhood memory. Instead, it delivered horror and emotional trauma.

The main tent was an enormous affair. At 550 feet long and 250 feet wide, it was large enough to seat 12,000 people. On that July day, between 7,000 and 8,000 were on hand to see acrobats, trained animals, trapeze artists, and all the portable and exotic delights of the circus at its finest.

However, in the throng of the crowd and the thrill of the entertainment, very few noticed the small fire that erupted in the corner of the tent near the men's restroom. Once they did, it should have been relatively manageable. But, unfortunately, the tent canvas was coated in a mixture of paraffin wax and gasoline to waterproof it from the elements. The coating accelerated the fire so fast that within 10 minutes, the circus was a toppling inferno, with 19 tons of flaming canvas falling on the spectators. In the end, 168 men, women, and, of course, children were killed. In fact, it was mostly women and children. Hundreds more were hospitalized. Strangely, no circus workers or animals were harmed in the making of that tragedy.

In the aftermath, it was generally theorized that someone must have carelessly thrown a cigarette, and, although there were many heroes that day in the ranks of the circus staff and performers, six circus officials received prison sentences for involuntary manslaughter. Tragedy goes down best with a chaser of officially assigned blame.

Then, in 1950, an Ohio man named Robert Segee came forward and confessed to the circus arson. He claimed that an Indian on a flaming horse told him to do it and that a burning woman told him to confess. Although he had a history of arson, his story was doubted due to his history of mental illness and the lack of proof that he was even in the state on the day of the tragedy. He was convicted that same year in his home state for other acts of arson, though, and was sentenced to 40 years. Decades later, he recanted his confession concerning the Hartford fire.

Accident or arson, the results were the same.

Sixty years later, the people of Hartford had built an elementary school at the site of the fire, but still couldn't get their minds off it. As a result, on the July 6, 2005, on the anniversary of the event, they dedicated the Hartford Circus Fire Memorial right on the site of the fire.

Located behind Wish Elementary School at 350 Barbour Street, the memorial starts at the northeastern corner of the school. There, a series of stone markers inlaid with plaques bearing explanatory text and images counts down the short timeline of the disaster by the minute.

The markers end at a large bronze circle inset into concrete and red brick. In its center, it bears a golden schematic of the original circus tent, radiating from which are the names of all the victims. The circle is in the exact location of the center ring of the circus. In addition, and as a nice touch, dogwood trees on the perimeter of the field around the bronze circle trace the outline of the actual circus tent, giving a sense of physical scale to the tragedy.

All in all, the Hartford Circus Memorial is a unique, well-planned, and fitting memorial in a world where memorials are usually unimaginative and inapt. Of course, few have the opportunity to memorialize something so haunting as a circus fire.

Of the 168 victims of the fire, three adults and three children were never identified. They were buried in the same plot in Northwood Cemetery on Matianuck Avenue, a former soldiers' cemetery just a few miles from the site of the memorial. Because the cemetery contains mostly identical headstones of soldiers, it's easy to spot the large horizontal rectangular slab of the plot. The slab tells the story of these six victims of the Hartford Circus Fire whose identity is "known but to God," while nearby, six small stone plaques mark their actual resting places.

These days, though, only five bodies remain. The sixth, formerly and famously known as Little Miss 1565 (the number assigned to her body at the morgue), was claimed by researchers in 1991 to be identified as Eleanor Emily

Cook. Her body was, as a result, removed and interred elsewhere with members of her supposed family. The decision was a controversial one, and many, including some of Eleanor's family, believe the identification to be erroneous. The text inscribed in the sixth stone tells only the positive side of the story of its former occupant's identification.

With a horrible tragedy, sometimes you have to force anything close to a happy ending that you can.

# Graves of the
# Smuttynose Murder Victims
## PORTSMOUTH, NH

IN NORTHERN NEW ENGLAND, a pair of matching, adjacent tombstones both bear the epitaph, "A sudden death, a striking call / A warning voice that speaks to all / To all to be prepared to die." It's probably exactly the advice that the pair of ax-murdered sisters-in-law who are buried beneath them might posthumously give.

The story of the Smuttynose murders has achieved a level of intrigue beyond the strange name that describes them. Just off the coasts of Maine and New Hampshire is a small archipelago of nine islands called the Isles of Shoals that is divvied up between the two states. On the Maine side is a pickle-shaped island called Smuttynose, about 25 acres in size. Its name sounds like that of some mythical sea beast or local bogeyman, but in reality, it has become synonymous with something more horrific.

About 140 years ago it was populated by just six people, an interrelated group of Norwegian fishermen made up of three men and three women. On March 5, 1873, the population dropped by two.

On that frigid night, a man named Louis Wagner rowed the 10 difficult miles to Smuttynose to rob the house of John Hontvet while the three men of the island were away fishing. For some reason, he didn't expect to encounter the three women who lived there. He ran into Hontvet's wife; Maren; her sister Karen Christensen; and Karen's sister-in-law Anethe Christensen. Wagner beat and then axed to death both Karen and Anethe, but somehow Maren managed to escape undetected and hid somewhere on that tiny rock of

an island. In fishermen's terms, she was the one that got away. The authorities eventually caught Wagner, and with the help of Maren's testimony, hung him for the brutal double murder.

Of course, since stories that are told numerous times get boring in the telling after a while, the facts are sometimes stretched to accommodate the idea that Wagner was an innocent man and that it was Maren herself who went all Lizzie Borden on her own family. Either way, the end result was a pair of dead, mutilated bodies and a local legend.

The Hontvet house burned down in 1885, and these days the island is privately owned, with nothing on it but a pair of buildings, a lot of rocks including one called Maren's Rock, a monument to a bunch of Spanish sailors who shipwrecked there at some point, and a Blackbeard legend about the infamous pirate's marooned fourteenth bride and the treasure she still guards to this day (it's the East Coast after all, and every bit of it claims its own Blackbeard lore).

There's no real way to get to get to the island without permission and access to a private boat, but various Isles of Shoals cruises do go by there with tour guides that regale the passengers with the story of that bloody night so many years ago.

The graves of Karen and Anethe are more accessibly located on the New Hampshire mainland, if still a little hard to find. The women are buried in the conglomeration of cemeteries that is collectively known as South Cemetery in Portsmouth, right on the coast. The best directions I can give are to parallel the short rock wall that delineates the cemetery at Sagamore Avenue until you find the rather unnoticeable tombstone of James M. Pickering. Once you've found his last trace on this earth, take the green path to the left of it. The Christensens' matching graves are a few hundred feet down and facing this path on the left.

You'd think that a few dozen acres of rocky turf of questionable worth out in the cold ocean could survive the entire history of the world without ever seeing any violent bloodshed. Instead, it almost seems as if the human race is on its second coat of painting the Earth in that shade.

# The Station Fire Site
## WEST WARWICK, RI

WHEN THE MENTION of a dredged-directly-from-the-devil tragedy causes the 1980s radio-filler "Once Bitten, Twice Shy" to start playing on an endless loop inside your head, the phrase "conflicting emotions" takes on a whole new meaning.

On February 20, 2003, 472 people gathered at a small nightclub called the Station in West Warwick, Rhode Island, to do all the more hedonistic things people do at nightclubs, on this particular night to the strains of 1980s one-hit-semiwonder band Great White. Mere seconds into the concert, the band's ill-thought-through pyrotechnics display burned the place down into ashtray leavings so quickly that it makes one wonder why the phrase "fast as fire" hasn't yet become a cliché in our language.

The nightclub fire killed an absurdly round number of people (100) and injured twice as many. It was a grimy, horror-filled night that most victims and participants would like erased from their memories. For the rest of us, there's the infamous footage of the night on the Internet to rewatch over and over again.

However, the case of the Station fire has something that most other tragedies don't have: a strange sheen of hair band rock 'n' roll. Some people lose their lives protecting others, some people lose their lives attempting to explore the world for posterity. These people lost their lives to relive the Day-Glo Decade.

Pictures of the club before the fire show a small, one-story, wooden building, its façade covered in a van art–style mural of giant rock star portraits against the backdrop of an American flag. Little more than a hand-painted sign announced its name. If these details were any indication, the Station couldn't have been much more inviting in its heyday than the pile of burnt rubble that it became. Of course, when we visited six years after the fire, all that had been bulldozed away, leaving a bit of gently sloping bare land and a blank marquee out front with a handwritten sign taped to it that read, NEVER FORGET 02.20.03."

Outlining the vacant lot where the nightclub stood is a large group of handmade crosses decorated with pictures, beads, stuffed animals, notes—all the usual accoutrements of roadside memorials. A few folding chairs and a shrine or two are also present, and a small green Dumpster off to the side completes the scene.

According to Chuck Klosterman in his book *Killing Yourself to Live,* the memorial was improvised by a few cokeheads and lesbians using the floorboards of the razed club. Normally, due to my sloppy scholarship, I would cite that insight without sourcing it, but it just seems too remarkable to steal.

When we visited, just a few weeks before the sixth anniversary of the disaster (seems like a real flaw in the English language that both the best moments and worst that happen in life have anniversaries), the tableau was covered in snow, much as it was on that February night. The snow made the place seem tranquil and holy, and it betrayed the footprints of recent visitors. I've seen pictures of the memorial in other seasons, when the area is just a dirt plot; it makes the place seem sadder, if that's even possible.

Anyway, by this point in the timeline, multimillion-dollar lawsuits have been settled, blame has been assigned, jail time has been served, regulations have been altered, and support funds have been raised. But the former location of the Station has remained for the past few years a glaringly blank spot of land. And that song just won't leave my head.

# Art of Jack Kevorkian
## WATERTOWN, MA

TECHNICALLY, HE'S A KILLER, and, technically, he's a criminal, so technically he belongs in this section of the book. However, I did balk at putting him here alongside the horrific perversity of the likes of the Boston Strangler and H. H. Holmes. His name is Jack Kevorkian. We know him as Dr. Death.

Jack Kevorkian was born in 1928 in Pontiac, Michigan, and received a medical degree from the University of Michigan in 1952. His specialty was pathology, the study of dead tissue, and it was the first official step in a career that exhibited a marked fascination with death in a profession that's supposed to be fascinated with life. In fact, his medical career was so idiosyncratic, he earned the nickname "Dr. Death" long before the media was trying to fit his name into their headlines.

For instance, he photographed the eyes of dying patients to document the moment of death, experimented with blood transfusions from corpses, advocated euthanasia and organ harvesting of death row inmates, and attempted to experiment on them during their executions. Eventually, his interests turned to assisted suicide, first promoting it philosophically and then promoting it actively with homemade contraptions called the Thanatron and the Mercitron, the former being a multiple injection device involving potassium chloride and the latter a mask and a canister of carbon monoxide.

Starting in 1990, he assisted a range of suicides, with a final tally being possibly more than 130, many of them in his home state of Michigan. His acts caused multiple state legislators to pass laws on the legality of assisted suicide. He was stripped of his license to practice medicine and then eventually arrested and acquitted multiple times.

However, footage from one case in particular showed him actively pushing the plunger on his Thanatron, instead of leaving the final act to the patient/victim/client. In April 1999, he was convicted of second-degree murder after representing himself and was sentenced to 10 to 25 years. He was released for good behavior eight years into his sentence. These days, he's made a run in state politics and so far has generally left death to the Grim Reaper.

Kevorkian has an interesting tie to New England. His oil paintings. So I guess technically he's an artist, as well, meaning he could have gone into the first section of this book. However, I also balked at putting him alongside the brilliant likes of Edgar Allan Poe, José Orozco, and . . . um . . . Elizabeth Montgomery.

Kevorkian's paintings are housed at the Armenian Library and Museum of America (ALMA) at 65 Main Street in Watertown, Massachusetts. ALMA preserves and displays works of Armenian history, culture, and art. Their interest in Kevorkian's work stems from his own genealogy. His parents were Armenian refugees during World War I.

ALMA is a surprisingly large museum, with four floors that hold history and ethnographic exhibits, a contemporary art and performance gallery, and a library, all dedicated to the 3,000 years of Armenian culture.

In fact, the ALMA venue is another reason I ended up categorizing Kevorkian's contribution to the macabre in this section. The Armenian Library also holds a collection of artifacts from the Armenian Genocide, a seven-year period of history during which the Ottoman Empire attempted to eradicate the entire Armenian population. More than a million Armenians died as a result of the atrocity.

Although ALMA has had large exhibits on the tragedy in the past, currently they have a small display that's more memorial than anything else. A small, spiral corridor lined with quotes and images concerning the genocide lead to a single large glass case. In it is a menacing-looking metal dog collar that one particular victim had been forced to wear after being castrated and enslaved, the tattered outfit of a dead child, an Armenian Bible, and a handful of bone fragments from a massacre. Tellingly, they've set the memorial up in a loft area that overlooks and overshadows the rest of the museum floor.

Back to Kevorkian, the museum has put on full exhibits of his oil paintings in the past in its contemporary art gallery, but usually only has one or two on permanent display. Gary Lind-Sinanian, curator at ALMA, was kind enough to give me a tour, as well as remove Kevorkian's paintings from storage so that I could see them.

Had these paintings been of sunrises and lighthouses, I might still have included them in this work just based on the grim nature of Kevorkian's reputation. However, the subject matter of his paintings is, itself, drenched in the macabre.

According to Lind-Sinanian, the paintings are more political and social cartoons that anything else. He also told me, "If one were to ignore the subject matter, they'd fit right in on the wall of a children's nursery." I agree. They are brightly painted, cartoony, and make use of visual puns and overt symbolism ... for instance, the iris blossom that grows through the eye socket of a skull in his painting *Very Still Life* or a broken scale of justice that throws the shadow of a cross on the wall in *Double Cross of Justice*.

The more than dozen paintings feature mostly grisly images, including a decapitated man about to feast on his own head, a shirt made up of Satan's face, and a corpse wrapped in Christmas garland. Children's nursery, indeed. Kevorkian also has a series of works utilizing medical themes, in which he attempts to portray conditions such as coma, paralysis, and fever in metaphor. A third vein of his works seems to be musical themes, including a straightforward portrait of Bach, whose music Kevorkian favors when ALMA does official exhibits of his collection.

One work in particular wasn't a painting at all, but more like a 3-D mixed-media piece. It's called *1915 Genocide 1945*. In it, two arms hold a Styrofoam head by its hair. One arm bears a swastika, the other an Ottoman Empire sigil. The entire piece is framed in barbed wire, while blood drips down from its neck and past the frame. Apparently, Kevorkian used actual blood for that latter part that he was able to procure during his medical laboratory days.

Just as Kevorkian's life has been controversial in society, so have his paintings been controversial for the museum. On the one hand, orthodox Armenian beliefs emphasize the sacredness of life; on the other, Kevorkian is a modern-day Armenian who has definitely impacted culture.

Nothing's simple with Jack Kevorkian . . . but everything's morbid.

# Colebrook Murder Victims Memorial
## COLEBROOK, NH

NO TOWN IS SMALL ENOUGH to avoid tragedy. Some towns, though, are small enough to be hurt a bit more deeply by it.

Colebrook, New Hampshire, is one such town. Located just 10 miles from the border of Canada and near pretty much nothing else, it boasts a total population of fewer than 2,500 people. However, because it is a border town, Colebrook has had more than its fair share of brushes with evil, although usually indirectly.

In 1906, the criminally insane millionaire Harry K. Thaw was arrested in Colebrook after escaping from an asylum where he had been serving a sentence for publicly shooting and murdering Stanford White, the prominent architect of the 1890 Madison Square Garden in New York City. Thaw shot him during a musical revue on the rooftop of that same building, in effect causing the architect to have designed his own murder scene.

In 1984, after an appalling national, and perhaps even international, crime spree, serial killer Christopher Wilder committed suicide during an altercation with police at a gas station in Colebrook. These days, the gas station is abandoned. It can be found at the northwestern corner of the intersection of Bridge and Main streets.

However, in August 1997, evil found a way to hit the citizens of Colebrook more personally.

Carl Drega was one of those hermetic paranoids whom we'd all do well to be terrified of. He lived in the nearby town of Bow, New Hampshire, but on this summer day found himself in Colebrook, where he was pulled over by state police at a supermarket and cited for driving a rusted-through pickup truck. Drega shot and killed both officers, whose names were Les Lord and Scott Phillips.

Perhaps at that point he decided that damnation was not something you earned half-assedly, or maybe he misunderstood the "glory" part of the "going out in a blaze of glory" idea. Perhaps it had been his original intent all along to go on a shooting spree. For whatever reason, he went to the nearby downtown area and shot a judge named Vickie Bunnell, against whom he'd had a minor grudge.

His final murder victim was local newspaper editor Dennis Joos, who had rushed out on hearing the shots that killed Vickie Bunnell and tried to wrestle Drega to the ground, dying in the attempt.

From there, after shooting and wounding another police officer, Drega took off for his house, burned it to the ground, and then fled to Vermont, where he died in a police shootout. On his property were found the remnants of various assault rifles, a large cache of homemade bomb parts, and surveillance equipment. Yes, he was one of those.

The violent deaths of these four prominent citizens left a ragged wound that desperately needed dressing. That dressing came in a lot of forms. Memorial land preserves, highways, plaques, and awards all now bear the names of those victims. Most directly, that dressing came from the somber slab of a small memorial.

On Bridge Street, just down the road from the aforementioned abandoned gas station, is a small garden park area. The park is located just outside the *News and Sentinel* offices of which Joos had been the editor and near which he was killed. Set prominently in that park is a small rectangle monument of mourning-black marble dedicated to the tragedy. Not content with just the mere names of the victims, the town had the portraits of all four etched into its obsidian surface, which looks for all the world like a dark bruise on the landscape of the town. At the bottom of the stone is the somewhat ironic phrase, "Their deeds are their memorials." Even for one who never knew the people whom the monument memorializes, staring into the faces of the victims is a bit unnerving, especially when you can see your own reflecting back at you in the shiny blackness of the stone.

In the machinery of society, sometimes a piece wobbles and dangerously flies off, damaging the mechanism of which it is supposed to be a part. Sometime it means a good bit of the machine needs to be repaired before it can continue working. Sometimes it means that the machine must keep working in its newly impaired state. I'm not sure how it is with Colebrook . . . only they do, really. All I can do is visit the memorial that they erected.

# Deerfield Massacre Mass Grave
## DEERFIELD, MA

MASS GRAVES ARE A LITTLE BIT HARDER to whistle past than the average grave. They're more unsettling, as they immediately point to some tragedy that forced somebody to preclude the usual sacred interment rites that we afford our dead on an individual basis regardless of religious or philosophical belief. The Deerfield Massacre grave, in Deerfield, Massachusetts, is one such disturbing example.

In the winter of 1704, during one of the more obscure pre–Revolutionary American wars, a group of about 300 French soldiers and Native American warriors of various tribes attacked the English settlement of Deerfield. Around 50 colonists were killed, half of which were children, and more than 100 were taken captive and forced to march 300 miles through the harsh New England winter to Quebec, Canada. Many died on the way. Of course, the exact numbers vary depending upon the source, but the bottom line is that a ton of people died that day. Enough that a mass grave could be the only closure.

The mass grave of this Massachusetts massacre is located in the corner of a small cemetery at the end of Albany Road in Deerfield that is sometimes called Deerfield Cemetery and other times Old Albany Cemetery. At the top of a small hump of land is a squat, pointed monument with inscriptions on two of its four sides. On one side is the succinctly dramatic phrase, "The Dead of 1704." On the opposite side, it states, "The grave of 48 men women and children, victims of the French and Indian raid on Deerfield. February 29, 1704."

There's not much else to say about this monument. The historical element of it is very much outweighed by the sheer morbidity of it. I mean, walk into any graveyard and you're standing above lots of dead. The ground is sown with them. Stand on this point of Deerfield Cemetery, though, and it feels as if the world is made of the dead.

Of other macabre interest in the cemetery is a single, simple headstone

located near the entrance on the opposite side from the Deerfield Massacre memorial. It is the grave of Mary Harvey, the wife of Simeon Harvey, who died at the age of 38 in 1785, along with her stillborn infant son who is buried with her.

That is the information communicated in the epitaph of the headstone at least, but at the apex of that tombstone is a far more expressive image. In the place that would normally be reserved for an angel or a pair of praying hands or some other such symbol of comfort, is a coffin is on its side, with the upper portion open to reveal the rudimentary image of the upper half of a woman and a small child, forever at rest together in their coffin bed.

All graveyards are memento mori, but the Deerfield Cemetery, with its mass grave and its monument to the tragic bond of a woman and her child, seems a bit more memento of the mori than most.

# Grave of Sarah Ware
## Bucksport, ME

THE HUMAN RACE has a long tradition of murder. Actually, we have a long tradition being aghast at murder, and then being fascinated by it. Murder fills our history, our fiction, and our news stories. Heck, even the Good Book couldn't go four chapters without having one. Of the untold numbers of bloody murders that the Earth has had to absorb into its brimming soil, only a small percentage is remembered throughout the ages. The reason for the remembrance is sometimes random, other times due to the fame of the victim or the infamy of the killer. Often the context plays a part.

However, one of the best ways to have a murder stick disconcertingly to posterity is for it to go unsolved. And that's why the residents of Bucksport, Maine, still remember the murder of Sarah Ware.

Other than the glaring fact that no one was successfully brought to justice for it, Sarah Ware's murder actually offers very little intrigue. In September 1898, the 52-year-old divorcee was walking home from a friend's house when she disappeared. Two weeks later, her body was found decomposing in a field, her head bashed in and almost completely severed from her body.

Investigators eventually found a bloody tarp and hammer that seemed to be the round peg for the round hole in Ware's skull. The implements belonged to a store owner named William T. Treworgy. That plus the testimony of a man named Joe Fogg who claimed to have been paid by Treworgy to move Ware's body was enough to send him to trial . . . where he was acquitted when the witness recanted his testimony and, some say, the murder weapon was lost. Nothing further came of the case. One strike and they were out. Nothing left to do but bury the body, which, like the investigation itself, also went awry.

Ware's final resting is Oak Hill Cemetery at the intersection of McDonald and Franklin streets in Bucksport. Her headstone can be found in the Ware family plot at the back of this small cemetery.

In a final bit of grisliness to punctuate the general grisliness of the case, Ware was actually buried without her head, the skull of which remained in evidence lockup for 100 years before finally being buried near that head-stone, supposedly reunited with her body. However, there seems to be some uncertainty whether her headless corpse was actually interred in the spot marked by her headstone or moved somewhere else by the family of the violently deceased. It's a niggling uncertainty compared to her unsolved murder, though.

The small, white stone that marks at least the location of her skull is over-shadowed by the row of vegetation that demarcates the back edge of the ceme-tery. The stone itself merely bears her name, the date of her birth, and the date of her death, which looks completely innocuous in that context. Death dates on tombstones rarely tell stories. All in all, it's certainly the type of grave for someone who should've been forgotten by history. Instead it's her membership card in a tragic club of people who won't be forgotten for a very long time.

# Josie Langmaid Monument
## PEMBROKE, NH

PEOPLE REACT IN DIFFERENT WAYS TO TRAGEDY. The people of Pembroke, New Hampshire, were so appalled at their particular brush with it that they decided they wanted all of us to be similarly appalled . . . in perpetuity.

In October 1875, 17-year-old Josie Langmaid was savaged, killed, and decapitated (in no particular order) while hurrying alone through a wilderness shortcut on her way to school. Her body was found later that night in the woods. It took a little more time and effort to find her severed head.

The killer turned out to be a nomadic Canadian-born workman-for-hire named Joseph LaPage. Despite being a family man, LaPage apparently had a few history books' worth of violence on the shelf of his life, including one other possible murder in the neighboring state of Vermont, and was pretty much the kind of guy that makes you want to throw out the bathwater, the baby, and the bathtub when it comes to the human race.

LaPage was eventually officially convicted of the crime. Two years after Josie's death, LaPage was executed at the end of a rope in the state capital of Concord.

The people of Pembroke then erected a tall granite obelisk memorial to Josie at the location of her death. So far, so civil. However, instead of remembering Josie as she was, they decided to remember Josie as she ended up. In addition to the normal platitudes one would expect of a memorial of this nature ("Death lies on her like an untimely frost upon the sweetest flower of all the field") and a second inscription that gives more detailed information,

including the fact that she was murdered, a third inscription gives precise directions to the pair of nearby locations where her body and head were found, I guess in case anybody wanted to honor her memory with a CSI reenactment.

On top of that bit of TMI, in each of those two macabre spots are set simple granite posts. The first, representing the bloodied stretch of sod where her body was found, is easily discovered only 90 feet behind the memorial. The second, which marks the piece of forest where her head was found is, according to the memorial, "82 rods north." I'm not sure how far a rod is, but it might as well be equivalent to 10 light-years. After a bit of bushwhacking through almost impassably tangled undergrowth, I gave up looking for it.

The memorial is located on the side of Academy Road, directly across from Three Rivers School. Her actual grave can be found in her family plot in Buck Street Cemetery on Pinewood Road, just a street or so away from the marker. LaPage was buried, as well, but the whereabouts of his gravesite is obscure to the point of being nonexistent. Much like the second granite post, I gave up on this bit of information, too. In his case, the research isn't worth the effort for the information.

# Birthplace of Ted Bundy
## BURLINGTON, VT

SOMETIMES IT'S SAD when a grandly aged historic location is bulldozed for a blandly constructed commercial building. Other times, it's pretty easy to be okay with it. For instance, the birthplace of Ted Bundy.

Not everyone knows that Norman Borlaug is credited with saving billions of people from starvation, but we all know that Ted Bundy was one of the more notorious serial killers in U.S. history. His nationwide animalistic rampage extended throughout most of the 1970s. At his capture, he confessed to the rapes and murders of more than 30 woman, some of them as young as 12 and 13. Of course, you can't trust a serial killer, so the actual number is unknown. After a decade in prison, he was put to death on January 24, 1989, by means of the electric chair. The stench of his sizzled flesh still wafts within our culture.

Although such a fiend might seem hell-sprung, he was actually woman-born like the rest of us. In Bundy's case, it was in a women's shelter in Burlington, Vermont, on November 24, 1946. After he was conceived out of wedlock by a father who then disappeared, his mother, Eleanor Cowell, fled to the sanctuary of the Elizabeth Lund Home for Unwed Mothers, a large Victorian-style house located at 346 Shelburne Road that had housed the Lund Home since 1893, back when it was called the Home for Friendless Women.

After his birth there, Bundy was brought up by his maternal grandparents in Philadelphia, Pennsylvania, although he was raised to think that they were his parents and his biological mother was his sister. He eventually learned the truth, and although that revelation can seriously hurt someone's good day, it still doesn't go even an inch toward explaining his vicious crimes.

A couple of decades after the birth of Bundy, the Elizabeth Lund Home for Unwed Mothers built a new building on a different part of their property at 76 Glen Road, renamed itself the Lund Family Center, and has prospered greatly in its mission of helping troubled women and children live healthy lives.

These days, Shelburne Road is a busy commercial strip, although a few old homes do still line it here and there. The 346 Shelburne Road site, though, is now the location of a six-story, multitenant office building, set like a giant tombstone on the spot where the original house once stood. The property still backs up to the new Lund Family Center site that is accessible by Glenn Road.

For me personally, the existence of street sludge like Bundy makes me imagine God puzzling over a set of upside-down cosmic blueprints and saying, "What did I miss here?" After all, with a face, an education, and a seemingly well-adjusted life that makes you suspect everyone of being a serial killer, Bundy adds quite a few variables to the whole problem of evil that humanity always seems to be trying to solve on its collective blackboard regardless of whatever cultural advances we take pride in. And even though the Lund Family Center moved sites for completely practical reasons, I like to imagine otherwise. I like to imagine that it was part of the process of razing the ground, and that the act of erecting a mundane office building on the spot was an attempt to drain any possible meaning from it. It's very Biblical. Like sowing accursed land with salt.

# Boston Massacre Site and Mass Grave
## BOSTON, MA

IN BOSTON MATH, five deaths equal one massacre. And while "Boston Massacre" is a great name for a momentous historical event the remembrance of which is meant to last as long as there's a country to print history books about itself, in this case I think it's pretty much just iffy word choice. I mean, the term *tragedy* can stretch like a gym full of 18-year-old yoga enthusiasts to encompass everything from sports accidents to genocides, but *massacre,* well . . . massacres take mass. Possibly acres of it.

On March 5, 1770, during the fomenting unrest that would soon yield the American Revolution, five people died as a result of a mob scene in downtown British-occupied Boston. Granted, all five were civilians, all five would have probably fallen under the aegis of U.S. citizenship had it had happened six years later, and all five were killed by armed foreign soldiers, but still . . . hardly a massacre, and for reasons beyond mere number.

Not to go all Tory, but I think I might side with the Brits on this one. Imagine a violent mob of 350 angry, projectile-chucking, tax-hating brawlers and rabble-rousers bearing down on your vastly outnumbered group of duly authorized men in the middle of the night. I mean, sure, the soldiers were armed better than the rioters, but just with single-shot muskets. You don't get to make warning shots with those.

Things escalated, confusion and chaos ensued, shots were fired in what could legitimately be seen as self-defense on the part of the Britons, and in the end five civilians were dead and 345 were not. See? Not exactly a massacre . . . except to propagandists like Paul Revere, who sold misleading engravings of the event mere weeks after its occurrence. I mean, it's not like the soldiers leveled a submachine gun at a crowd of peaceful students and protestors or spent a lifetime skinning and eating teenagers in a dilapidated Texas home.

And it's not just me. Voluntarily representing the eight soldiers and captain who were singled out and put on trial for the colonial deaths was, among others, John Adams, a patriot leader and future second president of the United States. All eight were found by the jury to be not guilty of murder in the first degree, while two were found guilty of manslaughter, the penalty for which was a mere branding of the thumbs.

Of the five victims, Crispus Attuks is the only name really remembered due to the fact that he was a black man, or possibly a man of mixed race.

At least, that's what the history books say. Of course, this ignores the way more obvious and powerful reason that he simply had an outlandishly cool name.

There are three major sites in Boston connected to the Boston Massacre. The first is, naturally, a traditional memorial. Located on the Tremont Street side of the Common, a few blocks away from where the event occurred, the statue depicts a robed woman in front of a pillar with various symbols of liberty and freedom from tyranny incorporated. Beneath her is a brass relief version of the aforementioned Paul Revere engraving.

More interesting is the actual site of the Boston Massacre, which is located in front of the Old State House on State Street. It's basically a large round grouping of cobblestones with a star in the middle set in a concrete median. A plaque on the side of the Old State House is the only place that points out that the site is anything but a random piece of concrete and worth crossing traffic and risking another massacre for. Each year on the anniversary, the event is reenacted on the spot.

Most interesting, is the final resting place of the five victims, located in the historic Old Granary Burying Ground at the intersection of Bromfield and Tremont streets, right on the Freedom Trail. For some reason that I assume to be political, they were all buried in a mass (acre) grave under a single headstone listing the names of the five victims. Interred with them was a sixth, and some believe the first official, martyr to the cause . . . 12-year-old Christopher Snider, who had been shot by a Loyalist less than two weeks before the Boston Massacre.

Despite my cynicism about some of the jingoism surrounding the event, that doesn't mean I'm not basking in the aftereffects to which this tragedy contributed. After all, it did help us escape dread British tyranny and, even more dreaded, having to learn the rules of cricket.

# James Allen's Book of Skin
## BOSTON, MA

THERE ARE FEW WAYS TO MAKE A BOOK bound in human skin creepier. But how about for that skin to have once covered the skeleton of a convicted felon . . . and for the book to be his autobiography?

In horror stories, books bound in human skin are as common as mass paperbacks at a used bookstore, but rarely does one come across them anywhere in real life. However, you can find an actual human-bound volume in one of the most hallowed libraries in Boston, Massachusetts.

The Boston Athenaeum as an entity dates back to 1807 and its current location, just off Boston Common at 10½ Beacon Street, to 1849. Besides being an historical site, the massive stone building is a working independent library. Much of it is only open to dues-paying members, but the first floor and exhibition galleries are open to the public, as are the regularly organized tours of the facility that the Athenaeum hosts.

In one of those areas not open to the public, in the Special Collections Department, is the self-penned and self-wrapped story of James Allen, also known as George Walton, also known as Jonas Pierce, also known as James H. York, also known as Burley Grove. All those aliases should be enough to tell you that Allen was a criminal. In fact, he was a highwayman. It's all in his book . . . if you can get past the front cover.

Born in Massachusetts in 1809, Allen spent the few days allotted to him in life between serving jail sentences and doing things throughout New England and Canada that warranted serving jail sentences. One of his first crimes was breaking into a store on the corner of Charles and Beacon streets . . . just a couple of blocks from where his hide-bound autobiography is kept now.

He died of tuberculosis at the state prison in Charlestown in 1837 at the age of 27, but not before he recorded his life and then somehow arranged for the account to be bound in the skin of his own back after he died. As a result, his body was donated to medical science, according to the law at that time, while his skin was secretly donated to literature.

Apparently Allen had enough back skin for two copies. The first was given to his attending physician, Dr. Henry Bowditch. The second was given to the one victim of Allen's who stood up to him during a robbery, John Fenno, whom Allen would have killed were it not for the random deflection of his bullet off Fenno's coat button.

There's actually a long history of anthropodermic bibliopegy in human culture. Most often the hide comes from criminals to wrap around confessions, as was the case with Allen, but there are also examples of medical cadavers wrapped around works of science, priests around theological tomes, dissidents around political treatises, and sometimes just people with a flair for the dramatic, around their own biography. As you can see, there is almost an aesthetically appealing thematic quality about it.

After being granted permission by the Athenaeum to see Allen's book, I arrived for my appointment. Once there, I had to sign in and get escorted to an upper-floor reading room, where the book was laid in front of me in a hinged black case while a librarian stayed within 5 feet of me at all times.

It was a step-back moment for me. There I was, sitting in a private room in an exclusive 200-year-old library, a "guest researcher" badge clipped to my lapel and a book bound in human skin laid out inches from my hand for my visual inspection. If I hadn't been typing my notes on a laptop, I'd have felt like a character in an old horror story.

I had been told in advance that, due to the deteriorating binding, I wouldn't be allowed to touch the book (no skin-on-skin contact), which is of course the first thing I wanted to do. The librarian did, however, provide me with some supplemental materials and the full text is available on the Athenaeum's Web site. Seeing the book with my own eyes, the book definitely

doesn't look creepy . . . there's no way for the naked eye (and, I assume, hand) to tell that it's bound in anything but socially acceptable animal hide. According to the story, even the bookbinder didn't know it was human skin . . . it had been tanned and disguised to look like deerskin.

The book is smaller than a standard sheet of paper and about half an inch thick (Allen led a succinct life). The cover is faded and of a color light enough to be almost colorless, with various stains (who would be eating while reading this?) and worn places here and there. A small black rectangle with a gold-embossed Latin phrase, HIC LIBER WALTONIS CUTE COMPACTUS EST, adorns its cover, which loosely translated, I think, is either, "Stop touching me," or "A little to the left." Actually, it translates to something along the lines of, "This book is bound in Walton's skin," with Walton, of course, being one of Allen's aliases. The title found inside the book is *A Narrative of* [insert all the aforementioned aliases], *the Highwayman. Being his Deathbed Confession to the Warden of the Massachusetts State Prison.*

It is unknown which of the two previously mentioned copies of the book is the copy that the Athenaeum holds, nor exactly when the volume entered the collection. However, it is believed to be Fenno's volume, donated by his daughter to the library sometime before 1864.

Besides redefining the term *autobiographical,* Allen's work seems like a smart bit of legacy marketing. He should have died anonymous and despised for his life of crime. Instead, his story lies in a revered spot alongside some of the rarest works of literature. Crime doesn't pay, but binding a book in your own leather apparently does.

# Great Boston Molasses Flood Marker
## BOSTON, MA

THE IDEA OF A 15-FOOT-HIGH, 160-foot-wide flood of molasses flowing down the street of a major American city does more than border on the hilarious . . . it shares a four-lane highway and a thriving trade industry with it.

But it happened . . . and it was far from funny.

On January 15, 1919, a towering wall of thick, brown syrup poured down Commercial Street in North Boston at an estimated 35 miles per hour, killing 21 people and injuring another 150.

The 2.5 million gallons of molasses burst from a defective 50-foot-tall storage tank on an unseasonably warm winter day at the nearby Purity Distilling Company. The ensuing wave was powerful enough to destroy buildings and toss automobiles as it inundated two city blocks and stained Boston

Boston Molasses Flood

On January 15, 1919, a molasses tank at 529 Commercial Street exploded under pressure, killing 21 people. A 40-foot wave of molasses buckled the elevated railroad tracks, crushed buildings and inundated the neighborhood. Structural defects in the tank combined with unseasonably warm temperatures contributed to the disaster.

Harbor for months afterward.

Among other things, the event is called the Great Boston Molasses Flood of 1919, but that seems unnecessarily specific to me. After all, I can't believe that such a tragedy was ever repeated in the annals of human history. Actually, the fact that it happened even once makes me rethink a few of my views on reality.

I know I started this entry out amused, but the thought of men, women, children, and animals writhing in deep tar pits of sticky brown goo, trapped beneath the crushing weight of the flood and suffocating as the viscous liquid filled their mouths and noses, is absolutely the stuff of nightmares. Certainly mine will be molasses-flavored for the rest of my days, even as my conscious thoughts are evermore haunted by the phantoms of molasses-glazed dead men.

The company that owned the tank was eventually found liable for the architectural deficiencies of the structure, although from the sound of it they deserved more than mere reprobation and fines. They deserved infamy. Apparently, the company had gone so far in the past as to paint the large storage tank brown to disguise its many leaks and then attempted to divert attention to their culpability immediately after the disaster by blaming bomb-planting anarchists. Then again, I'm thinking that a deadly tidal wave of molasses is a difficult thing to foresee, even if you're in the business.

These days, the tragedy is commemorated by a small green plaque with white letters at the entrance to Puopolo Park on Commercial Street, although it is one of the few sources to describe the height of the wave as being 40 feet tall. Honestly, when you've got a story like this one, you don't need exaggeration to tell it. The plaque faces Commercial Street and is set in a low stone wall along the street near the baseball fields.

I don't know about you, but I come away from this story knowing full well that I will never be able to use the phrase, "What a way to go," for anything else ever again.

# Cocoanut Grove Fire Plaque

BOSTON, MA

ON THE EVENING OF NOVEMBER 29, 1942, a nightclub in Boston, Massachusetts, called the Cocoanut Grove burned to the ground. A total of 492 people were killed. Entire cities have burned and killed fewer.

When Christianity needed an eternal torment, they could think of nothing worse than fire. History itself is hellish with decimating flames. The three mentioned in this section of the book have a total mortality of 760. Most of that number comes from the Cocoanut Grove fire, one of the worst fire disasters in not just New England, but in the entire country.

The Cocoanut Grove was located on 17 Piedmont Street in downtown Boston. It was tropical-themed, with all the flammable decorations that go along with that. It was a popular place. On that cold November night there were around 1,000 occupants, about twice as many as the official capacity allowed. There were soldiers on furlough from the ongoing World War II, a pair of newlyweds celebrating their matrimony from earlier in the day, a party of undertakers looking to get away from dead bodies for the night, and movie star Buck Jones was making an appearance. His final one, it turns out. The final one for a lot of people.

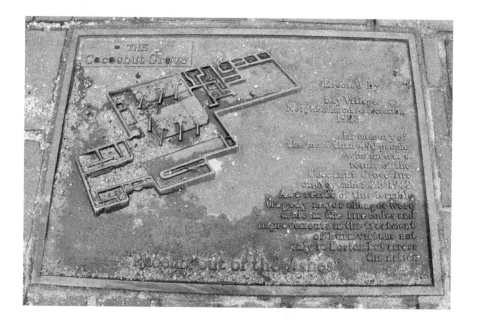

The fire began in the basement, in what was called the Melody Lounge. According to the accounts, a busboy was trying to tighten a lightbulb that had apparently been loosened by a soldier looking for some privacy with his girlfriend. While trying to rescrew it, the bulb popped out, and to see the socket better, the busboy struck a match. That's all it took. A match and a fake palm tree.

Still, more of the tragedy could have been averted had better safety precautions been taken in advance. The main entrance was a single revolving door, the worst type of exit for a mass stampede. Windows were boarded up and other doors were bolted shut for various reasons that dated back to the time when the club was a speakeasy.

There were a lot of stories that night, too many to recount in just a few hundred words. There were ironies, close calls, heroic deeds, but mostly there were tales of sorrow, grief, and pain. In the end, nearly 500 people died from burning, trampling, smoke inhalation, and all the other demons that ride along with every fire. More would have died if the local hospitals had not have been well stocked and trained as part of the war effort.

The club's owner was eventually found guilty of involuntary manslaughter and sentenced to 12 to 15 years, of which he only spent four due to cancer, dying from it mere weeks after his release.

However, if there is a silver lining to that horrible, viscous cloud of black smoke that stained the Boston sky that night even darker, it's that the tragedy caused a overhaul to fire codes and their enforcement across the country, ensuring that uncountable future tragedies were averted.

Boston has only a single square foot of space dedicated to memorializing the massive loss of life from the Cocoanut Grove fire. A small bronze plaque is inset into the red brick of a sidewalk outside of a parking lot near where the club once stood, created by the youngest survivor of the tragedy, Anthony P. Marra. The plaque bears a schematic of the club layout with seven palm trees, an explanation of the fire, and the phrase, "Phoenix out of the Ashes." According to the plaque, it's a reference to the changes in fire codes and advances in burn treatments that occurred as a result of the tragedy. In this particular case, I think, "Salvage from the Wreckage" might've been a more accurate epitaph. Or maybe just "Ashes."

# THREE

# Horror Movie–
# Filming Locales

A S IF THE WORLD didn't naturally have enough evil, dread, and terror in it, many often seek it in their movies as well. And I'm assuming that includes everyone who is reading this, plus myself. Actually, a more accurate way to phrase that first sentence is that because the world so naturally accommodates evil, dread, and terror, we need for it to be dealt with in our movies, as well. Thus, the horror genre of film.

When the filmmakers of Hollywood scuttle across the borders of their native California to find other sources of visual and cultural character to serve as physical locations for their stories, one vein that they mine regularly is the unique offerings of New England. Especially for horror films.

The reason for that is pretty much elucidated on every page of this book and involves history and climate, age and influence. But the short of it is that New England is just an ideal place to set a scary story.

And many of them have been filmed here. These movies include stories of witches and warlocks, psycho killers and monster sharks, vampires and voodoo, ghosts and gypsy curses. It's as if it's the rare monster that doesn't feel at home in the mise en scène of New England. Horror stories taken from the pages of such writers as Ray Bradbury and John Steinbeck and then directed by such legends as Tim Burton, Stephen Spielberg, and Wes Craven have all called New England home. And famous actors and actresses such as

Jack Nicholson, Bette Midler, Harrison Ford, and Nicole Kidman have all enacted or suffered horrors on New England soil.

In selecting the movie locations listed in this section, I tried to stick to movies that made prominent use of New England towns, buildings, and landmarks in their filming, and not just as B-unit shots to establish place . . . although I did make exceptions when I really wanted to write about a particular movie.

Regardless, this section offers the opportunity and directions for an intense movie marathon followed by a spectacular New England road trip. Or, at least, just a good read (I hope) when you have some time to kill between movies.

# *Beetlejuice* (1988)
## East Corinth, VT

L EAVE IT TO TIM BURTON to create a New England ghost story with a calypso soundtrack. And to make shrimp cocktails both hilarious and terrifying.

In the 1988 comedy *Beetlejuice*, the Maitlands, a recently deceased couple played by Geena Davis and Alec Baldwin, find their house "haunted" by the very much alive Deetz family that buys it after their death. Frustrated with the bureaucratic morass of the afterlife and their own inability to scare the family off their property (despite the handy *Handbook for the Recently Deceased* they're given), they call a bio-exorcist, an entity skilled in the removal of the living . . . and they call him three times.

Beetlejuice. Betelgeuse. Beetlejuice.

Burton's strikingly original movie owes half of its success in popular culture to its director's unique visual sense and the other half to the energetically vile performance of Michael Keaton as the black-and-white-stripe-suited Ghost with the Most—a phrase I have not heard in too long a time. (I plan on remedying that with the next person I see and hope they pay it forward.)

Although the film takes place in Connecticut, it was actually filmed in Vermont, in the town of East Corinth, right on the New Hampshire border. The main street that bisects the town takes you by most of the featured locations. The town's Mason Hall stood in for Lydia Dietz's schoolhouse, a general store stands in for a hardware store, the town library makes an appearance ("Nice building . . . bad roof . . . goooood parking"), and the whole town is shown in the usual overview, as well as in a custom-made scale-model version that plays a prominent role in the film. As to that town model, it has long been Internet-rumored that it was given to the local library after filming, where it was put on display. However, after inquiring at the library, I was informed otherwise.

The movie includes two locations in particular that you're going to want to find if visiting East Corinth for this reason. The bridge where the Maitlands die still exists, but was given a makeover to become the picturesque covered bridge seen in the movie. In real life, the actual bridge is not only not covered, but is just a handful of planks and a pair of guardrails . . . hardly worth a death scene. It can be found on Chicken Farm Road, close to where the street intersects with Village Road. Be careful going over it.

The second location doesn't exist, unfortunately. The delightfully mashed-up 1980s Victorian-style house where most of the movie takes place and which is featured on the (then) VHS box and (now) Blu-ray case was specially constructed on-site for the film and was mostly just façade anyway. The hill where it was built, however, can be seen on the main road at the southern edge of the downtown area. A closer view of it can be found off Jewell Lane, which is basically a glorified driveway to the farm where the hill stands.

As you can tell, the filming of *Beetlejuice* didn't really leave any kind of mark in East Corinth. But then again, most of the most iconic shots happened in the afterlife, and there's only one way to see that. Be sure to consult the handbook after you go.

# Dark Shadows (1966–1971)
### NEWPORT, RI, AND NORWALK, CT

SOAP OPERAS HAVE LONG BEEN A DISPARAGED GENRE in our culture for all kinds of valid reasons. However, the short history of television has shown that there is a way to make soap operas cool . . . stuff them full of monsters.

On June 27, 1966, ABC debuted a new kind of daily serial. The darkly atmospheric program began with the story of an orphaned governess who had found employ at a spooky mansion in a small town on the Maine coast. The show was called *Dark Shadows*. You can find it under *D* in the cultural phenomenon encyclopedia.

*Dark Shadows* tells the tale of the Collins family at the Collinwood Mansion in Collinsport, Maine. The mistress of the mansion, Elizabeth Collins Stoddard, was a recluse whose husband had mysteriously disappeared years earlier. She was played by Hollywood star Joan Bennett, whose grave is included elsewhere in this book.

Once the gothic atmosphere had been set, *Dark Shadows* eased its audience into the idea of a monstrous soap opera with a few ghosts and a mysterious phoenix woman. However, a year into its run, it exploded with popularity when it introduced an unlikely star . . . a sympathetic centuries-old vampire named Barnabas Collins, played by an even more unlikely 42-year-old Canadian stage actor named Jonathan Frid. After his debut on the show, Barnabas Collins became a legitimate television icon, complete with screaming teenage girls. After that success, the show's producers ushered in a line of zombies, werewolves, witches, and ghosts, among other dark souls . . . every creature one needs for a melodramatic monster mash.

And while the show retained all the elements that made soap operas laughable (and somehow successful), the supernatural context freed the stories up to go in new, surprising directions, including time travel, parallel universes, and all the twists that a simple dash of monsters can add to a recipe. In addition, due to the low budgets and grueling daily schedule, the show was filmed with an Ed Wood–type disregard for flubbed lines, equipment intrusions, and all kinds of things that ended up making it more endearing than amateurish.

Finally, after five years and a staggering 1,225 episodes, *Dark Shadows* ended its original run in April 2, 1971, and was replaced by a game show.

However, as a testament to the level of acclaim it achieved over more mundane soap operas, *Dark Shadows* birthed two movies. The first, *House of Dark Shadows,* was released in 1970, and the sequel, *Night of Dark Shadows,* in 1971, the year of its demise.

The show took place in Maine, but the exterior of Collinwood Mansion was filmed in Newport, Rhode Island, famous for its many gigantic mansions. A large sprawling castlelike edifice currently known as the Carey Mansion was chosen. The image of this mansion introduced episodes and was used as a transition between scenes, sometimes in black-and-white or silhouette, and then when the show went color, in washed-out, fog-enshrouded tones . . . and always with the signature high-pitched and unnerving theme song playing.

Carey Mansion was built in the 1920s, and incorporated parts of another building from 1885. Sections of the original building were supposed to have been transported from France and Washington, D.C. It's located on Ruggles Avenue, near a section of the Cliff Walk in Newport. The mansion is privately owned and, in recent years, has been leased to Salve Regina University and used as an academic facility and student dormitory.

For the two movies, a mansion in New York was used. However, some scenes in *House of Dark Shadows,* which followed a continuity outside that of the series, took place at the 62-room Lockwood-Mathews Mansion in Norwalk, Connecticut. It was here, in fact, that a much more vicious movie version of Barnabas Collins met his end . . . in that continuity, anyway. This 1868 mansion resides in a public park called Mathews Park on 295 West Avenue. It was also featured as the Stepford Men's Association building in the 1975 horror film *The Stepford Wives.*

*Dark Shadows* always seems on the brink of entering back into popular consciousness, with television syndication, comic books, and various themed merchandise available even to this day, as well as an attempt at a revival series in the 1990s. In addition, a Hollywood movie is currently on the horizon (the one either before you or behind you, depending on when you're reading this), directed by Tim Burton and starring Johnny Depp as Barnabas Collins.

*Dark Shadows* was a strange and unique phenomenon. I mean, there are soap operas that have run continuously for decades that aren't as beloved. We just like our shadows dark, I guess.

# *Flowers in the Attic* (1987)
## IPSWICH, MA

THE TOPIC OF INCEST IS REVOLTING, taboo, harmful to the genetic pool and, apparently, full of dramatic potential.

The 1987 film *Flowers in the Attic* tells the story of four siblings imprisoned and mistreated in an attic by their mother and grandmother. Believe it or not, it's a very short road that gets them there.

At the untimely death of their father at the beginning of the film, the Dollanganger children, who are all extremely blond and all extremely tender toward one another, are forced to move in with their maternal grandparents . . . who are extremely wealthy and extremely estranged from their daughter. It turns out, the patriarch of the family never approved of the man his daughter married (for good reason), and for his newly widowed daughter to get back into his good graces (i.e., will), he must not learn of the existence of the children.

Quite sensibly, then, they're hidden in an attic, where they're neglected by their mother, slowly poisoned, and constantly abused by their grandmother, who is played by Louise Fletcher in another Nurse Ratched–type performance in another type of cuckoo's nest.

I've ignored specifically pointing out the incest plot points both to keep from ruining certain surprises and to avoid giving you the impression that the movie is a vulgar redneck-fest, since it isn't. In fact, the movie is only softly incestuous. I actually almost wrote *tactfully incestuous* there, but the phrase creeped me out. As a result, you could watch this movie with your own family members without feeling too uncomfortable.

Believe it or not, this gothic horror film with the sadly evocative title was actually panned as not being incestful enough because it wasn't true to the much more overt source material, a 1979 book of the same name by V. C. Andrews, who also has a brief cameo in the movie.

I, personally, don't have a gauge for how much incest belongs in a story, so I'll focus on the filming location. Almost the entire story takes place in the palatial estate of Foxworth Hall, which in real life is actually the palatial Crane Mansion on Castle Hill in Ipswich, Massachusetts. The mansion was used as the exteriors for Foxworth Hall and can be found at 290 Argilla Road.

Incidentally, the Crane Mansion also played the part of the palatial estate of Jack Nicholson's diabolical character in the 1987 film *The Witches of Eastwick*. Oh, the salaciousness that place has fictionally seen.

Built in 1928, the 59-room Stuart-style mansion was erected by Richard T. Crane Jr., a wealthy businessman. The entire estate currently sits on 165 acres and is a national historic landmark open to the public for a variety of activities.

It's a beautiful building, both inside and out. Most mansions are, I guess. When I visited, there was a public art show on the first floor of the mansion, for which the usual fee for entrance had been waived. The estate around the Great House, as it is called to differentiate it from the other buildings on the property, contains rolling hills, gardens, a trail system, Atlantic Ocean beach access, and various other attractions. Everything that a poor man could want and a rich man must have. Worth pointing out specifically is a pair of large black griffin sculptures located behind the house that were created by Paul Manship, whose most famous work is probably the golden *Prometheus* statue at Rockefeller Center in New York.

Although the Crane Mansion is a grand place well worth touring, picnicking at, or using as a filming location, I doubt I'd want to be imprisoned for a year in one of its attics with my sister. No matter how hot she was.

# *Friday the 13th, Part 2* (1981)
### NEW PRESTON AND KENT, CT

ONE MOVIE BEFORE HE FOUND THE HOCKEY MASK that helped him find himself, and one movie after his mother bore all the slashing and heavy lifting, Jason Voorhees made his official debut in *Friday the 13th, Part 2*.

Released in 1981, just a quick and dirty year after its predecessor, the story takes place five years after the events of the original. Like the first movie, *Part 2* still involves the systematic, consonant-soundtracked, and gory deaths of a bunch of barely supervised teenage camp counselors. This time, however, the film features a grown-up, plaid-shirted, backwoods, sack-headed Jason as the killer.

A few familiar faces from the first film return for this sequel. Jason's previously decapitated mother makes appearances as a flashback, a hallucination, and a preserved corpse head. Crazy Ralph returns with more of his patented doom-predicting . . . and to die. Alice, the sole survivor of the group of counselors from the previous movie, comes back to establish continuity . . . and to die. The rest of the characters are newcomers, though, fresh and ready to train for their summer jobs . . . and to die.

The first movie was filmed in New Jersey, but this time the moviemakers decided to make Jason a New Englander and moved filming up a couple of states to western Connecticut in the neighboring towns of New Preston and Kent.

The few buildings that make up downtown New Preston show up near the beginning of the movie. It is here that the couple that ends up jointly speared postcoitus (with the *Friday the 13th* films, it's easier to reference most characters by their manner of death instead of their names), make a phone call, meet Crazy Ralph, and are pranked by a tow truck. The town hasn't changed much in the past 30 years. A couple of the buildings have been repainted or changed businesses, and the prominent Exxon station is gone, but it's still pretty much instantly recognizable.

Elsewhere in New Preston was the casino where some of the counselors hung out and conversed drunkenly about the possibility of Jason, while the counselors that stayed back at the lodge got gutted by the reality of him. The casino was the Lake Waramaug Casino, located on West Shore Road, but it burned down a year or two after the filming. These days, a house occupies the spot.

This time around, Crystal Lake is played by North Spectacle Lake in the town of Kent, and most of the rest of the movie is filmed in the area. Packanack Lodge, the centerpiece of the film, was actually a 65-year-old hunting lodge (95 years old, these days) and can be found on Kenmont Road, which circles the lake.

In this modern era of *Friday the 13th* remakes, the lodge is now a private residence and, according to the welcomingly painted sign at the end of its gated driveway below the unwelcoming NO TRESPASSING sign, it's called Laurel Ledge. Located at 164 Kenmont Road, the building itself isn't visible from Kenmont, which is variously unpaved and wends through Kenwood/Kenmont Camp, so you can't see it unless you trespass or possibly go in the depths of bare-treed winter. However, if it pleases the court, I suggest holding off on risking frostbite or arrest just to experience a filming location from a movie with a sequel number after it.

# *Ghost Story* (1981)
## WHITE RIVER JUNCTION AND WOODSTOCK, VT

T HERE'S NOT A WHOLE LOT TO SAY about the 1981 movie *Ghost Story*. It's a ghost story, certainly, if a relatively unremarkable one at that, despite the fact that I'm going to try to wring 500 words of remarks from it. In this case, the movie's inability to evoke anything more than ambivalence is particularly unfortunate because the film has such a strong cast. It stars Fred Astaire, John Houseman, Douglas Fairbanks Jr., and Melvyn Douglas, all respected

veteran actors, as well as the delightfully enigmatic, creepy, and often nude (at least in this movie) Alice Krige.

Based on a book by Peter Straub, the story centers on the Chowder Society, a group of four lifelong friends in their golden years who dress in tuxes, meet regularly, drink brandy, and exchange ghost stories . . . exactly the way retirement should be. Eventually, and I supposed it's not much of a spoiler to reveal this plot point, they become embroiled in one when a group secret they have kept for 50 years starts affecting those close to them.

The most memorable part of this movie are the great makeup effects by Dick Smith, who is responsible for some of the best makeup in cinema, including for *The*

*Exorcist* (in which a head spins) and *Scanners* (in which a head explodes), as well as such impressive nongenre fare as *The Godfather* and *Amadeus*. In *Ghost Story*, he's tasked to render multiple versions of a living, decayed corpse, and each one is worth at least one rewind while watching the movie. (Is "rewind" still the correct term in this digital age?)

Still, with such positives as the cast and the special effects, the story's still a bit too scattered and uneven for it to be a good film, with half of it being made up of long flashbacks, and not enough of the story focusing on the present-day Chowder Society.

All averaged out, the movie's not the type to incur such interest to make you want to rush out to see where it was filmed; however, the scenery in the film is also great, being set mostly in snowy Vermont, and filmed there, as well.

Besides a few scenes set in Florida and New York, the rest was filmed in the Vermont towns of White River Junction and Woodstock. The Woodstock location was the more central one, with its downtown area featured prominently, including a statue of a Civil War–era soldier that is used as a visual reference point throughout the film.

On the day I visited Woodstock, tourists were everywhere in this picturesque little town, visiting the quaint shops and restaurants that line the main street, which changes names every other block but is basically Route 4. Of course, only one of those tourists was looking for a soldier statue for its appearance in a ghost movie, and you're reading him.

The town seems to have moved the statue since the filming, though. A comparison of movie footage and Google Street View reveals that in the movie it was centrally located right at the intersection of Elm and Central streets. When I went, that location featured merely a streetlight and a median. However, I did find the soldier statue at the end of the main street. It had been given a higher pedestal at the intersection of Central and Pleasant streets, on a bit of green toward the quieter end of the downtown. It's a Civil War memorial, dedicated to all those in the area who "served in the army and navy of the nation in the War of the Rebellion of '61 to '65."

Back to the film: Despite *Ghost Story*'s flaws, it's still great to be reminded of a time when film stars were older than 25, as well as comforted by the fact that there are not more scenes of full-frontal naked men plummeting out of buildings in the world of cinema.

# *The Good Son* (1993)

CAPE ANN, MA, AND JACKSON AND NEWINGTON, NH

IF HORROR FILMS ARE TO BE BELIEVED (and why wouldn't they be?), then our children really will be the death of us.

*The Bad Seed* in 1956, *Village of the Damned* in 1960, *The Omen* in 1976, *Children of the Corn* in 1984, *Joshua* in 2007 . . . it seems as if no decade has been able to avoid having projected onto a big screen the deep-rooted fears we have of kids.

In 1993, it was Macaulay Culkin's turn to make us regret settling down and raising a family.

Fresh and fresh-faced off a pair of Home Alone movies, Culkin was ready to stretch his prepubescent acting chops with *The Good Son.* In it, he plays Henry Evans, a demented boy who secretly terrorizes his Maine family and openly terrorizes his cousin, played by Elijah Wood, with all sorts of mayhem, including fratricide, canicide, and whatever else adults would never believe an innocent young child with a strangely measured diction could do.

*The Good Son,* although a pretty hackneyed idea by this point in cinema history, is still almost worth the watch for the mere reason that it showcases some amazing scenery, having seemingly been filmed in what could only be the most beautiful parts of Nevada, Minnesota, and New England.

The astounding desert parts of the film took place in Nevada; the cliff that was central to the plot arc was actually filmed in Minnesota and then made to look like an ocean cliff through the magic of movies; and the rest was filmed in New England—specifically, New Hampshire and Massachusetts.

The Jackson area in New Hampshire surrendered up its Mirror Lake to play the part of a frozen pond for Henry to attempt to add sororicide to his list of crimes. Two hours south in Newington, New Hampshire, is the Route 16 overpass where Henry threw "Mr. Highway" into traffic, causing a pretty violently filmed 10-car, no-fatality accident.

The Cape Ann region of Massachusetts featuring prominently throughout the movie, including the towns of Rockport, Annisquam, and Marblehead, each of which, like the three Wise Men of old, offered up their treasures for a child, even if the Wise Men chose their child a little better.

Rockport donated to the movie the visual of the Peg Leg Inn on 2 King Street, which stood in for the psychiatrist's office. (There always needs to be

a psychiatrist on hand in any demented child film.) Annisquam gave the film the Evans house and the harbor that is the downtown area of the film. In Marblehead, the historic Old Burial Hill on Orne Street was the cemetery that contained within its borders the well where Henry stashes first his cigarettes and then, later, a crossbowed dog corpse. The well is still there, although these days it's used a flower box instead of a body disposal unit. There's enough body stashing going on in the rest of the cemetery.

Anyway, after witnessing yet another member of this large subgenre of horror film, all I can say is thank God for the brain-rotting and soporific effects of television, or the fiend apparently present in every precious and softly skulled noggin of our children would be totally out of control.

# *Hocus Pocus* (1993)
## SALEM AND MARBLEHEAD, MA

BETTE MIDLER WILL ALWAYS BE A WITCH TO ME, and it's all because of her role in the 1993 Halloween film *Hocus Pocus*. And even though I don't think I've seen another Bette Midler movie in all the thousands of films that I've seen and stored in all the places of my brain where knowledge is supposed to go, *Hocus Pocus* is enough to make me visit her grave when she dies. Actually, that's a forward-looking statement, so don't hold me to it. I can definitely say, though, without fear of my shareholders, that *Hocus Pocus* is at least enough to make Bette Midler a part of my Halloween traditions.

This Disney film tells the tale of a trio of witches known as the Sanderson Sisters, who are played by Bette Midler, Sarah Jessica Parker, and the other one.

The three aging crones are magically imprisoned during colonial times for attempting to ensnare children for use in a spell to regain their youth, but are then accidentally resurrected in modern times by a virgin with a black-flamed candle. Besides witches, the film has a zombie, an enchanted talking black cat, and the requisite Halloween costume party.

While obviously not a horror film, *Hocus Pocus* is one of those workable Halloween kids movies, the kind you need to have running while you carve pumpkins and await trick-or-treaters, or if you're just generally as disturbed by a switched-off television as I am.

The film takes place in both colonial and modern Salem, Massachusetts (mostly in the latter), so the filming crew decided to film in both colonial and modern Salem. Someone gets paid a lot of money to make those kinds of decisions. By modern Salem I mean, well, just Salem, and by colonial Salem I mean the Salem tourist attraction known as Salem 1630: Pioneer Village.

As with pretty much every single movie production, most of the interiors and such were shot in Los Angeles. The house exteriors that were shot on location in Salem, though, include the homes of both Allison and Max, the teenage protagonists in the film. Specifically, Ropes Mansion on 318 Essex Street, a large historic white house with black shutters operated by Salem's Peabody Essex Museum, stood in for Allison's house; and a less notable but still unique house near Forest River Park stood in for Max's. Salem Common and the defunct Phillips elementary School were also used as a park and a high school, respectively.

The beginning of the movie featured a witch-on-broomstick's view of colonial Salem, which as I mentioned is actually a reenactment attraction in one of Salem's coastal parks. Nothing says, "automatic production value for a period piece" like a reenactment attraction. Most states have them. Massachusetts has a couple. This particular one is a recreation of Salem (natch) at the time of the Salem witch trials (double natch). In the attraction's heyday, it featured period buildings and live actors speaking Old English, dressing in black wool, and doing whatever people did before they had Bette Midler movies to watch. These days, the attraction is open infrequently (it had been completely closed for many years), but you can still see the buildings through the fence that surrounds it in Forest River Park at the end of West Avenue. The series *Bewitched* filmed here, as well, about two decades earlier.

So if you want to see Bette Midler in a distracting mouth prosthetic over-acting with all her fellow cast members and singing the old Screamin' Jay Hawkins standby *I Put a Spell on You*, this movie's for you. If you want to see two Bette Midlers in the same movie, you're looking for '80s gem *Big Business* . . . it's an aisle or two over in Comedy.

# *The House by the Cemetery* (1981)
## Scituate and Concord, MA

JUST BECAUSE AN '80S ITALIAN HORROR MOVIE was filmed in the state of Massachusetts doesn't mean it had to omit all the trademarks of that sub-genre, and *The House by the Cemetery* (or *Quella villa accanto al cimitero*) has all the requisite bad dubbing, high-intensity gore, and blatant laxness of plot to firmly place its country of origin as the boot-shaped one that cools its heels in the Mediterranean.

It won't take a horror fan long to recognize the infamous work of Lucio Fulci, one of the stars in the Italian horror firmament, whose renown is mostly derived from his willingness to dive headfirst into over-the-top ensanguined scenes, much to the consternation of various international ratings boards. And *The House by the Cemetery*, although not the most disturbing example of his work in this regard, is still no exception.

*House* is the story (I think . . . I've seen it a couple of times and could still be wrong) of a New York researcher who moves his family to an old house (by the cemetery) in the fictional town of New Whitby, Massachusetts, to continue the work of a recently deceased colleague who killed himself after living in that same house (by the cemetery).

The house is a large, ooky bit of architecture whose front lawn is mostly scattered headstones from some old, tiny cemetery. All kinds of confusing and nonsensical horrors occur once they move in, including a ghost child full of halfhearted warnings, a strange and eventually beheaded nanny, an immortal mad scientist named Dr. Freudstein who leaks maggots, an excruciatingly long bat attack sequence, half a dozen locked-in-the-basement scenes, and all manner of scenarios that end in dark red pools of blood.

I'm not going to lie to you. There are 3.2 million problems with this film. The one strong point, however, is the house itself, with its unique architecture and woodsy New England setting.

Most of the town exteriors for New Whitby were filmed in Concord, Massachusetts, but the titular house itself can be found in the coastal Massachusetts town of Scituate, about 30 miles southwest of Boston and 50 miles southwest of Concord.

The house is part of a town-owned historical property called the Ellis Estate and is set on 120 acres of publicly accessible forest and trails. Located on 709 Country Way, it is set back from the main road, accessible by a dirt track that wends through a forest veined with public hiking trails. Currently, the house is the headquarters of the Scituate Arts Association.

Unfortunately for us morbidly inclined, the cemetery surrounding the house in the film was fake, although the nearest cemetery, Groveland Cemetery, is less than half a mile away, so technically it's still a house by a cemetery. These days, although it maintains the same structural appearance, newer paint and a general not-in-a-cemetery-ness makes the house look a bit homier than its 30-year-old celluloid version.

Interestingly enough, Lucio Fulci wasn't the only Italian horror director to set a horror film at the Ellis house. Seven years after the release of *The House by the Cemetery*, the notorious Umberto Lenzi of *Cannibal Ferox* infame lensed *Ghosthouse* there (also known for underhanded marketing reasons as *La casa 3*). In that film, a dead girl and her doll terrorize and murder in grotesque ways any interlopers who dare set foot in her house.

As a result, although I can't say it's the most famous (ghost) house (by the cemetery) in Italian horror cinema, the Ellis house still has a snug place in its annals.

# *I Spit on Your Grave* (1978)
## KENT, CT

I'M OKAY WITH HAVING MY HEAD thrust occasionally into the horrible pig trough of humanity at its worst. It's one of the reasons I come to the horror genre. However, with the 1978 exploitation film, *I Spit on Your Grave* (a.k.a., *Day of the Woman*), you come out disgusted more with the movie itself than with the world.

I honestly wouldn't have minded skipping this movie's inclusion in this book, as horror culture itself should've initially skipped the film back in the '70s, but then I'd lose the opportunity for a diatribe. Actually, horror culture would probably have skipped it, itself, had the movie not received mainstream attention due to the fact that it was somehow released in mainstream theaters, giving it the chance for mainstream critics to pour their deadline-enhanced bile on it. And they should have. Unfortunately, the critics made the mistake of lambasting it mostly for its vulgarity, its obscenity, and its misogyny . . . all descriptors that get the attention of horror fans. Not because we're depraved, but because we are always up for a challenge. Horrify us. The critics should have just focused on how much the movie sucked, and then most of the rest of us would never have been tempted to watch it.

*I Spit on Your Grave* is the blandly filmed story of a caricature of a woman who is brutalized repeatedly in an extended scene by four caricatures of men, and then exacts her revenge in 50 parts seduction and 50 parts brutal murder, including castration, hanging, axing, and mutilation by motorboat propeller. Now, you shouldn't be able to "get" a movie from a single-sentence synopsis, but there you go. You also shouldn't be able to "get" a movie by watching it in fast-forward, but there you go again.

The movie was filmed in Kent, Connecticut, and the moviemakers thank the town in the credits. I'm not sure how many townsfolk would return a "you're welcome" to that. In addition to a shot at the center of town near the beginning of the movie, the three main locations in Kent are the lake house that the woman rents to write her novel, the church where she asks forgiveness for the atrocity that she's about to wreak, and the gas station hangout that pops up throughout the movie.

I couldn't discover where the gas station is located, but judging from its condition in the movie, there's a chance it probably doesn't exist anymore. The house, though, is the last one on Birch Hill Lane, a short dead-end strip of road that is barely such. It's not a lake house, but the side of the house faces a bit of wilderness, making it easy for the filmmakers to fake the location.

Church-filming locations are usually pretty simple to find due to their often being centrally located and having an Internet presence of some sort, whether they are still functioning as a house of God or a historical building. In New England, however, every other church is painted white and has a tall pointed steeple, and moviemakers often specifically choose these types of churches to quickly establish a New England setting. Fortunately, this film pretty much stayed within the confines of Kent, so it was easy to narrow down the options. The church used in *I Spit on Your Grave* is the First Congregational Church, located at 97 North Main Street.

In exasperated conclusion, what I want from a horror movie is to assault my sensibilities to keep myself from getting too comfortable with what I think I know about the world. I don't want the little bit of intelligence that I have assaulted. It's too weak to fight back.

# *In Dreams* (1999)
## MASSACHUSETTS AND NEW CASTLE, NH

*I*N DREAMS sounds like it would be the title of a romantic comedy, an uplifting fantasy, or one of those inspiring dramas based on a true story. It's not any of those, though. It's the title of a movie about a child killer.

Released in 1999, *In Dreams* is based on the 1993 book *Doll's Eyes* by Bari Wood, with the story altered substantially and renamed after a Roy Orbison song. The movie begins in the drowned town of Northfield, which had been flooded decades earlier to make a reservoir. The scene depicts in an exquisitely beautiful and exquisitely creepy fashion scuba divers swimming into cafés, above cars, and through graveyards. The scale tips decidedly to the creepy side, when it's revealed minutes later that these divers are looking for a missing girl.

Actually, beautiful and creepy is this movie in a poster blurb. Everything from a child's school play to an abandoned cider mill to a decrepit hotel is filmed to be both beautiful and terrifying. In addition, *In Dreams* goes to great length to ensure that *Snow White* isn't the only movie to make the apple a completely ominous symbol.

Directed by Neil Jordan and starring Annette Bening and Robert Downey

Jr., the story revolves around a woman whose psychic connection to a child killer tragically entangles her family and buffets her sanity. It's an easy plot to make trite, but, with *In Dreams,* Jordan and his actors create an unsettling, vivid, and compelling strip of horror film.

The film takes place in Massachusetts, and in the credits, the filmmakers thank the towns of Northampton, Easthampton, and Northfield, the last of which apparently wasn't drowned in real life under 2 billion gallons of water. They also specifically credit the Veterans Administration in Northampton and the Northfield Mount Hermon School in Northfield.

However, the credits list the movie as being filmed in Northampton, North Carolina, Tennessee, and at a studio in Baja, Mexico. No mention of the other two Massachusetts towns in that section of the credits, though other sources include even more filming locations in that state. At the very least, one particularly important filming location in New Hampshire was left uncredited, which I feel should be rectified. . . if a mention in a minor regional book about death-related sites counts as anyone's definition of *rectified.*

One of the more visceral scenes takes place in a giant, decaying ocean liner–shaped hotel on the coast. In the movie it was called the Carlton Hotel, and Annette Bening's character has a premonition of wandering around its decrepit grounds and interior to eventually find her dog eating the corpse of her husband in one of the rooms (see, not a romantic comedy). This hotel is the Wentworth by the Sea, which was built in 1874 and is located at 588 Wentworth Road in New Castle, New Hampshire, which is barely an island anymore. When *In Dreams* was filmed, the hotel was exactly as it was portrayed in the movie, abandoned and dilapidated. The peeling paint of the weedchoked exterior was the reality of it. However, since that time, it has been purchased by the Marriott hotel chain, refurbished, and reopened as the impressive resort hotel it once was.

Now, instead of a haunted inspiration for horror filmmakers, it's a vacation destination worth kicking back at while listening to some Orbison and making sure the dog is well fed.

# *Jaws* (1975)
## MARTHA'S VINEYARD, MA

SHARKS SHOULD HAVE ALWAYS TERRIFIED US to a maximum amount. But somehow it took a monosyllabically titled movie released in 1975 to make us really afraid of them.

With only a short television resumé and a Goldie Hawn movie under his belt, 27-year-old Steven Spielberg attacked *Jaws,* a film based on Peter Benchley's book of the same name. For the story, he needed a vacation island with nice beaches full of bikini'd bait to stand in for the fictional Amity Island. He chose Martha's Vineyard, an island off the coast of Cape Cod in Massachusetts.

For five months, Spielberg's film crew, with their 24-foot-long robot shark, took over the town of Edgartown on the island's west coast. The making of the movie and the sagas involved with filming on water with a malfunctioning shark at the height of Martha's Vineyard's very high tourist season has become as legendary as the film itself. Regardless of the effort it took to complete, the important thing is that the cinema world got *Jaws.*

Although the movie might have made people afraid to get in the water, it didn't scare them away from Martha's Vineyard. Now it's a pilgrimage spot for Spielberg and *Jaws* fans . . . as if folks didn't already have enough reason to go to this vacation island.

To get to Martha's Vineyard, you have to either fly or ferry, as no bridge connects it to the mainland. You can pay extra to bring a car over on the ferry, but the island is small enough to traverse with bicycles and the town's efficient bus service.

Edgartown, as well as the various other places on the island that the filming leaked over into, does less than you'd think to commemorate the fact that one of the landmarks of cinema was filmed there, and by *less* I mean nothing at all. Perhaps this is because no resort beach wants to be famous for a shark just as no park wants to be known for its ants, even if they are fictional and everybody has them in DVD version in their film collection. Still, it's not very work intensive to see all the specific sites. In fact, just visiting Edgartown is visiting *Jaws.* Many of the streets, stores, and houses of the downtown area made it into the movie.

However, one location in particular should be on any *Jaws*-themed itinerary. . . . Jaws Bridge. Actually called the less intriguing American Legion Memorial Bridge, as well as Big Bridge, it helps Seaview Avenue (also variously known as Beach Road and Edgartown Oak Bluffs Road) connect Edgartown with the town of Oak Bluffs and divide the Atlantic Ocean from Sengekontacket Pond. In the movie, the shark swims toward it for a few panicking shallow-water morsels. In real life, people just like to jump off it for kicks.

Despite its nickname, the bridge is a small one, just a few car lengths in total. In fact, we drove over it three times before realizing it was the bridge from the movie, despite the loud proclamations of, "You have arrived at your destination," from our GPS unit. Also complicating matters was that the bridge was under construction when we went. I guess they needed a bigger bridge. The stone quay that runs perpendicular to the bridge where Roy Scheider ran during the scene is there, as well, while the beach area on the ocean side, called Joseph Sylvia State Beach, was where the rest of the scene was filmed.

Although it's not there anymore, for the past three and a half decades a second must-see *Jaws* sight rotted on the shore of a pond on the opposite side of the island from Edgartown. The *Orca 2,* the stunt boat that stood in for the original *Orca* during the sinking scenes at the end of the movie, was left derelict on the shore of Menemsha Pond in Menemsha and could be viewed at a distance from the shore on the town side. It was also possible to get to the wreck, but, because it was located on private property and you had to have a boat or were willing to make a 40-mile round trip around the circumference of the pond, it was able to quietly decompose without too many souvenir hunters picking at its corpse. Only in the past few years did the owner of the property have the wreckage dismantled and completely removed.

Filming *Jaws* on Martha's Vineyard apparently worked out well enough, that, despite the fabled hardships, scenes from two of the sequels to *Jaws* were also filmed on the island. In the interests of comprehensiveness, I should cover those movies in this section as well, but in the interest of both your and my lack of interest in those films, I'll refrain.

You'd think that it wouldn't be too hard for pretty much any moviemaker to make sharks scary. Yet somehow, 35 years after its debut, *Jaws* has quite literally remained the last word in shark movies. There isn't even a second place in the category.

# *The Last House on the Left* (1972)
## Westport, CT

WHEN YOU FIND THE VERTIGINOUS STONE STEPS where was filmed the climactic scene of *The Exorcist*, you lie down at their base broken-boned and in need of last rites. When you find the biker bar from *Pee-Wee's Big Adventure*, you arm-dance to the brass-fueled strains of "Tequila." When you find any of the locations where they filmed Wes Craven's *The Last House on the Left*, you merely look shamefully at your shoe tips. At least, that was my reaction.

*The Last House on the Left* was released in 1979, during a pivotal time in horror film history when genre filmmakers started facing and portraying the unabashed brutality present in the world. This was the era of Tobe Hooper's *The Texas Chainsaw Massacre.* The era of George Romero's *Night of the Living Dead.* The era of William Friedkin's *The Exorcist* and Cronenberg's *Rabid.* Of those, only *Last House* was filmed in New England . . . Westport, Connecticut, to be exact.

I find it hard to call *Last House* a classic. Hard to laud it at all, really. It isn't the kind of movie that you marvel at and heartily recommend to your

Netflix buddies. The film is so brutal that this entry was almost more accurately filed in the "Infamous Crimes and Killers" section of this book than in "Horror Movie–Filming Locales." But it is a milestone in horror and holds an important place both for the reasons mentioned in the previous paragraph and because it was the film debut of the director who would go on to create Freddy Krueger and introduce *Scream* to a stagnating genre.

The film is based to the point of plagiarism on an actual classic, Ingmar Bergman's *Virgin Spring* . . . minus the spiritual paradox and redemptive beauty. In *Last House,* a group of fiends kidnap a pair of teenage girls and then do everything that can be done to someone weaker before ultimately killing them. Later, they find themselves taking shelter at the home of the parents of one of their victims, and the cycle of violence continues, with the fiends finding themselves lower down on the evolutionary tree.

The film has very few filming locations, none of which are really iconic of the film. Most of the movie takes place in either the woods or a single, ordinary house, but one that stands out a little is a cemetery. At one point in the action, one of the victims momentarily eludes her captors but is chased down, caught, and killed in a cemetery, which becomes symbolic of her own immediate and her friend's eventual doom, as well as being a way to break up the visually monotonous scenery of trees and dirt.

The cemetery that was used is called Poplar Plains Cemetery and can be found on Wilton Road in Westport. I doubt it has a street address, but it's located adjacent to 287 Wilton, just down the way from restaurant called the Red Barn. Although it's not out in the wild, there are enough trees around it to fake it . . . and there were even more back when *Last House* was filmed. It's a small cemetery, sparsely studded with old markers and surrounded by a low stone fence. Because it's such a tiny graveyard, it's easy to match up the individual stones with those shown in the movie (which is most of them), even after all these years

I wanted to see the house, as well, but couldn't find it, even after the explicit directions in the title of the movie. I guess it's just as well. You don't want to spend too much time in the world of *The Last House on the Left* . . . regardless of how horrifically well it might mirror our own. Also, those grapes are probably sour anyway.

# *Let's Scare Jessica to Death* (1971)
## Southern CT

WHEN I STARTED WATCHING *Let's Scare Jessica to Death*, I was afraid that for the first time in the history of cinema, a title would spoil the ending of the movie, that it would be the type of tale where all sorts of spooky shenanigans turn out to be caused by people literally trying to scare Jessica to death. It would be kind of like titling *Carnival of Souls* as *She Died in a Car Accident* or *Psycho* as *He Thinks that He's His Mother* or *April Fool's Day* as *April Fool's Day*. Okay, second time in the history of cinema.

Fortunately, that wasn't the case with this 1971 horror film. Unfortunately, the eye-catching title also had nothing at all to do with the movie itself. *Let's Scare Jessica to Death* is the story of a woman, recently released from a mental ward, who with her husband and a friend has just bought a house out in the country and is attempting to start a farm. Soon, Jessica begins to see strange things and hear voices, and eventually doesn't know whether she's crazy or if the place is haunted. Turns out, neither is the case. The area's infested with vampires. (It's not a spoiler if the movie is 40 years old.)

The film is rather bland in parts, but does sport a nice hippie sheen that

doesn't get too annoying, as well as a few solid scare scenes that might be worth a random night in the DVD player. For instance, I never realized how under-utilized gaffer hooks are as implements of violence, or how spooky a bass case really is, like a cross between a coffin and an iron maiden.

*Let's Scare Jessica to Death* was filmed in a few towns on the shore of the Connecticut River in southern Connecticut. For instance, the prominently featured intersection of Main and Maple streets, where all the strange VFW-types hang out, is located in the town of Chester Center.

The old Bishop House, with its unique and old-fashioned architecture, is the centerpiece of the movie and the most worth finding. It's rather prominent, located off a major highway, but is still extremely hidden for all that. It's just off Middlesex Turnpike, somewhere around address 230 between Interstate 95 and Reservoir Road in the town of Old Saybrook. It took me a while to find the tiny, weed-choked, almost secret driveway that really has no business coming off a turnpike in the first place.

However, I didn't stay too long in that driveway. When I visited, the house seemed abandoned and overgrown to such a degree that it was actually much scarier than it was in the film. And I visited during the day. To cap it off, a NO TRESPASSING sign was placed in a location blatant enough to get its message across in no uncertain terms: "You will be consumed by cannibals if you linger."

However, across the highway is a large car dealership, and from its parking lot there is an excellent view of the house, with its distinctive tower that looms above the tangled trees on the little rise that is the reason you can't see it from the lower-set highway. As a result, you could live your whole life in that town and not know the house is there, or you could buy a Kia on a single visit there and be in the know from day one.

The interiors of the old Bishop House were filmed elsewhere, at the E. E. Dickinson Mansion on 34 North Main Street in the nearby town of

Essex, and I assume the graveyard featured in the movie is also in the general area of those towns, but I didn't really look for it. New England has so many cemeteries just like that on every corner, it really should reconfigure its economy to make the dead one of its larger exports.

So let's scare Jessica to death? Sure, why not. Also, I realize that *April Fool's Day* was filmed a decade and a half after *Scare Jessica*. I'm okay with messing up timelines for punch lines.

# *The Serpent and the Rainbow* (1988)
### BOSTON, MA

W HEN YOU'RE MAKING AN AUTHENTIC-LOOKING voodoo film on location in Haiti, there's really no reason to film any scenes in Boston, Massachusetts . . . unless the protagonist in your film is being sent to Haiti with the backing of a large pharmaceutical company, in which case the headquarters would probably be located in that city.

Such is the case with Wes Craven's 1988 *The Serpent and the Rainbow*. The company is called Boston Biocorp, and the protagonist is an anthropologist played by Bill Pullman, who is being sent to Haiti by the firm to find a rumored compound that can "put somebody in and then back out of death," not realizing in the naive epoch of the late 1980s that corporations messing around like this is how zombie plagues start. Fortunately (or unfortunately), it never really comes to that, as the company is basically forgotten about once that plot point is established, with the movie from then on focusing on Pullman's own personal odyssey into the darkness and terror of voodoo.

Horror movies are notorious for claiming to be based on true stories, and *The Serpent and the Rainbow* is no exception. In this case, the claim centers on the fact that the story is an adaptation of the published account of a Harvard scientist who investigated anesthetics in Haiti. The film industry kind of has a minimal standard when it comes to what it designates as a true story, though, so I'm pretty sure the verity of this one stops at "voodoo is practiced in Haiti."

Anyway, *The Serpent and the Rainbow* has all the stuff you'd hope would be in a movie about voodoo, including cryptic rituals, the walking soulless, wild

hallucinogenic sequences, and multiple live burial scenes. None of which, of course, happen in Boston.

The one scene filmed in Boston was basically just an establishing shot. Or at least should have been, except that the moviemakers went ahead and filmed Pullman there as well, walking across the camera lens for a good five seconds on his way to Boston Biocorp's headquarters. The shot has Pullman sharing a frame with the famous Trinity Church and its neighbor, the 60-story glass-paneled John Hancock Tower, where the pharmaceutical company head-quarters is fictitiously located.

This architectural odd couple is located in Copley Square, a well-traveled Bostonian plaza where people get the opportunity to simultaneously marvel at two very different and equally impressive types of architecture, a centuries-old church and the tallest building in New England.

It's actually a good shot, albeit one that's always there for tourists to see, but it does make one pay more attention to it as opposed to just seeing the usual second-unit shots of Boston landmarks. I mean, not to overanalyze a movie in which an eyeless corpse in a wedding dress shoots a python out of her mouth, but the 140-year-old Trinity Church, with its 280-year-old parish, dark stone exterior, clay roof, gargoyles, and various sculptures not just juxtaposed against the sleek, modern façade of John Hancock Tower, but actually reflected mirror-perfect in its glass panels, is kind of exactly what this movie is all about. Well, that and zombies.

But I think you know what I mean. The old versus the new, tradition versus extradition, religion versus commerce. Yup, in the time it takes for somebody to look at their watch and wonder, "When are they getting back to the voodoo?" Craven succinctly sums up his whole movie in a single image.

Or maybe he just needed a cool, quickly identifiable shot that screamed "Boston" louder than naming the company Boston Biocorp.

# *Session 9* (2001)
## DANVERS, MA

IT WAS NIGHT-PLUS-CLOUDS DARK, and the tropical storm that had been moving steadily up the East Coast all weekend was fire-hosing whitewater rapids all over my windshield, rendering it almost opaque instead of just the usual dirty. The bald tires of my car were doing their best to achieve the only cool verb they could on the skim of water that covered the road, and my usual night blindness that's bad enough to kick in even during the day was making everything look like I was driving through hyperspace. I had as many appendages as I could spare on the wheel, and I was squinting to the point of flattened eyeballs and ejected contacts and hoping that none of the wavering red lights in front of me were brake lights.

I was on my way to watch a horror movie. More than that, I was on my way to watch a horror movie on the very spot where it was filmed. More than that, I was on my way to watch a horror movie on the very spot where it was filmed, which happened to, in the past, have been in this order: an insane asylum, an abandoned insane asylum, a movie set, and an apartment complex.

That's right. Once it was a place where lobotomized patients shuffled in white slippers down never-ending corridors, the criminally insane drew caricatures of old victims on the walls with crayon stubs, and trembling lunatics gibbered alien syllables into slobber-drenched pillowcases. Now it's a suburban luxury apartment complex complete with swimming pool, fitness center, and billiards lounge, all within easy commute of Boston.

The Danvers State Hospital in Danvers, Massachusetts, was completed in 1878 during the big sanitarium boom of that century. Also known as Danvers State Insane Asylum, Danvers had a central administration building with two staggered wings that made the entire construct seemed shaped like a "giant flying bat," to quote the horror movie I've yet to name except in the header.

The building was red-bricked, many-gabled, and set like an evil queen's castle on the crest of Hathorne Hill. At its most crowded, Danvers housed 2,400 inmates plus support staff, whose main jobs were to care for the insane. This care sometimes included shock treatment, hydrotherapy, prefrontal lobotomies, and whatever else was the latest fashion of the psychiatric community.

Eventually, the second law of thermodynamics set in for most of the sanitariums from that era, and the conditions of these giant asylums worsened due to budget cuts, the basic expense of keeping such expansive things running, and general overcrowding. Most of them shut down after a century or so. Danvers lasted until 1992, although it had been experiencing death spasms regularly over the preceding years.

For the next decade, Danvers sat decaying on Hathorne Hill like a stubborn, cancer-ridden vulture, daring the state to put its crumbling interiors to some purpose other than as a playground for urban explorers and fodder for local spook stories. Meanwhile, it grew to a new height of popularity over its sister establishments when the horror movie *Session 9* was filmed within its rotting halls in 2000. This was the movie I was going to see at the apartment of a friend who had recently started renting at Danvers.

Starring David Caruso during the limbo between his *NYPD Blue* and *CSI: Miami* phases, the film is a solid and subtly unnerving story of strange events that befall a small crew of asbestos removers preparing a long-abandoned asylum for demolition. Danvers Insane Asylum played itself in the movie.

In its current incarnation as an apartment complex, most of the original building and its outliers are now gone. The only relics that are preserved are the façade of the iconic main building, a wooden gazebo-like structure, and a cemetery . . . of the dead Danvers insane. I know. Sounds like a badly translated Lucio Fulci film title. But just because they were lunatics doesn't mean

they didn't die and need to be buried, and somewhere in the neighborhood of 700 to 800 of the unclaimed ones had been interred on the grounds.

The cemetery is certainly not as spooky as one would think a boneyard of dead lunatics would be. There are no old headstones set at jarring angles or broken-open mausoleums harboring ghouls or ex-patients who just can't leave, and I didn't see one giant rat. Instead, it is nicely kept, with a few trees, a low stone fence running along two sides, and stone plaques inlaid into the ground with the name and date range of the interred. In the center of the graveyard is a stone bench that faces a trio of commemorative stone markers with plaques listing all the names of the dead that could be found in the asylum's unfortunately incomplete records.

Of course, that's during the daytime, and, even though I have visited the cemetery during the day, I had to also drop by after we finished watching the movie at my friend's apartment (located in the area that would have been encompassed by one of the sanitarium's bat wings), even though that put me out there sometime around the witching hour. After all, nothing opens the sinuses like standing in the middle of the night in a cemetery filled with the dead insane during a rainstorm after watching a horror movie that took place on that exact spot.

# Something Wicked This Way Comes (1983)

## Northern VT

JUST ABOUT EVERY blood-drenched horror aficionado has, still surviving within them, a dark child characterized by a strong affection for the innocently spooky, and sometimes those dark children escape from their basements demanding sustenance . . . or else. To keep those dark children satisfied, we've been feeding them on a diet of Ray Bradbury literature for decades.

Disney's 1983 *Something Wicked This Way Comes* is notable foremost because it's based on the Ray Bradbury classic of the same name. In fact, the screenplay for the film was also written by Bradbury, and even with the usual heaping helping of studio meddling, it still managed to be one of the darker Disney children films ever made.

In *Something Wicked,* a strange carnival run by a mysterious Mr. Dark comes to Green Town, Illinois, in early autumn, setting on course a series of events that force a pair of 12-year-old friends to quickly learn how to navigate that ominous space between carefree childhood and soul-crushing adulthood, while an aging father, whose soul has long been crushed, learns how to mount over its debris. And all of this while the three of them combat the supernatural evil that the sinister carnival hides.

Although a weak shadow of its literary inspiration, the Disney adaptation ranges from passable to delightfully Bradbury-esque in various parts, often due to the period and seasonal setting of the film. The studio custom-built the 1930s town of Green Town on a large outdoor set at Walt Disney Studios in California and then, to capture the Illinois that every Bradbury fan has visited so often in his or her imagination, shot all the establishing exteriors in . . . New England. Still, they did shoot those exteriors in the autumn, and a New England autumn can be absolutely Bradbury-esque, as well.

The establishing shots were all filmed in northern Vermont, in the rural areas of Waterville, Morrisville, and Jeffersonville. Unfortunately, the filmmakers often combined those shots with matte paintings, so it's difficult to determine exactly where the shots were taken. Although that's not much of New England connection to include in this chapter, *Something Wicked* is the

only chance I've got to invoke Ray Bradbury in this book, and that's just something I really wanted to do.

Waterville, Morrisville, and Jeffersonville are all located near one another, right above the more famous Vermont town of Stowe. As a result, regardless of the movie that featured them, they make for a fantastic autumn road trip full of soft hills covered in colorful foliage, quaint towns with bright white churches in their centers, farm stands with autumn delectables, and everything else you need for the season.

It might seem kind of strange that in putting together a book filled with horror, atrocity, and morbidity like the one you're now reading, I'm featuring two Disney films made for children. Truth is, when it allows itself to access it, Disney has a pretty deep dark streak somewhere underneath all the fairy dust and princess arias. Of course, the other movie I'm referring to is *Hocus Pocus,* which actually isn't really all that dark in comparison with *Something Wicked,* and I'm sure you've already skipped over that entry for more interesting ones. That's okay. *Something Wicked,* though, you're going to want to rewatch, whether you have dark children of your own to share it with these days or you still must keep your inner one fed.

# The Stepford Wives (1975)
## DARIEN AND NORWALK, CT

Y OU KNOW WHAT MOVIEGOERS found scary in 1975? Primly dressed housewives who cook well and sexually satisfy their husbands.

Billed philosophically in its trailers as a "very modern suspense story," *The Stepford Wives* is about a balding husband, a defiantly bra-less wife, and two minor plot points who move from the crowded, dirty high-rises of

Manhattan to the sprawling paradise of suburbia that is Stepford, Connecticut, only to discover a few shades of darkness that even New York City at its blackest must strive to match.

Actually, as you already know, it's about a lot more than mere suspense. It's a story about the loss of identity, gender relations, family roles, the price of perfection, the perils of reveling in our flaws . . . oh, and spooky automaton women with grocery carts.

Based on a book by Ira Levin, who also wrote the novel upon which the film *Rosemary's Baby* was based, this film is pretty creepy no matter what your gender, although one of the flaws of the film might be that it's too far a horror story for women and too far an escapist fantasy for men, when the basic idea is fully capable of being equally horrific to both.

Regardless, the idea behind *The Stepford Wives* is such a compelling one that it's hard to mess up completely (unless you're Nicole Kidman and Frank Oz), and as such has become an instantly recognizable cultural metaphor, even 35 years later, outliving even the recognition of its casting of Ginger from the one-time popular culture touchstone *Gilligan's Island.* I'm assuming current generations are losing touch with that stone, at least.

*The Stepford Wives* was filmed in an area of southwestern Connecticut that, with its lavish houses, high-end shopping, and general New England picturesqueness, needed its own special adjective. *Stepford* fit that high-priced bill nicely.

Two locations in particular stand out from the usual run of house exteriors normally filmed in any movie. The first is the strip mall that makes a few key appearances throughout the story. Named through some quirk of reality the Goodwives Shopping Center, it's located at 25 Old Kings Highway in the town of Darien. Its appearance and retail tenants have changed over the years, of course, but it still has a supermarket, although it's now a Shaw's instead of the Grand Union shown in the movie.

The second location is the ominous-looking Stepford Men's Association building. In real life, this extravagant castlelike building is the 62-room Lockwood-Mathews Mansion in Norwalk. Built in 1868, it sits in the middle of a public park called Mathews Park on 295 West Avenue and is open for tours. The mansion was also featured in the 1970 film *House of Dark Shadows,* based on the television series *Dark Shadows.*

The afore-referenced 2004 comedic remake of *The Stepford Wives* was also filmed in the same areas of Connecticut, including at the Lockwood-Mathews Mansion, but that's two more mentions than that film really should have, despite being directed by the voice of Yoda and Miss Piggy.

# Stephen King Film Adaptations
## Various Locales, ME

IF IT WEREN'T FOR STEPHEN KING, Maine's representation in this part of the book would be a heck of a lot smaller. Actually, it would be nonexistent. However, because of Stephen King, Maine more than holds its own when it comes to horror filmmaking locations. And while it might be unfair to roll all these movies up into a single, albeit long, entry (especially when I dedicated whole entries to such celluloid wasters as *Warlock* and *I Spit on Your Grave*), there's just so many times I want to write the phrase, "Based on a Stephen King story . . ."

Now, Maine's not a preferred filming location by the movie industry, for a pair of major reasons. First, it's pretty much the farthest point in the country that you can get from the studio hub of Hollywood and all the supporting industries it takes to make a film these days. I mean, even Alaska and Hawaii are closer. Second, although Maine's harsh, snowy climate looks beautiful on film, it's also terrible to film in.

However, when the author is an international best-selling superpower who frequently sets his stories in Maine and then lobbies to have the movies adapted from those stories filmed in Maine, movies are going to be filmed in Maine.

## *Creepshow 2* (1987)

LIKE ITS BETTER-RECEIVED PREDECESSOR *Creepshow, Creepshow 2* is an anthology film based on Stephen King works. Whereas the original was directed by zombie legend George Romero and was based on a screenplay written by King, *Creepshow 2* merely featured a screenplay by George Romero based on some Stephen King ideas. Michael Gornick, who previous to this movie pretty much just directed a few *Tales from the Darkside* episodes and banged around Romero films in various crew roles, was the one who took over the director responsibilities for the sequel.

In it, the stories involve a murder-avenging wooden cigar mummy ("Old Chief Wood'nhead"), a black lake–dwelling flesh-eating blob and a raft of swimsuit-wearing college kids ("The Raft"), and a determined and ghastly hitchhiker with a penchant for saying "Thanks for the ride, lady" ("The Hitchhiker"). Stephen King cameos in this latter episode as a truck driver.

The scenes for "The Raft" and most of "Old Chief Wood'nhead" were filmed in Arizona, but "The Hitchhiker" was filmed in Bangor, along with some of the interiors for "Old Chief Wood'nhead." In addition, the main street of the town of Dexter, Maine, was used for some of the wraparound story, which involved a creepy newspaper delivery monster, a boy, some bullies, and a man-eating plant, the narrative of which was parceled out between and around the main tales.

## *Pet Sematary* (1989)

YOU DON'T WANT TO BE BURIED in a pet cemetery. One of the more famous film adaptations of Stephen King's work, this movie focuses on the lengths a father goes to bring his dead two-year-old child back to life. Those

lengths include digging up his child's grave and burying him in an old pet cemetery/Native American sacred ground, even though the father knows full well it will only bring back a crazy, demonic version of his child. If you're a parent, you understand. I guess.

Featuring a few creepy scenes genuinely worthy of your most violent wince, *Pet Sematary* had its most central scenes filmed in the towns of Hancock and Bangor. For instance, the red-roofed, yellow-sided house where most of the film takes place, and in front of which the aforementioned child violently dies at the grille of a tractor trailer, can be found at 303 Point Road in Hancock. It's still red-roofed and yellow-sided. Surreally, a CHILDREN AT PLAY sign is also posted across the street from it. There is no NO KITE FYING sign, though.

The human cemetery featured at various points throughout the movie is Mount Hope Cemetery on 1048 State Street in Bangor. It was here that Stephen King cameos in the movie as a minister presiding over a funeral. The exact spot can be found on the State Street side of the cemetery, right up against a steep hill with a stone staircase cut into it. It was on the side of that steep hill, to the left of a set of stairs if you're ascending them and around the vicinity of the Bragg plot, where the father single-handedly disinters his child.

I like a cemetery with some history.

# *Graveyard Shift* (1990)

IN *GRAVEYARD SHIFT,* the filmmakers turned the rather compelling image of a giant, legless, blind queen rat found in the 1970s-era Stephen King short story of the same name into a more pedestrian giant bat . . . and it's only in bad horror movies that a giant bat can be pedestrian.

The story involves a bunch of grungy textile mill workers who spend a few nights of overtime cleaning out the basement of their mill. They soon discover that the basement hides hordes of rats and a giant bat. Then they die. Stephen King doesn't cameo.

The coolest part about the movie is its location centerpiece, the Bartlett-yarns Mill in the town of Harmony. It's a 200-year-old mill that looks absolutely creepy even without having any connection to a horror movie. Seemingly located out in the middle of nowhere (in this case, nowhere does have an address . . . 20 Water Street), right on Higgins Stream, the mill looks abandoned, haunted, condemned, possessed, and every other related adjective that my thesaurus can throw at me. However, the mill is still in business, producing wool and wool products. I hope for their sake that they actively keep their basement clean.

# *The Langoliers* (1995)

THE ENTIRE THREE-HOUR-LONG MINISERIES *The Langoliers* pretty much just takes place on airplanes and in airports, but it's an interminable experience for more reasons than that. Featuring a crazy, paper-ripping Bronson Pinchot of *Perfect Strangers* fame and a bunch of time-chomping, trijawed, badly computer-generated Pac-Men (the titular Langoliers), the film tells the story of a group of airplane passengers who awaken midflight to find themselves in an empty plane, which they then land at an empty airport to discover that they've somehow experienced an unscheduled layover in the nether regions between moments of time. It's a lot like watching the miniseries from start to finish, actually.

The story was filmed predominately at Bangor International Airport, a single-runway, extremely limited-destination airport that, in reality, you'd still have to get yourself twisted up in a time rip to ever find yourself at. Stephen King cameos as a hallucination.

# *Thinner* (1996)

IN *THINNER,* an in-car middrive sexual favor causes the death of a jaywalking gypsy woman. As a result, the obese driver gets cursed by the father of the gypsy woman . . . to rapidly lose weight until he dies of emaciation. The dwindling protagonist eventually and violently wrangles the help of the gypsy, who can't quite remove the curse from the semiprotagonist, but can put it into a moral dilemma—causing strawberry pie. Because that's the way the universe works, I guess. Sounds like a comedy, but it really belongs in the genre of "Should have never been a movie in the first place."

If for some strange reason you ever need to know where it was filmed, the answer is all over Maine, including the towns of Appleton, Belfast, Camden, and Rockland. In fact, in the credits of the film, the producers "wish to thank" a sizeable list of very specific towns and businesses that were either used as filming locations or provided support for the crew in some way. Specific sites include the Augusta House of Pancakes at 100 Western Road in Augusta, the Whitehall Inn at 52 High Street in Camden, and the Knox County Courthouse at 62 Union Street in Rockland. Oh, and Stephen King cameos as a pharmacist named Dr. Bangor. You don't really care about this one, do you? Onward, then.

# *Storm of the Century* (1999)

STORM OF THE CENTURY is another of Stephen King's television miniseries, although this time, it's based on an original King screenplay and not on any of his previous works. In it, a mysterious supernatural stranger named Andre Linoge comes midblizzard to the snowbound island of Little Tall, kills random people, spouts meaningless catchphrases, and in general just acts mysterious and random.

Surprisingly, this movie is the only one of these Stephen King/Maine movies listed in this entry to feature snow, so it at least has that going for it, even when the snow is fake and falls like thin pieces of polystyrene foam and then stains white the shoulders of the actors' coats no matter how long they stay indoors. Nevertheless, I'm a big fan of stories that take place in the snow, and if the worst movie in the world took place in a snowstorm, it would still be fun to watch on a wintry night by the fire.

Filmed in a few non–New England places, including Canada and California, the Maine portion was filmed right in the center of the town of Southwest Harbor, a small locality outside of Acadia National Park on Mount Desert Island that, unlike the island it plays, is large, completely accessible by car, and a pretty big tourist destination. Stephen King cameos as a lawyer in a television commercial.

# *Warlock* (1989)
## PLYMOUTH, MA

I'M NOT SURE HOW OBSCURE the 1989 film *Warlock* is. I've never heard anybody praise it, blast it, or really bring it up in conversation . . . even when those conversations happen to be about movies starring male witches. Normally, I would definitely call that obscure, but the fact is, just about every video rental store I went to growing up had this movie in its horror section without fail. I know *Warlock*'s box cover better than I know my own wedding pictures, and those are hanging up in my house as I write.

*Warlock* was directed by Steve Miner, the man most famous in the horror genre for his involvement in the early Friday the 13th films, for which he acted variously as producer and director. In this movie, the titular character,

played by Julian Sands, escapes imprisonment in colonial Massachusetts through a portal that drops him out in modern-day Los Angeles. Well, late-1980s L.A., anyway.

Julian Sands's warlock is a bit different from other cinema witches. He doesn't wave magic wands, fly on a broom, or wear a conical hat. Instead, he bites out tongues, gouges out eyes, and skins children, all while trying to track down and unite the disparate pieces of a satanic book so that the Dark Lord himself will accept him as his son. Father issues can really take over a person's life.

Despite taking the easy way out by setting most of the movie in L.A. (except for the Boston ending that they obviously still filmed in L.A., despite the Celtics paraphernalia they tried to plant in the scene), the filmmakers did go on location across the country for the colonial Massachusetts prologue. All the way to the town of Plymouth, in fact, the site where the Mayflower pilgrims first came ashore.

And the reason they suddenly went all vérité despite their laziness in location scouting throughout the rest of the movie is because, located in Plymouth, is a ready-made 1600s village tourist attraction called Plimoth Plantation (colonial Americans were notoriously bad spellers) that easily doubles as a period film set.

Plimoth Plantation is featured in a scene that only goes on long enough to fit in all the opening credits. In it, a group of austere, black-clad Puritans walks down the center of a village road to a giant medieval tower wherein is imprisoned the warlock, in magic thumb and toe cuffs.

Located at 137 Warren Road, Plimoth Plantation bills itself as a living museum. This village reenactment showcases a working, peopled, and animal'd colonial village from the 1600s. Also, just down the path is a Wampanoag village from the same period that features actual descendants of the Wampanoag tribe, although according to the rules of the place, neither you nor they have to pretend that they're from another time as in the neighboring colonial village.

Your admission to Plimoth lets you walk around on your own, enter houses, and interact with the actors who portray the stuck-in-time residents. It can be about three times as awkward as you think, especially if you walk into a house and accidentally corner an actor when all you wanted to do was look around. I'm a pretty bad time traveler.

Because it's stuck in time, the village pretty much looks the same as when it appeared in *Warlock*. Thatched-roof buildings line a central dirt concourse, and people do salt-of-the-earth-type work while being followed around by sheep. However, instead of that concourse's leading to a stone medieval tower, it actually leads to the entrance of the village, which is a wooden fort full of cannons. If you've seen the movie, with its brazen 1980s special effects, it's not really a surprise that the medieval tower was added with special effects after this scene was shot.

If you've seen the movie . . . now, that's a surprise.

# *What Lies Beneath* (2000)
## CHIMNEY POINT, VT

**B**URIED SECRETS ARE SOMETIMES HARD TO KEEP BURIED. Especially when that secret is a dead body. Even more especially when that dead body wasn't buried in the first place.

That's probably about as much as I can say about the 2000 ghost flick *What Lies Beneath* without spoiling too much of the story, because there are a couple of plot twists. Then again, the movie is a decade old, so we're probably past the statue of limitations on spoilers. As a result, my conscience is completely guilt free when I say that in the end they all die in a horrible global nuclear holocaust caused by extraterrestrial invaders who play the alien equivalent of violins on Mars while they watch us burn to an orbiting cinder. Now you don't need to watch it.

Starring Michelle Pfeiffer and Harrison Ford and directed by Robert Zemeckis of, well, 4,000-big-budget-movies-starring-Tom-Hanks fame, *What Lies Beneath* is the story of a woman who is pretty sure that her house is possessed, although she's a little confused as to by whom or why. The film features a spooky bathroom, a red-herring neighbor, and, for some reason, tons of shots of Pfeiffer's bare feet.

According to the filmmakers, *What Lies Beneath* was an attempt to make a Hitchcock-style thriller with the added dimensions of ghosts and reality-impossible computer-generated camera shots. As a result, the camera goes in unique places, such as under bodies lying on the floor or through the doors of moving cars. Also, as a result, a lot of the scenes you think are on location are actually studio-shot with green screens and computer augmentation.

The movie takes place in Vermont, and most of the exteriors that weren't computer-generated were actually filmed there, with all the usual Los Angeles caveats. Most of the movie takes place in a house that was specially constructed by the filmmakers in DAR (Daughters of the American Revolution) State Park in Addison, Vermont. According to a "Making Of" feature included on the DVD release of the movie, the filmmakers wanted to create their own house because they wanted one specifically designed to look pleasant in the daytime, using regular camera angles, and then menacing in the nighttime with more skewed camera angles. I'm not sure whether that worked or not, but I do know that the house was torn down after filming.

Now, my next paragraph was supposed to start, "Although you can't visit the house, you can visit another nearby landmark that plays prominently in the film." It was a true statement when I originally conceived it, but circumstances have deemed it otherwise.

I'm referring to what used to be called either the Crown Point Bridge or the Champlain Bridge, an 80-year-old, 2,184-foot span that connected Vermont and New York and which was pretty much the only way to cross the southern end of the almost-a-Great-Lake Champlain without taking a ferry or training for the Olympic swim team. It was on this bridge (and its facsimile back in the studio) where the climactic scene of *What Lies Beneath* takes place, as telegraphed earlier in the movie by the not exactly subtle establishment of the fact that cell phone service only kicks in once you're halfway across it.

The Vermont end of the Champlain Bridge was located at Chimney Point, an unincorporated site within the town of Addison, Vermont, at the intersection of Routes 17 and 125. When we visited it on October 4, 2009, it was still there, although they had closed down one lane of the bridge for reasons I had no clue of at the time. Turned out it was for safety reasons. On October 16, mere days after our visit, we learned that the cautious powers that be had completely closed down the bridge due to erosion of its concrete piers, controversially stranding a lot of people on both sides of the enormous Lake Champlain.

Then, on a snowy day in late December, they actually destroyed the half-mile bridge in a massive controlled explosion that briefly left a ghost of the bridge outlined in black smoke before reducing the whole construction to mere empty air, debris-strewn water, and the memory of a Harrison Ford film. A new bridge is planned for sometime in 2011, but the new span will be just a mere bridge, not a movie artifact.

It's too bad. For what lies beneath lied beneath that bridge. Okay, that seriously was a spoiler.

# *The Willies* (1990)
## VARIOUS LOCALES, CT

THE STRANGE FEELING KNOWN AS "THE WILLIES" occurs at the lower end of the fear spectrum, somewhere between startled and spooked. Akin to and maybe even the same thing as "the shivers," the willies creeps up the ladder vertebrae of one's spine, causing a brief moment of panic to flood one's body in response to extremely minor stimuli, such as a spider's legs brushing against the back of one's hand or hearing a vague tale about some distant serial killer of crimes past.

And I assume it was this feeling that the makers of the 1990 film *The Willies* were going for.

*The Willies* is an anthology movie that involves a trio of boys telling one another various stories in a tent in their backyard. Some of the stories are extremely short, no more than urban legend anecdotes, really, and include a microwaved poodle, a Kentucky Fried rat, and a heart attack in a haunted house attraction.

The two main tales of the anthology that follow these nonappetizers involve a monster that preys on schoolyard bullies in a bathroom and the sometimes surreal tale of a glob of a boy obsessed with catching flies, killing them, tearing their wings off, and gluing them into dioramas of scenes from everyday (human) life.

Despite some legitimately creepy scenarios and special effects, the stories aren't well put together, unfortunately. However, the film does almost inadvertently succeed as a time capsule of the period. For instance, the film features cameos by two *Twin Peaks* alums, Dana Ashbrook and Kimmy Robertson. The David Lynch series debuted that same year, and both actors look as if they just dashed off its set in costume for their quick roles in *The Willies.*

The film also has a specially written *Growing Pains* segment starring Kirk Cameron and Traci Gold (Jeremy Miller, who played the youngest Seaver sibling in the series, actually plays one of the aforementioned schoolyard bullies in the film), as well as a *Goonies* joke at the expense of Sean Astin, who stars as one of the boys telling the stories. Appearances by such popular culture ephemera as High-C Ecto Cooler juice boxes and Garbage Pail Kids stickers are also included.

The movie was filmed in both California and Connecticut. Honestly, a lot of it was probably filmed in California, but the filmmakers did at least incorporate cut footage of various of the signature scenery of New England . . . old graveyards, covered bridges, white churches. As a result, most of it is pretty difficult to find with only screenshots and an entire state to explore. That is, except for the covered bridge.

Because the movie shot of it actually included the highway sign, it wasn't difficult to learn that the bridge was the West Cornwall covered bridge, which carries Route 128 over the Housatonic River. Built in 1864, this local landmark is 172 feet long and is on the National Register of Historic Places. That's pretty much all I have on this bit of bridge. I really just wanted to write about 1990.

In the end, the movie is definitely extremely minor stimuli, but it might be worth letting your child sneak downstairs after bedtime to watch. Fortunately, the willies rarely leave scars.

# *The Witches of Eastwick* (1987)
## NORTHEASTERN MA

GOD HAS NO CHANCE IN A WORLD where Jack Nicholson is the devil, and the devil has no chance in a world where his consorts are Michelle Pfeiffer, Cher, and Susan Sarandon.

Based on the John Updike novel of the same name, the 1987 film *The Witches of Eastwick* tells the story of three lonely women who on one martini- and pity-fueled night somehow accidentally conjure a mysterious stranger named Daryl Van Horne—not exactly an anagram for the devil, but close enough. Van Horne seduces, vixenizes, and impregnates them, and then is victimized by them in return. Meanwhile, all sorts of supernatural shenanigans transpire as the women discover their latent magical abilities and Van Horne unleashes his own special brand of witchery.

Plenty of exteriors and outside shots were used in this movie, and the majority of those are located throughout the east coast of Massachusetts. Even though the 1984 source material and the movie itself are set in Rhode Island, it does make a couple of kinds of sense to transplant the scenery to Massachusetts. Aside from the reputation that Massachusetts has for historical witchery, Pennsylvania-born John Updike had also by that time in his life chosen that state to be his own.

For the most part, the town of Cohasset, with its centrally located New England–white church and quaint business district, stood in for Eastwick. However, other locations throughout Massachusetts were used, as well, for both interior and exterior sets. These locations include Abbott Hall in Marblehead, the Wang Center in Boston, Milton Academy in Milton, and, prominently, the Crane Estate in Ipswich, which stood in for the Lenox Mansion in the film. Incidentally, this same mansion stood in for Foxworth Hall in the movie *Flowers in the Attic,* which I cover elsewhere in this section of the book. Because I discuss that location in detail in that entry, I'll focus more on the town of Cohasset itself here, and by focus, I of course mean include a few vague sentences about it.

The classic New England white church is actually Cohasset's first Parish Meeting House and was built in 1746. It's located on 23 North Main Street, and it, along with the stores and houses in the immediate area, served as back-

drop for some of the more memorable scenes, including the one where Van Horne, bewitched by his three companions, is blown down the street, across a lawn, and into the church by a hurricane of feathers before involuntarily spewing cherry juice while voluntarily railing against God and women in front of an aghast church congregation.

I've watched *The Witches of Eastwick* twice in my life, and, honestly, I still don't quite get it. It's not really a movie about witches, not really a movie about romance, and only kind of a movie about its actual characters. Maybe one day I'll read the book. When I do, in my head, Van Horne will still be Jack Nicholson; Cher, Pfeiffer, and Sarandon will still look hot; and, now that I've visited it, Cohasset will still be Eastwick.

# FOUR

# Notable Cemeteries, Gravestones, and Other *Memento Mori*

O UR DEAD WILL LONG OUTLIVE US. We only spend a small number of decades mobile, conscious, and getting excited about television line-ups. We spend centuries to millennia, however, in mounds, tombs, graves, crypts, or whatever your culture's preference is for disposing of empty canisters. There, in the darkness, we quietly molder to our basic elements or, if preserved by design or through random alignments of environment, await for that fine line between grave robbery and archaeology to be crossed.

For most of us, the only mark we'll really leave on this planet is a piece of rectangular stone above a human-size plot of grass. Sure, we'll have descendants, but they've got their own lives to attend to, and as the generations pass, our memory will be forgotten by everyone but the cemetery caretaker.

As a result, if you want to be remembered, it's almost better to have an interesting gravestone than to be an interesting person. And New England has had more than four centuries to collect a diverse range of remarkable cemeteries, tombstones, and other memento mori.

Although this section of the book does discuss some fascinating death-related sites other than graves and the cemeteries that gather them, it's filled mostly with final resting places. The reason for that is cemeteries are everywhere in New England, in the glass and metal heart of its biggest cities to the roadsides of its smallest towns, many made up of just a few dozen headstones that continue to obstinately stake their claim throughout the centuries regardless of the way the world changes around them.

The memorials mentioned in this chapter are notable for their history, the myths that they have inspired, their artwork, their location, and anything that makes them stand out from the commemorative yet less memorable earthy drawers where we file our dead. And they are all completely worth visiting. In some ways, apart from the stories about them that are told in this chapter, cemeteries in general are the perfect spot to spend some time. It is there and almost there alone that one can simultaneously imbibe nature, history, culture, and art in solitude, with the only crowds being six feet below.

If there is a single message that comes from all the entries in this section of the book, one shared epitaph on each of the stones presented herein, one unified placard on each museum exhibit, it's that death itself is to always be remembered . . . while we're all still capable of remembering. Start designing your tombstone now.

# Grave with a Window
## NEW HAVEN, VT

I SPY IS NOT A GAME that you're supposed to be able to play from the grave. However, in one small cemetery in New Haven, Vermont, it's an option. Evergreen Cemetery, just off of Town Hill Road, is generally unremarkable as far as cemeteries go. At least, it would be if it were not for one fascinating interment.

His name was Timothy Clark Smith, and he was a doctor during the 1800s, meaning he saw, and in those days of bloodletting and lack of sterilization, probably caused, quite a bit of death. Enough, in fact, that he developed a phobia. Not of death, though. He was afraid of not being dead. That's a special type of phobia called taphephobia (from the Greek *taphē*, "grave"). In other words, he was afraid of being buried alive.

Actually, because of the time period, it might not have been a phobia. It

might have been a completely rational fear. You don't have to read very many Edgar Allan Poe stories to know that back then death was such a probability for everyone that doctors didn't take too long to "call it," much to the eventual chagrin of the temporarily comatose. In addition, lack of modern embalming practices caused corpses to get planted much quicker back then . . . sometimes before they had a chance to wake up and protest.

I'm thinking that Dr. Smith must at one point have been on the diagnosing end of one of these unfortunate situations and was therefore terrified of its happening to himself. I say this based solely on the fact that he designed and rigged his own tomb in an attempt to prevent that undesirable outcome.

For instance, he installed a set of stairs for easy ingress, egress, and access underneath a large square capstone beside his burial mound. He is also supposed to have been buried with a bell in his hand and a breathing tube somewhere, although I couldn't verify the latter when I visited. I guess I couldn't verify the bell, either.

Most interestingly and verifiable is the horizontal window he installed at the surface of his grave, 6 feet above him and centered squarely on his face, so that people could check on him to see whether he was politely moldering away in the manner that nature intended or screaming hoarsely for rescue.

These days, visibility only extends a few inches down the 6-foot-long cement shaft due to moisture and the age of the glass, and its being a thin, dark, long tunnel. However, more than being a disappointment to me, this investigation was an absolute nightmare. Much more freaky than seeing an actual skull is only being allowed to imagine the skull that's grinning up at you at the bottom of this shaft. In the darkness. Staring. In my nightmares.

Between you and me, Dr. Smith's plan sounds sort of flawed in a few places. Most notably, someone would have to be whistling past this graveyard at the exact right time and then be able to hear a bell going off under 6 feet of earth. I don't even hear the alarm during fire drills at my office. The breathing tube would have bought him some time, I guess, but the only thing worse than being buried alive is to survive being buried alive for days.

But there you go. One man's phobia is all of our amusement. Wife, please bury me with my cell phone.

# Center Church Crypt
## NEW HAVEN, CT

YOU EXPECT SOMEBODY TO TELL YOU that the bodies are in the basement when you're in a mortuary or at a murder scene. You do not expect to hear that in church.

I mean, sure, Europe has been crypting bodies beneath its holy places for centuries, but in America, we've always favored planting our corpses over storing them. However, the Center Church on the Green in New Haven, Connecticut, has a crypt. But it's not like any European one.

Center Church, also known as the First Church of Christ in New Haven, dates back to 1638 with the founding of New Haven, and the current building at 311 Temple Street was built in the early 1800s. New Haven is one of New England's many history vortexes, so old buildings are just mossy with the past. For instance, Center Church parishioners have included such history-book celebrities as Eli Whitney and Noah Webster, and its visitors auspiciously included U.S. presidents Rutherford B. Hayes and James Monroe.

But these days, its crypt is its claim to fame. The cemetery in the basement of the church actually predates the building. The land that the church is built on was the old burial ground for New Haven. In fact, most of New Haven Green was a graveyard. Eventually, when the funeral needs of the city outgrew its cemetery, the townsfolk moved the headstones to the nearby Grove Street Cemetery and then raised the land to make the 16-acre park called New Haven Green. Only the headstones beneath the church were preserved in their original location, although *beneath* is a relative term here, as the basement level of the church was actually the original ground level of New Haven.

The church allows free tours on a limited basis, for two hours between 11:00 am and 1:00 pm on Thursdays and Saturdays during the meteorologically congenial months of April through October. When you visit, you are first shown the interior of the church itself, with its large Waterford crystal chandelier, large Fisk pipe organ, and large Tiffany stained-glass window, all three of which dominate the relatively small auditorium.

Next, you're led down a small stairs right into the basement cemetery, which is well lit and not very cryptlike. In fact, the room looks exactly like what it is, an indoor graveyard. The crypt has 6-foot-tall ceilings and red-bricked floors that are broken here and there by protruding slate, granite, and brownstone tombstones and tables. Many of the markers are well preserved due to the protection of the church building from the elements. According to the church, the remains of 137 identified people are buried there, although there could be as many as 1,000 unidentified interments.

The oldest labeled tombstone dates to 1687; and buried in the crypt are the relatively famous, including Benedict Arnold's wife and Rutherford Hayes's grandmother and aunt. Another interesting marker belongs to a trio of young children memorialized with a single, triple-crowned tombstone, with the face of a girl at the top of each and the whole thing forming a bed of sorts, with a matching footboard gravestone a few feet in front of it. Here, as well as elsewhere in the cemetery, is evidence of the period practice of reusing the chosen first name of a child who died early until one finally survived the high mortality rates of colonial-era children.

The teachings of the Good Book upon which Center Church is based says that the dead in Christ shall rise first. There's no mention of the dead in church. I'm guessing, though, that the dearly departed in the Center Church crypt can wait their turn for the Resurrection. With a roof over their head, a consistent stream of visitors, and a unique station in the annals of American funerary arts, they seem to have it pretty good.

# Grave with a Glow
## PORTSMOUTH, NH

THE WEATHER CONDITIONS WERE CLEAR AND COLD, with more than a hint of skepticism in the air. I was in the middle of a graveyard many hours past dark. I had my camera and a tripod with me, although I'm not sure why. I'm really bad at taking night pictures, and I certainly can't take pictures of things that probably don't exist.

I was at South Cemetery in Portsmouth, New Hampshire, checking out a local legend about a tombstone that glows. It's not the first time I've been in a graveyard at night, and because I plan on dying like everyone else, it won't be the last.

South Cemetery is large cemetery located on South and Sagamore streets. It's actually a combination of five different cemeteries that sort of merged together at some point . . . our graveyards will soon overtake us all. I had visited the cemetery before, in the daylight hours, both to see the graves of the Smuttynose murder victims (see the "Infamous Crimes, Killers, and Tragedies" section) and to scout out the location of the glowing tombstone so that I could locate it at night.

The directions themselves were easily found, with most sources pointing to Joseph Citro and Diane Foulds's book *Curious New England*, which contains a brief and at least secondhand account of the phenomena. Entering from the main entrance on South Street, you're supposed to follow the path a short walk until you get to the bottom of the hill. On your right is a pond. Across the pond is a grouping of three similar, squarish tombstones. The middle one glows.

When I followed those directions during the day, I saw a really obvious set of three tombstones right on the pond's shore and facing it. Walking around the pond, I got a closer look at the stones. They were originally white but had been darkened by age and weather, and they lacked the polished surface of newer stones. They were joined at the base and bore the family name of Burns. I assumed it was these tombstones that were referenced in the directions, although I figured that it didn't matter because at night the right one would be highlighted anyway. I took pictures of other possible trios of gravestones, just in case, since I knew I'd have to scan the entire far shore of the pond if the Burns didn't burn.

The night I visited, which happened to be months after my day visit, snow blanketed the ground and the tops of most of the monuments. Besides giving a pretty cast to the graveyard, the snow also meant that the crunch of my boots was very loud and borderline unnerving. In addition, the snow made every small copse of trees stand out darker than usual, making them look as if they hid something terrible and soul-consuming. Fortunately, any fear I should have experienced was kind of swallowed up in the low-burning annoyance I felt over having to chase a dubitable legend with what I was sure would be little, if any, payoff.

I followed the path down the hill from the main entrance on South Street until I got to the pond. There was plenty of light from the half moon in the sky and, even though it's a pretty large cemetery, I could see the lights of passing cars, houses, and street lights all around the short wall that delineates the area.

As I walked, I actually caught a flash of light from the other side of the pond. It wasn't anywhere near the three stones previously mentioned, but more off to the side closest to South Street and farther back from the pond. Turns out it was from a tombstone, and it took less time than the flash of light itself to see that the source was obviously a street-lamp reflection on a polished surface. I mean, I could almost make out the shape of the lamp in the tombstone, and the light moved and disappeared from the surface depending on my angle to it. No way someone could mistake that for a preternaturally glowing tombstone . . . no way. Well . . . no. No way.

The rest of my experience in the cemetery can be summed up in four words: freezing my ass off. Also in three: no glowing tombstone.

Now, the only caveat I have to offer in defense of the glowing tombstone legend is the snow. The pond was invisible due to the ice and snow cover, so if reflections from the water ordinarily contributed to the phenomenon, any glows would have been snuffed that night. In addition, the snow cover itself was pretty much glowing from the ambient light, so it might have drowned out the meager glowing of the tombstone.

Also, God and my optometrist know, it could well be that I just missed it. Accounts seem to indicate it's difficult to miss, but I'm usually up for that type of challenge.

# Skull Cliff

## LYNNFIELD, MA

I'VE SHELLED OUT 40 BUCKS to get into an architecturally elegant, highly acclaimed museum to see renowned pieces of art and have felt gypped. I've also hiked a sweaty half mile into the woods and up a quarry to see a bit of graffiti and have been awestruck. This is the story of that latter occasion.

The Lynn Woods Reservation in Lynnfield, Massachusetts, is a 2,200-acre park in the suburbs of Boston. Among its 30 miles of trails are quite a few landmarks, including a 60-year-old stone tower, a cave where a man spent his life and fortune digging for pirate treasure at the behest of ghosts (see the section on ghosts in the "Classic Monsters" portion of this book), and a set of pits rumored to be wolf traps.

But you won't come across Skull Cliff on any of the official maps for the place. And that's too bad.

Actually, Skull Cliff is not the oddity's real name. It doesn't have one, in fact. The few places on the Internet that mention it barely do that and instead just include an image. Honestly, despite these 800 words, that's really all you need. After all, it's a 30-foot-tall rock cliff face completely covered in brightly colored bands of skulls and bones. What good are words for that? Well, I guess they come in handy for similes, so here you go, then. Overall, Skull Cliff looks like some kind of two-dimensional Technicolor archaeological dig or a rainbow, the leprechaun at the end of which you wouldn't want to meet.

Very little is known about the artwork, and that very little is pretty much only gleaned from the signature that the artist left on the image, so basically my source on this is a rock. But according to that rock, it was painted in 2001 by a graffiti artist named Ichabod, who along with his signature and date, also included the trite advice, "Take the knowledge that you will someday be these bones and enjoy now all that is precious."

Ichabod has a little bit of fame in the small circles that include people who care about graffiti. Mostly he's known for tagging freight train cars with his name and skulls, so it's apparently his motif of choice. I can't blame him. Skulls are cool, whether they are vertiginously painted on the side of a cliff or on the side of a rusty boxcar.

Anyway, armed with some terse directions dug off the Internet and a dubitable starting point, I went to check it out. The unmarked trail head is behind the Bostonville Grille, located at 325 Broadway. I know that doesn't sound right, and I had my reservations about it as well, enough in fact that I outwaited a waitress having a smoke behind the restaurant, before starting down what I hoped was a path and not just a random break in the foliage. I didn't want to have to explain what the heck I was doing.

It actually did turn out to be a path. At the beginning, it parallels a bit of swamp on the right and a large outcropping of rock on the left. At one point

it even wended through an open pair of barbed wire–topped gates . . . no fence, no signs, just some freestanding gates. Eventually the path and the swamp veer right, but to find Skull Cliff, continue to keep the outcropping close on your left. After clambering up a bit of a rise, you'll find it. And in fewer wrong turns than I took.

That's how I got there, anyway. It's a forest, so there are obviously multiple ways to find this thing, only a few of which involve getting lost on the way. It's definitely worth it no matter how you get there. Skull Cliff is surprisingly vibrant for being almost a decade old and, although various other rocks in the overgrown quarry have been covered in graffiti from less-inspired spray painters, the cliff face has been left respectfully untarnished.

But seeing it is not enough. You're going to want to get to the top of it.

A barely discernible forest path loops around behind it for that purpose, or you can climb up some of the rocks to the side. Once at the top you'll be further rewarded with an amazing view of the city of Boston in the distance. Oh, and if you turn around you'll see Lynnfield Commons, a newly built apartment complex located at 375 Broadway that I didn't come across in my research. It might be easier to get to the cliff from there or the roads nearby, but separating the cliff from the complex is a steep incline, a tall fence, and a few dozen yards of brush.

It doesn't really matter how you get there. In this rare instance, being there is all the fun.

# Grave of Midnight Mary
## NEW HAVEN, CT

THEY SAY YOU'RE NOT SUPPOSED TO GO TO BED ANGRY, and I assume the same principle applies to your deathbed, as well. Somebody forgot to tell Midnight Mary.

At least, thanks to her tombstone, that's her name in death. In life, she was known by the name Mary E. Hart. The story goes (and goes and goes) that one day Mary was misdiagnosed with the condition of death and was, as a result, given the normally appropriate treatment of interment in the earth. The night of her burial, her sister or aunt or some such relative had vivid enough nightmares about Mary that she had Mary's body exhumed.

Upon doing so, the exhumers found . . . well, let's just say grisly confirmation that Mary had been buried alive. The story is documented in detail with eyewitness testimony, photographs, county records . . . just kidding; no evidence of the truthfulness of any aspect of this story exists. There is a grave to hang it on, though.

It can be found in Evergreen Cemetery on Ella Grasso Boulevard in New Haven, Connecticut, the same cemetery where Sarah Winchester of Winchester Mystery House fame is buried. Mary's tombstone is a giant brick of rough pink stone the size of a foosball table. On its forward surface is a large oval, in which the following story is inscribed, give or take a few punctuation marks for flow reasons:

"At high noon just from, and about to renew her daily work, in her full strength of body and mind, Mary E. Hart, having fallen prostrate remained unconscious, until she died at midnight October 15, 1872 . . . born December 16, 1824."

I guess you could definitely read "buried alive" somewhere between those lines if you assume an epitaph composer expert at understatement. However, a single line of emphasized black text above the rest is what really made this tombstone famous and worth inventing a backstory for: "The people shall be troubled at midnight and pass away."

Over the years, locals and spook story spinners have somehow interpreted that phrase to mean that Mary hated the world enough to curse it with her final epitaph and that anybody caught in the graveyard after midnight or who desecrates her grave would suffer death shortly thereafter.

Of course, if they'd just go to Sunday school once in a while (or the church of Google), they'd know the phrase is from book of Job in the Old Testament. In that passage, a character named Elihu is in the midst of a lengthy monologue directed at a tragedy-worn Job and his less-than-comforting companions, the content of which centers on . . . well, short story, it's not a curse, although there is a bit of the apocalypse inherent in it. With that context in mind, the funereally used phrase seems more like a statement about being resigned to fate, with shades of looking toward the end times . . . which is pretty much the intent of every tombstone inscription ever inscribed. Mary Hart's commemorators just dove more deeply into the official book of epitaphs than most.

If you want to see the inscription for yourself, her grave can be found at the back of Evergreen Cemetery, right on the path that parallels the wrought-iron fence that separates the graveyard from Winthrop Avenue. The stone is well preserved despite its age due to some touchup work at some point, and looks thoroughly modern . . . except for the lengthy and cryptic inscriptions. Besides Mary's final resting place, the stone also marks the interments of relation-of-some-sort James P. Hart and his wife, Fidelia Pierpont. Unfortunately, they didn't receive epitaphs that would turn them into immortally famous bogeymen, as Mary did. Some people are just buried lucky.

# Phineas Gage Landmark and Skull
## CAVENDISH, VT, AND BOSTON, MA

ALBERT EINSTEIN BECAME FAMOUS because of his brain. So did Phineas Gage. Just in a different way.

Phineas Gage was a 19th-century, New Hampshire–born construction foreman. In 1848, at the age of 25, he was working in Cavendish, Vermont, blasting through boulders to prepare for a railroad line. To do this, he would bore a hole in a rock, fill it with gunpowder, insert a fuse, throw in an insulating layer of sand, tamp it down with a heavy iron bar, light the fuse, and then, I assume, run for cover waving his arms and screaming like a seven-year-old girl. It's the kind of job the benefits of which include knowing how you're going to die.

Well, at some point, something went amiss in the procedure. Speculation is he forgot the sand layer, and the iron tamping bar hit the gunpowder, igniting it, and rocketing the more than 3.5-foot-long bar of iron directly through his cheekbone, brain, and skull, before landing some 25 yards behind him, all slimy with frontal lobe.

It should have killed him, but instead it made him immortal. How's that for a superhero-origin story? Not only did he survive, he pretty much maintained consciousness and sensibility directly after the accident. He was treated by the resident physician of Cavendish, Dr. John Martyn Harlow, and, after about 10 weeks, pretty much fully recovered, with only a bad eye and some scarring, belying the fact that at one point Gage had been fit to be looped with twine and hung on a Christmas tree branch.

The interesting thing, other than that he survived, are all the reports that float around about a personality change that occurred as a result of the damage. He apparently went from being a paragon of level-headed hard work to a Hyde of antisocial and flighty character. Not sure how much of that is true. I am sure just by common sense that he was a changed man in a lot of ways. I've gone through some pretty drastic changes myself in my life, even without the trauma of a piece of iron going through me first.

Phineas gained some fame for his accident, both in the medical community, due to the physiognomy of the incident, and in the public, due to the freakishness of it. He even displayed himself at Barnum's famous New York museum. Eventually, after a few jobs that included coach driving in Chile, he moved in with his mother. Finally, in 1890, 12 years after the accident, he died of an epileptic fit.

In the town of Cavendish, Gage has his own memorial. Or his injury does, I'm not sure which. A large rock striated on its sides with its own bore holes is set in a small park in the middle of town at the intersection of Pleasant Street and Highway 131. On that rock is a large bronze plate that tells Gage's story. It's actually one of the most detailed memorial plaques that I've encountered in my journeys. It includes an image of his skull showing the "placement" of the tamping bar; an image of Dr. Harlow; a map of the area showing the location of the accident, Dr. Harlow's house, and you (are here); the story itself; and a detailed chronology of the events of Gage's life.

But wait . . . it gets even grimmer/better.

Much like Einstein's aforementioned brain, Gage's skull has become a holy relic of sorts. After his death, his body was exhumed and his skull sent to Dr. Harlow. These days, it's on public display at the Warren Anatomical Museum, a few cases of elegantly displayed medical oddities and implements on the fifth floor of the Countway Library of Medicine at 10 Shattuck Street in Boston, Massachusetts.

In addition to the skull itself, the hole in which is clearly visible with its ill-fitting bit of fused bone over it, the Gage exhibit includes a life mask of Gage, some old pictures, and the actual tool that has become synonymous with him. In fact, typing the generic phrase "tamping iron" into a search engine yields mostly images of Gage's skull and references to his story.

Passage of tamping iron through Phineas Gage's head marked by arrow

In my own hole-less cranial dome I'd always imagined this tamping iron to be vaguely crowbarlike, even after having read its dimensions. Instead, on seeing it in person, it's more javelin-like and those dimensions really mean something. Here they are in print, anyway. It's about 3 feet, 7 inches long and 1.25 inches in diameter. It weighs more than 13.5 pounds and tapers to a pretty vicious point at one end while being flat on the other. All told, that's bigger than one would think could go right through the brain of a man without immediately killing him. It's big enough to bear the following error-filled inscription on its surface in large, flowing script:

> This is the bar that was shot through the head of Mr. Phinehas P. Gage at Cavendish, Vermont, Sept. 14, 1848. He fully recovered from the injury & deposited this bar in the Museum of the Medical College of Harvard University. Phinehas P. Gage Lebanon Grafton Cy N-H Jan 6 1850.

There are pages in this book with less text on them.

# Sugar Hill Cemetery
## SUGAR HILL, NH

THE APOCALYPSE IS A LOT LIKE A WATCHED POT. It just never boils. Throughout history, a lot of groups have found that idea out the hard way . . . in publicly embarrassing fashion. One such sect of Adventists located in the far-north town of Sugar Hill, New Hampshire, found themselves humiliated in this particular fashion both in front of their peers . . . and their dead.

It all started in New York with a 30-something Baptist preacher named William Miller. Like most Baptist preachers, he believed Jesus Christ was returning to Earth to pluck the faithful, judge the unbelievers, and end the world like every action movie . . . in fiery destruction, complete with the requisite shot of a slow-motion Christ walking away from a planetary explosion without looking back.

Unlike most Baptist preachers, though, he thought he'd cracked a hidden Biblical code that gave the date for that world premiere . . . which happened to be somewhere between March 21, 1843, and March 21, 1844 . . . coincidentally, just a few years from when he discovered it. In those pre–Las Vegas days, the only business a prophet could get into was religion.

For reasons that say uncomfortable things about the basic makeup of human beings, his beliefs began to gain a real popularity in the areas of New England and New York. His followers were called Millerites, of course, and these acolytes waited with intense anticipation for the day they wouldn't have to work, hurt, or make awkward small talk with boorish people.

For reasons that say even more uncomfortable things about the basic makeup of human beings, when that time period came and went without either a bang or a whimper, the fervor didn't abate. Instead, a second close-at-hand date was established: October 22, 1844.

Because an exact day is much more compelling than a mere range of 365 of them, Millerites really started getting into this one.

One such group was located in Sugar Hill, New Hampshire, a small community chiseled out of the neighboring town of Lisbon. These ardent Millerites enjoyed their last New England fall, arranged their earthly affairs, and then gathered in the town cemetery for what probably would be the best seats at an Apocalypse. Not only would they get to see the end of it all, but they could watch the dead rise, as well.

Some of the accounts of this little story even have these Sugar Hill Millerites dressing in white robes for the event. Although that's probably a caricature, I'm sure they put on at least some sort of finery. Meeting your maker's an auspicious affair, after all. However they were dressed, they perched themselves on some tombstones and sat there like Linus waiting for the Great Pumpkin.

And then, of course, they left in disappointment like Linus waiting for the Great Pumpkin.

The world and that cemetery eventually outlived those Millerites. The world you know, but the cemetery is called Sunnyside, and it can still be found on Cemetery Road at the intersection of South, Easton, Pearl Lake, and Sugar Hill roads.

It's a small cemetery built on the side of a hill, and none of the epitaphs that I could see from post-1844 allude to the event at all. No "Josiah Reynolds, here for the second time" or "Abel Danvers, still waiting." Would be a lot cooler cemetery if they did, though.

# Grave of Ocean-Born Mary
## HENNIKER, NH

THIS STORY STARTS with a naturally sea-legged infant, gets interesting with a sentimental pirate, and then ends with a grave and a con man. It is the story of Ocean-Born Mary.

In 1720, a group of settlers were sailing to the New World from Ireland when, en route, a girl was born to James and Elizabeth Fulton. That's pretty much all that had to happen for the infant to earn the nickname "Ocean-Born," but it took a little more to achieve local legend status in New England. Here's how that happened.

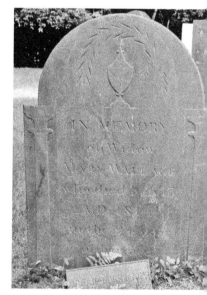

After the child's birth, the ship was waylaid by pirates. Upon seeing the newborn, the captain of the pirate vessel offered to let everyone live if the Fultons merely named the child after his mother, Mary. Such a good son, that pirate.

The plan seemed like a bargain to all and when the Fultons agreed, he gave them a bolt of green silk out of which to make the girl's future wedding dress, and left for other, less compassion-inducing targets.

The Fultons kept their promises, including Mary's name and turning the fabric into a wedding dress, when they finally arrived in New England.

The whole thing sounds too fairy tale to be true, of course, and everyone has a different opinion about which parts are and which aren't. We do know for certain that some aspects of the story have been embellished. For instance, that the pirate was this or that famous pirate. Or that the pirate eventually came to New Hampshire and married Mary, himself. Most anything that makes any story better is probably false.

But Ocean-Born Mary certainly lived, because, well, she died. Her grave is located in a cemetery behind the town hall at 18 Depot Hill Road in Henniker, New Hampshire. She's buried under her married name, Mary Wallace. The headstone can be found in a straight line from the front gate on the right. You'll know you're at the correct one because in front of the grave is a metal plaque staked into the ground upon which can be found the name "Ocean-Born Mary." According to the tombstone, she was 94 years old when she died in 1814. That is a long time to put up with being called "Ocean-Born."

Graves usually end a story, but this one continues for a bit. In 1917, more than 100 years after Mary's death, a man named Louis Roy moved with his mother to Henniker, after asking around for a house with some history. Something cozy and exploitable. He was directed to what had once been the house of Robert Wallace, one of Mary's sons.

He bought the house, and immediately starting calling it the Ocean-Born Mary House, despite the fact that she had never lived there. Not one much to concern himself with pesky facts, Roy immediately started filling the house with antiques he claimed were Mary's, offering tours, dressing his mother in period costumes, conjuring ghost stories, and claiming that pirate gold was buried on the property and selling shovels to tourists to go find it.

The house stands to this day, and, as a testament to the huckster prowess of Louis Roy, is still known as the Ocean-Born Mary House. Located on Bear Road, just outside of town, the house is brown with a pair of chimneys, and a low rock wall made of large stones surrounds the property. These days, the owners don't offer tours or shovels, but nicely situated just outside the privacy of their stone fence is a marker with a plaque that reads in a neutral fashion, "Homestead of Robert Wallace, also known as Ocean-Born Mary House, 1784."

And all that centuries-spanning craziness because of an awkwardly timed pregnancy.

# Adams Memorial
CORNISH, NH

I've seen armies of figural statues in my travels across the country. So have you. They're in every park, museum, and meeting square in every town, New England or not . . . and a good portion of them aren't worth being sketched on a dinner-stained table napkin, much less enduringly cast in metal or carved from stone. But I reckon I'd conga-line with all of them if said serpentine dance led to the Adams Memorial.

In Cornish, New Hampshire, on a beautiful estate designated a National Historic Site for reasons I'll get to in a bit, sits one of the most evocative figural statues I've ever had the pleasure of shoving a camera at. This dark, inscrutable form is a life-size work of funerary art and is a casting from an original form that is absolutely fabled in another part of the country. I'm not sure how many New Englanders know the story, as it doesn't start in New England but about 300 miles south in the nation's capital of Washington, D.C.

Boston-born Henry Adams was a member of the prominent and presidential Adams family and lived most of his life between his birth city and D.C. He was a historian and writer of voluminous output and impressive knowledge. His most enduring work, however, didn't occur until the untimely death of his wife, Marian "Clover" Adams, who committed suicide in 1885 at the age of 42 by drinking photography chemicals.

For reasons that it would probably take a psychotherapist (and a vivisectionist) a lifetime to tease out, Adams felt compelled to commission a grander grave memorial than usual for his wife. He chose Augustus Saint-Gaudens, an Irish-born American sculptor of considerable fame whose impressive works eventually adorned the Boston Common and Copley Square in Boston, Grant and Lincoln Parks in Chicago, Madison and Cooper Squares in New York, and many other prominent places and museums across the country and world.

Adams gave only vague direction to Saint-Gaudens for the design of the memorial, and the sculptor came up with an intense work of utter peace . . . or a peaceful work of absolute intensity. However you want to capture that wispy butterfly, the work was so compelling that it came to be called one of the finest examples of funerary art in modern times.

It is a simple depiction—an androgynous being wrapped from head to toe in a cloak sits, its eyes closed, its right arm lifted to its cheek. That's it. And

yet that simple form elegantly conjures images of death and thought and resignation and eternity as no religious text really ever has.

Adams didn't want it named, but in D.C. people started calling it *Grief*, as
unfortunately limiting a name as that title is. The statue still sits in its original location, on a pedestal across from a curving bench in its own private
spot of Rock Creek Cemetery, right above the otherwise unmarked graves of
both Clover and Henry Adams.

It took only a slight deformation to make the statue chilling.

In 1906, Civil War veteran General Felix Agnus hired a company to create
a copy of the Adams Memorial for his own final resting place. The company,
which did not own the rights but did pretend to, hired Eduard Pausch to create
a knockoff of Adam's famous piece for the general. The result was a close but
slightly off version of Saint-Gaudens's original masterpiece. The company
was successfully sued by the wife of the famous sculptor, but the general, when
he died in 1925, was still buried under it in Druid Ridge Cemetery in Baltimore, Maryland.

However, unlike the fame and awe that the original produced, the Black
Aggie, as the Pausch copy came to be known, inspired terror and occult lore.
Tales spread about the death stare of its glowing red eyes and the morbid fate
of any who sat on its lap, inspiring vandalism, adolescent initiation rites, and
all sorts of other Thomas J. Foolery.

In fact, its ominous reputation soon grew so burdensome to the cemetery
that sometime in the midcentury it sent the statue away to a Baltimore
museum, where it sat in obscurity for decades. Eventually, the knockoff statue
somehow found its way to the courtyard of the Dolly Madison House, a federal court building in Washington, D.C., just a block away from the White
House and close to the site of the Lafayette Square home and all the regular
haunts of Henry Adams himself.

But to bring this topic back to New England, the original sculptor Saint-
Gaudens had a summer home in the aforementioned town of Cornish that he
eventually permanently moved into, converting the barn on the idyllic property into a studio where he worked. After his death in 1907, the estate was
turned into a National Historic Site. Visitors can now tour his house, see his
studio, walk through its grounds, and appreciate various castings of his works,
all of which is worth it even without knowing a thing about the sculptor. It's
one of my favorite places in New Hampshire, actually.

And the full-size casting of the Adams Memorial sits right in the middle of it all, in a privacy of 10-foot-tall hedges beside a beech-lined path beside the studio and house.

Having spent most of my life in the D.C. area, I've seen both the original Adams Memorial and the Black Aggie, so when I moved to the Live Free or Die state, I was surprised to find out that the statue had, in a way, moved there years before me. Although it's not the

original, it still gives New Englanders and tourists the chance to be haunted in person by this haunting statue.

# Memorial Arch of Tilton
## NORTHFIELD, NH

I T SEEMS LIKE A MASSIVE, freestanding Roman-style stone arch is the must-have accessory for every city that wants to be fashionable. Paris has one, Dublin has one, New York has one, assumedly Rome has one, and, somehow, the tiny but apparently trendy town of Northfield, New Hampshire, has one. Some cities use their arches as stand-alone monuments, others as park entrances. The 55-foot-tall, 40-foot-wide granite Memorial Arch of Tilton in Northfield is a giant tombstone . . . kind of.

Charles Tilton got rich during the California Gold Rush. When he returned to his hometown of Sanbornton Bridge, New Hampshire, he decided to make himself more at home . . . town. In addition to various municipal projects he spearheaded, he donated various statues to the town, including one of a lizard-encircled, bare-breasted Indian queen that currently adorns its main street. He became so enmeshed with the area, in fact, that the people eventually named the town after him when they officially incorporated.

The Memorial Arch of Tilton, though, is his crowning achievement. Also his most embarrassing.

Apparently inspired by the Arch of Titus in Rome, Tilton had his own arch built in the early 1880s on a large hill with one of the best views in the area. According to Tilton, it was intended to be a memorial for his ancestors. Of course, mostly it was intended to be a memorial for himself. He planned on being interred in the large, lion-topped, pink-granite sarcophagus between the two columns at its base. He also planned on Northfield, the adjoining town where the hill was located, being incorporated into its Tilton neighbor. However, when Northfield refused to drop its maiden name, Tilton took his corpse and went home. He's now buried squarely but less grandly in Park Cemetery off West Main Street in Tilton.

To get to the arch, you basically just have to go to Northfield and look up. If you are less trusting of your ability to navigate using a soaring vanity project as a compass, the path leading up to the monument is off Summer Street, close to where it intersects both Bay and Elm streets.

The thing is absolutely massive and would be a surprising piece of stonework to come across if one is not expecting it . . . which would probably be anybody driving through central New Hampshire. The hill around it is cleared, making for a nice spot to picnic, especially since Tilton's dead body didn't make it into the edifice. Eating deli sandwiches in the shadow of a monument is probably more pleasant than eating deli sandwiches in the shadow of a tombstone. Of course, the absence of its original purpose does make the empty lion-topped box at its base a bit enigmatic. I'd suggest a few possible uses for it, but an unused sarcophagus makes for a good story.

Although there's less reason to place flowers there, the Memorial Arch of Tilton still stands as a monument to, well, unhatched chickens and obstinate rich folk, but it's nevertheless impressive and certainly serves as a mark of distinction for the area. Although not from Paris, Dublin, New York, Rome . . .

# Hope Cemetery
## BARRE, VT

HOPE CEMETERY IN BARRE, VERMONT, is touted as one of the more interesting cemeteries in New England. And it is. It'll just take a few hundred years before I find it that interesting a place.

Established in 1895 and covering an area of 65 acres, the cemetery displays more impressive works of funerary sculpture per square foot than probably any other graveyard in the country. And it's all because of the local geology.

The town of Barre (pronounced "Barry") rolled out of its collective bed one day to discover that the pea in their mattress was a mother lode of valuable and unique granite that was resistant to discoloration, disintegration, and all the other aspects that make old statues poignant.

The stone soon made the town famous worldwide and attracted sculptors and their families from all over the world to form the rocks into other than their natural shapes. More often than not, due to reasons of timing and economics in their home country, these immigrants were from Italy, as can be attested by the overwhelming majority of names ending in *i* or *o* that are carved into the gravestones of Hope Cemetery.

As this community of sculptors and their family members died, the sculptors did what they did best . . . made sculptures. In all, 10,000 monuments, all made of Barre granite, now decorate the land encompassed by Hope Cemetery.

From the classical to the cheesy, Greek colonnades and angels to race cars and soccer balls, the place absolutely gleams with uncorrupted white shapes, although you'd think with an Italian immigrant population that had been genetically exposed to the legendary works of such sculptors as Michelangelo, Donatello, and Leonardo, they'd have dedicated themselves to more than just sculptures of biplanes, beds, and easy chairs.

So why would I be so unenthusiastic about a place that seems pretty cool in the grand scheme of things? Well, death doesn't gleam, and neither should cemeteries. Hope Cemetery is just too nice a place. Graveyards need a shadow of morbidity to them, or they lose their meaning. In addition, because all the statues in Hope Cemetery are made from Barre granite, there is a uniformity to them that is somewhat unpleasing to the eye. Also, it's a pretty open cemetery, with few trees, emphasizing even more the unappealing freshness of the sculptures. You don't leave Hope Cemetery feeling as if you've just exited from peaceful and hallowed ground, but from an artisan show floor.

Still, on the plus side, Hope Cemetery is levels better than most modern cemeteries, with their ordered rows of rectangular pink and gray polished marble, ground-flushed plaques, and mausoleum shelves, all of which seem to steal the mystery and character from death and make it look manufactured.

But . . . when over time the soccer ball cracks in half like a destroyed planet, when the pyramids decay to look more like that shape's most famous representative, when the statues deform and turn ghastly from certain angles, when trees and vines start overtaking the place, Hope Cemetery is going to be fantastic.

# Blood Cemetery
## Hollis, NH

THEY SAY THAT BLOOD CEMETERY on Nartoff Road in Hollis, New Hampshire, is one of the most haunted cemeteries in New England. I'm not really sure who "they" are of course, nor how they can speak with such authority on such a dubitable topic, but I can say that since the inception of the Internet, "they" have become even more vague. Nevertheless, the rumor still persists.

If you're one to believe signs posted in front of graveyards, Blood Cemetery is actually called Pine Hill Cemetery. Of all the large, gothic, atmospheric cemeteries in New England, it's strange that the "most haunted" rumor would crop up about this particular one.

Sure, Pine Hill Cemetery is old—250 years old, in fact—but it's also tiny to the point of farce, with nary a mausoleum, statue, or ominous-sounding epitaph in sight. Far from being touted as one of the most haunted cemeteries in New England, it should be touted as one of the most vandalized, judging by the number of broken, knocked over, and missing headstones.

However, it's not that strange that this graveyard garnered such a cool nickname, when all the facts are known. Well, when one of them is. Now, you'd think being called "Blood Cemetery" would have an intriguing story to go along with it, a brutal massacre from histories past, an unsolved and enigmatic series of murders . . . maybe even a spectral flood of red ectoplasm seeping nightly from the epitaphs of the gravestones.

Instead, the reason it's called Blood Cemetery is simply that a family surnamed "Blood" is buried there.

There's a corollary in Cemetery Land that if somebody with the last name of Blood is fertilizing graveyard grass from the roots up, the place is going to be called Blood Cemetery, no matter what pleasant, nonthreatening name the place is incorporated under. In addition, that graveyard will be haunted, as stories about ghosts named Fritzwenger and Hershberger aren't as compelling as stories about ghosts named Blood. This is in addition to the corollary that for every graveyard that exists, there is somebody who will inevitably claim it's haunted. And the math gets complicated from there.

In the case of Pine Hill Cemetery, there are quite a few Bloods buried there, although only a few of their headstones remain. Around one of these tombstones in particular, that of Abel Blood, a legend has popped up.

Abel was born sometime in the late 1700s and died in 1867. Nothing's really known about the life of Abel other than the fact that he probably had a pretty cool set of vanity license plates and his wife was named Betty. That's right. Betty Blood. Maybe not as poetic as being named after the first recorded murder victim in ancient literature, as her husband was, but still good enough for a straight-to-DVD horror movie title.

Unfortunately, Abel Blood's tombstone does not exist anymore. The original was stolen and broken by vandals a few years back, only to be replaced and to have that replacement suffer the same fate. Now, a broken tooth of a stump in a line of Blood gravestones in varying states of disrepair is all that remains to mark Abel Blood and his legend . . . which I am getting to.

However, pictures of it can be found on the Internet, although seeing it is a tad disappointing. The original headstone of Abel Blood featured merely an inset carving of a hand with its index finger pointed upward. But that hand, with its worn-away finger and outdated cut of sleeve, was crucial to the myth. You see, when the moon was at the appropriate angle to the horizon, or when the wind blew from a certain direction, or just when the right person was telling the story, that hand (and you may want to skip a few lines down if you're squeamish) . . . pointed down. That's it. An entire New England tradition of demons, monsters, and human atrocity, and that's the chilling legend of Blood Cemetery that has been passed down from generation to generation in southern New Hampshire.

"They" owe me my money back.

# Grave of a Knight Templar
## WESTFORD, MA

WALKING DOWN THE SIDEWALKS of your own neighborhood, you'll probably see the usual stuff. Fire hydrants and chalked hopscotch grids. The initials of some random kid who got them in before the cement dried. Trash bins if it's that day of the week. However, if you walk down the sidewalks of Westford, Massachusetts, you might stumble across the grave of a pre-Columbus Scottish knight.

Legend has it that a Scottish earl named Henry Sinclair took a crew of explorers and discovered America in 1398, a whole century before Christopher Columbus, and explored regions of Nova Scotia and New England. According to the inscribed glacial rock that still stands to mark the grave of one of their fallen, they made it at least as far as what is now Westford, Massachusetts, a town northwest of Boston near the New Hampshire state line.

You can still see that engraving in the exposed rock beside a sidewalk

along Depot Street, near the Abbott School. Nowadays, it's called the Westford Knight, and people with almost supernatural eyesight claim that the engraving depicts a knight holding a downward-pointed sword in one hand and a shield in the other, the latter emblazoned with a coat of arms that apparently identifies him as Sir James Gunn of the Clan Gunn, who was apparently not just a knight . . . but a Knight Templar. I'm not sure exactly what a Knight Templar is, actually, but I've seen so many stories about them that I'm pretty sure they're just fictional creations, like the Founding Fathers, the 12 Disciples, and the Harlem Globetrotters.

Of course, like every other absolutely cool story, there is tons of evidence that points to it being absolutely false. You knew it from the first paragraph, though.

Most legitimate historians, archaeologists, and people who know from experience that the world's just not that cool a place think that the story does not have even an iota of credibility, that most of what is considered to be a carving is just natural scratches from glaciation and that the small T-shaped part (that some take to be an upside-down sword hilt) that really is punched into the rock was done so circa the 1900s. They have a lot more substantial evidence for their ideas, unfortunately, including the rather damning fact that the rock face would have been buried under feet of soil 600 years ago, when the effigy was supposedly carved. It's the circle of life, though. Some weave fanciful tales based on shoestrings and birds' nests. Others believe with a disproportionate passion. Curmudgeons then come along waving those horrible devices of torture called reason and evidence and make us cry "uncle." The process repeats with all of us switching teams at various moments.

Knight or not, all the above didn't stop locals from cordoning off the marking with chains, nor from erecting a plaque with an explanation (the cooler one) of the existence of the mark, which it calls a "punch-hole armorial effigy." The right words can make anything sound believable. When I visited, a white chalk or paint outline was just visible around the shape of the shield to help guide those whose eyes have difficulty matrixing random scratches into the form of a 14th-century Knight Templar.

Eventually, controversy notwithstanding, weather is going to turn this bit of horizontal rock face into a smooth surface to make it all moot and, possibly, finally ready for carving. However, inside the nearby Westford J. V. Fletcher Library on 50 Main Street is a stone that's supposed to be related to the Westford Knight and is in much better condition because it has been kept indoors for decades.

Called the boat stone, the 2-foot-wide rock bears the unmistakable images of a detailed boat, an arrow, and the number 184. It's supposed to be a waymark carved by Sinclair's party to get them back to the boat. There are plenty of doubts about this explanation, as well, including one of my own. Seems like if I were a knight wandering around an uncharted land and was entrusted with having to go through all the laborious effort and time of inscribing marks into boulders on the go, that I would skip the "boat" part of the message. I'd assume it would just be understood that the boat is where we all wanted to end up.

Back to the Westford Knight, I don't know if I get an expert opinion on it, but I have seen it with my own eyes, and to me it looks merely like a rock with some texture to it. Then again, I don't know that I've ever seen an old rock carving that I haven't said that about. My vision sucks.

# Boston Tombstone Skull Iconography
## BOSTON, MA

DURING THE DAY, the patriotically red stripe of the Freedom Trail in Boston, Massachusetts, takes tourists 2.5 miles through all the many landmarks that are central to both Massachusetts and Colonial American history. These sites include the meetinghouse where the Boston Tea Party was organized, the church from which Paul Revere received his famous lantern signal, and the monument near the spot of the Battle of Bunker Hill. However, from a different angle, under a different shade of sky, with a morbid enough

cast of mind, the brick-paved Freedom Trail becomes a blood-red streak that carries the unwary to some of the most macabre spots in Boston.

In other entries in this book, I write about the site of the Boston Massacre and the mass grave of its victims, the book made from the skin of a convict at the Boston Athenaeum, and the grave of witch hunter–general Cotton Mather. All these bits of ghastliness are located on the Freedom Trail. However, also found in various locations along the trail is some of the more ghastly skull iconography one will ever have the pleasure of finding on a gravestone.

There are three different cemeteries on the Freedom Trail: the Granary Burying Ground, King's Chapel Burying Ground, and Copp's Hill Burying Ground. All three of these boneyards are more than 350 years old and are tourist destinations for the prominent cadavers one can find buried there, including Paul Revere, John Hancock, Samuel Adams, and a whole slew of other names similarly buried in high school history books.

Interspersed among these historic notables are nonfamous graves decorated with a second helping of memento mori. As if the tombstone itself isn't enough of a grim reminder of our shared fate with these long dead, a whole stylistic range of skulls and skeletons adorns many of these Boston headstones.

Running the gamut from the simple Edward Gorey–type winged skull sketch that many Puritans seem to be so fond of and which can be found in cemeteries throughout New England, to more realistically styled versions, these skulls seem to taunt visitors with their eventual fate in the morbid game of Red Rover that, in our more optimistic moods, we like to call "the way it is."

Of particular interest is a series of skeleton motifs in the Granary Burying Ground. Along an outer brick wall are inset slate-fronted crypts depicting full-bodied skeletons in various poses. On one, a bony fiend dances with a scythe in one hand and an hourglass in the other as if happy that the next round of mortality's on it. On another stone, a skeleton leans demurely on a disembodied skull, its scythe thrown casually over its shoulder. On yet another, a pair of skeletons dressed in loose (of course) robes lean against a winged hourglass with their fists against their head, apparently contemplating somber thoughts that their ever-grinning teeth seem to belie.

The skulls and skeletons are everywhere in these graveyards, so there's no reason for me to point all of them out to you and one very good reason for me not to (laziness). Just visit the cemeteries on the Freedom Trail and you'll see them rising from the ground like the actual skeletons that they mark cannot. The great thing about visiting this diverse assortment of skull iconography is that due to the highly touristy nature of the Freedom Trail, you don't have to be self-conscious about your macabre interests. In this case, it's your patriotic duty to be morbid.

# Skull and Bones Tomb
## New Haven, NH

Yale College in New Haven, Connecticut, has more tombs than most graveyards, but this prestigious Ivy League college doesn't bury its dead in them. It inters secret societies in them.

Also called tomb societies, senior societies, and landed societies, these elite, secretive self-run student organizations have for more than 150 years been, well, elite, secretive, and self-run. Over the years, tomb societies have included such groups as Scroll and Key, Wolf's Head, Book and Snake, and Sage and Chalice, among others.

Each one of the landed societies has its own headquarters, which is called a "tomb," owing to the blocky, windowless appearance of most of them. Access to these enigmatic buildings is more or less only granted to initiates, and these structures have gone a long way to helping establish the aura of mystery that surrounds these societies.

Of course, the oldest and most famous of all is the Skull and Bones. Founded in 1832, it has inspired numerous stories due to its strange rituals and high-ranking roster of alumni. For instance, three U.S. presidents were members of the Skull and Bones (William Taft, George H. W. Bush, and George W. Bush), as were various media leaders, presidential cabinet members, congressmen, finance industry captains, university presidents, and Supreme Court justices . . . enough high-ranking members of society, in fact, to whip conspiracy theorists into a rapturous froth.

The Skull and Bones Tomb is located at 64 High Street across from the Linsly-Chittenden Hall. This bare, symmetrical, sandstone building is the quintessential Yale tomb—imposing, windowless—and it seems to squat mute and stubborn on its little bit of Yale campus turf. The tomb was built in 1856, and has had wings and other additions built onto it in the intervening years.

Aside from residing in a tomb, the Skull and Bones society is particularly renowned for just what you'd expect from a society with a name like Skull and Bones. This extends from strange rites and initiation rituals to the objects that they keep in their inscrutable tomb.

Death is apparently their décor of choice, with skeletons, skulls (both real and artificial), coffins, and other sepulchral artifacts, statuary, and artwork adorning the inside of the tomb. In fact, in early 2010, news was made when Christie's auction house advertised that it had been tasked by an unnamed European art collector to put up for bid an object that was supposedly from the Skull and Bones Tomb. That object was a human skull with an attached pair of crossed bones that had been turned into a ballot box, the nefarious purpose of which no civilized man could ever guess. Or it was used to cast votes. However, mere days after the announcement, the item was mysteriously pulled from bidding due to a "title claim." It was never seen again . . . in the two weeks between it happening and my writing this paragraph.

Most infamously, many have claimed that in the early 1900s the Bonesmen stole the skull and bones of Geronimo, the Apache warrior, Native American hero, and patron saint of jumping. The rumors became pronounced enough that the descendents of Geronimo recently sued to get it back. Similar rumors abound about other famous skulls and objects in the illicit keeping of the society.

Whatever the truth behind the goings on at the Skull and Bones Tomb, the reality is probably pretty mundane. It's just a club of college kids, after all. They just happen to have a very cool building in which they can do all the awesomely silly things that college kids do.

# Panarchy Tomb Room
## HANOVER, NH

M Y BASEMENT HAS A LEAKY WATER HEATER, a few boxes of badly organized Christmas and Halloween decorations, and a rusty weight bench/ clothing rack. The basement of 9 School Street in Hanover, New Hampshire, has a century-old subterranean ritual room complete with altar and thrones. One of these basements is cooler than the other.

Panarchy is a co-ed undergraduate society at Dartmouth University. It's housed in a large, white, column-fronted residence that dates back to 1835. Originally, the historic house was a private home. From 1902 on, though, it housed various Greek organizations until being taken over in 1993

by Panarchy, an officially school-recognized society outside the official Greek system.

At some point in the history of the place, somebody with a lot of time and concrete on his hands constructed an underground chamber in the basement of the house that is rimmed in concrete seats and thrones, with a concrete alter set at one end of the room. Nobody knows the original purpose of the room, although the most common guess is that it had to do with obscure fraternity rituals.

These days it's called the Tomb Room, and unlike the secret society tombs of Yale mentioned in the previous entry, visitors are welcome without their being initiates. Panarchy holds various meetings and events in its Tomb Room, many of which are open to the public. The rest of the Panarchy House is used for living quarters and all the things that Ivy League college kids do at Ivy League colleges.

When I visited, it looked like typical college housing . . . empty beer cans set on whatever random horizontal service was at hand at the time, music and political posters and stickers plastered on the walls, mislaid articles of clothing, ball-strewn pool tables . . . all the detritus of dorm living. A girl with a mouth full of foaming toothbrush let me in after only a minimum of barely comprehensible interrogation.

She led me down a flight of innocuous wooden stairs and into the Tomb Room before leaving me to finish her morning routine. (It wasn't that I'd arrived at an ungodly early hour; I'd just forgotten that by crossing the boundary of a college, I was in a different time zone. College noon and actual noon are not equivalent times.) The windowless room was smaller than I'd imagined it would be and was lighted by a quartet of bare bulbs that hung from the four corners of the ceiling. It was also plainer than I thought it'd be. Pictures that I had seen previous to visiting the room revealed gray cinderblock walls completely covered in graffiti. However, when I was there, a fresh coat of light paint had just been applied . . . taking the edge off the spookiness of the place. I believe the girl even apologized for that, but I couldn't tell with that toothbrush in her mouth.

It was winter time when I visited and the room was pretty cold, so it certainly had that part about its being a tomb right. The floor is paved with red bricks and, at odds with the rest of the house, was completely free of clutter, although that might have been because of the recent painting. All the cement furniture was well preserved and bore no trace of disfigurement. The surrounding row of concrete seats were all inscribed with either names or years, some as old as 1897.

At the head of the room, three of the seats were built more like thrones than were the more almost benchlike seating of the rest of the room. The thrones had clawed feet, higher backs with dividers that separated the seats from each other, and each one bore a different name: E. R. Anderson, Dunning, and W. L. McCorkle. I tried to sit in one, but due to the narrowness of the thrones I can only assume that whatever fraternity group built it must have been shoulderless.

Directly in front of those thrones, a simple, 2.5-foot-tall concrete box sculpted with flowers and a cloth sash gave the impression of an altar. In those same pictures of graffiti-covered cinderblock walls, I often saw candles melting on it. All that was being offered to the gods when I visited, though, was a paintbrush, primer, and a pair of gloves.

Although it contained no human-size slabs, the Tomb Room still certainly lived up to its name. I, my Halloween decorations, and my weight bench are absolutely envious.

# Mexican Tomb Figures Collection
ORONO, ME

EVERY TIME I GO TO A MUSEUM, I wonder whether ancient pottery gets boring even to anthropologists and archaeologists. I mean, the first piece they look at might be new and exciting, but after that, it's just so many sand-colored pots. And, sure, they reveal important information about the cultures that created them, but that has to have a limit, too. Although your boss's coffee mug says way more than makes me comfortable about our culture, it still says very little of value.

That said, pottery taken from the tombs of the ancient dead ought to be endlessly fascinating. After all, these pieces were made or chosen for interment, giving the items an interest far beyond any possible practical or flippant use. You give special gifts to kids going away to college. You give awesome gifts to family going into the afterlife.

In western Mexico, the ancients sent off their beloved ones with tomb figures, hollow clay effigies of creatures and humans in a wide variety of shapes. The more elite dead of western Mexico were often buried in shaft tombs, deep vertical pits dug anywhere from 10 to 60 feet into the rock, which then opened into multiple horizontal chambers at the bottom. In fact, the artifacts that filled these tombs are pretty much all we have left to reconstruct their cultures, as they left no monuments or other lasting works behind—merely tombs filled with these millennia-old effigies and vessels, most of which have been looted over the years.

Of course, you don't have to go tomb raiding yourself to be intrigued first-hand by these pieces, but you do have to take the long trek up to central Maine, where the Hudson Museum at the University of Maine in Orono claims the largest institutional collection of western Mexican funerary figures in the country. Which is even more impressive when you consider how far Orono is from western Mexico.

These burial effigies came from the personal collection of William P. Palmer III, an avid collector with the funds to match. There are some 550 of these pieces, all deriving from the Colima, Jalisco, and Nayarit cultures of western Mexico.

The tomb figures were created in a variety of forms wide enough to surely keep those aforementioned bored archaeologists and anthropologists excited. The shapes include men and women contorted into various positions, abstract pieces, and a few dozen kids shows' worth of animals . . . just about any image that an ancient race would have access to or could dream up. The actual artifacts range from urns, vases, and jars to incense burners, bowls, and figurines, from the extremely plain to the highly detailed. All in all, the set definitely looks like something one would rather be collecting than burying.

Portions of the collection are regularly displayed at the museum, although

you may want to call ahead before visiting, just in case. However, the entire collection can be viewed online at the Hudson Museum Web site at www .umaine.edu/hudsonmuseum.

Admission to the 9,000-square-foot Hudson Museum is free; the entrance is on the second level of the Collins Center for the Arts. You don't need directions to the college. It takes up most of Orono. But once on the campus, you'll want to get to the intersection of Flagstaff, Belgrade, and Sebago roads to find the Collins Center. When I visited, the center was in the middle of showing an opera, and the first floor was filled with attendees on their intermission break. However, a few large banners and signs announced the presence of the museum, and a long ramp close to the entrance led up to the second floor, where virtually no one was visiting the museum.

And that's their bad. I was expecting a small hallway filled with randomly assembled objects. What I found was one of the more aesthetically pleasing museum arrangements that I'd seen for a long time. Giant, almost room-size glass cases were filled with every kind of cultural artifact from the New World, including necklaces made from teeth; masks in the shapes of bats and demons; a giant bowl in the shape of a whale; and even a three-foot-tall, 1,500-year-old statue of a Veracruz Snake Apron Princess wearing a vampire bat mask and a pair of snakes for a belt. The placard beside her stated, "The iconography suggests that she is associated with human sacrifice and the underworld." Indeed.

Turns out, she was actually part of the Palmer collection that I had come to see, although none of the other tomb figures on display were as big as her. On a tiered display stand in a city-aquarium-size case were about 50 of them. I was actually expecting shelf tchotkes, but many of the figures were the size of garden gnomes. Most were clay-colored humanoids in various poses, some holding musical instruments, infants, weapons, or vessels.

They all seemed whimsically designed, but that changed when I envisioned them sitting in a dark stone shaft underground, silently overseeing the decomposition of a body and then, after that, just trying to find new ways to pass the millennia. Honestly, that made me dig them more. Of course, there were many items of interest at the Hudson Museum besides these tomb figures I went there to see, but they would have been worth the price of admission by themselves, had there been one.

In the end, my visit to the museum made me want glass floor-to-ceiling display cases for my own house. It also made me want to be buried with stuff. Cool stuff. The kind of stuff that would make people want to loot my grave.

# Grave with a Grudge
## MILFORD, NH

IN HORROR STORIES, unavenged murder is often set right by the victim's corpse rising from the grave to point a decaying finger at the guilty. Very rarely does the grave itself point the finger.

In the much less zombie-plagued arena of real life, however, such a case actually exists in a small cemetery in the town of Milford, New Hampshire.

The gravestone belongs to one Caroline Cutter, who died in the mid-1800s. It's simple, white, and rectangular, and upon its face is crammed about

150 words of painstakingly etched accusation, courtesy of her husband, Dr. Calvin Cutter, a prominent surgeon of the time.

Although the cramped inscription has weathered almost to the point of illegibility in places, you can still puzzle out the wording pretty easily . . . by looking it up elsewhere. I chose an 1887 issue of *New England Magazine.* I'm a little behind on my reading.

According to the gravestone, Caroline Cutter was "Murdered by the Baptist Ministry and Baptist Churches." Specifically, a deacon and a reverend accused her of lying in a church meeting and then another deacon somehow "reduced [her] to poverty," two instances in an apparent range of conspiratorial efforts to keep Cutter "down." These church staff members were called out by name, of course. The grave goes on to state that "The intentional and malicious destruction of her life and happiness, as above described, destroyed her life," and finished with a quote from Caroline herself, "Tell the truth and the iniquity will come out."

Honestly, the gravestone kind of reads like the paranoid screed one would find written on the back of a Chinese menu and shoved at you by the same homeless person who penned it, or which one would find on a random Web site on the 40th results page of a completely unrelated Google search. Still, we all deal with the death of loved ones in different ways. Calvin Cutter dealt with it by getting all finger-pointy. According to Fritz Wetherbee, the inveterate chronicler of all things New Hampshire, the Cutters were kicked out of the Baptist church denounced on the gravestone because Dr. Cutter was bullying members into funding the construction of another church in town that Cutter had pushed to be built and had so far funded all by himself on just his own empty promises. Caroline apparently took the expulsion pretty hard.

The grave is located in Elm Street Cemetery at the intersection of Elm and Cottage streets. It's easy to find. The tombstone is about 20 paces directly in front of the opening. In addition, a golden retriever–size memorial boulder with an inset plaque sits on the plot a mere foot or so in front of Caroline's headstone. The boulder is a memorial to Carrie Cutter, the daughter of Calvin and Caroline.

According to the plaque, Carrie was the "first female to enter the service of her country in the Civil War, the first that fell at her post, and the first to form organized efforts to supply the sick of the army." She was 20 at the time of her death. With all that going for her, you'd think we'd of all heard of her, but maybe her father set an unfortunate precedent for disbelieving anything that funeral plot spouts.

Still, even though the message on Caroline's headstone has survived 170 years or so, something tells me that she would rather have had some pretty roses or a nice pair of praying hands etched onto her grave . . . and that Caroline the Undead could've taken care of the Baptists on her own.

# Green Mount Cemetery
### MONTPELIER, VT

ONE OF MY FAVORITE CEMETERIES in all of New England is Green Mount Cemetery in Montpelier, Vermont . . . and I realize that it says something analysis-worthy about me that I have favorite cemeteries. I also realize that the insight would've been a lot more surprising if it were not in a book with a skull on the front cover.

Green Mount Cemetery has no famous interments, doesn't feature prominently in any movie that I'm aware of, is not huge to the point of getting lost in, and doesn't have a really intriguing history . . . all things that make cemeteries stick out to me. But it does have a few impressive pieces of funerary art that, combined with the cemetery's beautiful setting, make this a pretty spectacular graveyard.

Located at 251 State Street (also known as Route 2) in the state capital, Green Mount Cemetery began as a 35-acre purchase in 1854 at the bequest of a benefactor, who willed enough money for the purpose that the town was able to match it and secure a nice little piece of land for its dead citizens.

Set right in the rolling hills of Vermont, which light on fire in the fall—exactly the time I suggest visiting it—the cemetery crawls up the side of one of those hills, and the dead welcome you to Green Mount with a massive stone freestanding arch. Inside is a soldiers' lot for Civil War dead, a potter's field for the less-heralded dead, and a children's section, because even in the afterlife, children eat at the small table.

Meanwhile, many of the surrounding monuments and tombstones vie heroically for your attention like kindergartners straining their little arms into the air for a teacher. Among these are interesting statues of men, women, animals, and the minimum number of flared-winged angels.

One of the more unique grave markers is the William Stowell tomb, which features a tall set of hand-carved stairs cut into a single granite ledge. The stairs are visible from the road and twist up the tomb and the hill in which it is set, depositing the climber on an upper level of the graveyard.

At the top, and set far enough away from it that I assume it's not affiliated with the tomb, is a dead tree stump that has at some point been roughly carved into a throne. From that high vantage, you can sit and survey the realm. Unless it rained recently, in which case you can sit and get your seat wet.

Elsewhere, a life-size statue of a little girl leans against a flower-carved rail. The statuary marks the burial spot of seven-

year-old Margaret Pitkin, who died in 1900 and has a cooler monument than 60 percent of U.S. presidents. In the story that goes with it, a sculptor was commissioned to create the piece from a photograph (and a block of stone, of course). When the parents saw the finished piece, they were dismayed to discover that he had left off a button on her shoe . . . that is, until he showed them the picture, which revealed that one of the shoes of the girl in the picture also featured a missing button. Good thing, too, because "You missed a button" is a lot harder to correct with statues than with sweaters.

The John Hubbard grave is also a highlight and features a bronze statue of a seated, shrouded figure that seems to be writhing in the deep anguish of grief (see the photo on page 148). Sculpted by Karl Bitter to memorialize the grave of a local philanthropist who died in 1899, the image is similar to the much more serene Adams Memorial from Saint-Gaudens featured on page 168.

In fact, this statue has a local spook legend about it that bears an even more striking resemblance to the story of the Adams Memorial. According to lore, the Hubbard statue is called Black Agnes, and whoever sits on its lap ends up suffering bad consequences of various sorts. As I noted in the entry on the Adams Memorial, the Felix Agnus copy of that grave statue was dubbed Black Aggie and has a similar legend around it.

While I can understand the similarities of stories (since both sculptures have a lap and can easily seem creepy), the similarity of the name is a bit of a mystery . . . admittedly one whose solution isn't in my top 200 mysteries that I need solved to die satisfied. So that means I'll probably learn the solution at some point.

Finally, but not comprehensively, there's the Frederic Dieter grave. I couldn't find much information on this one, but firsthand experience might be all you need to know in this case. The grave is topped by an amazing life-size statue of a terrifyingly dead and prostrate Jesus, whose hollow eyes, jutting ribs, and various Biblically accurate wounds make you feel

uncomfortable taking pictures of it. Over him, leans a female mourner who I guess would be his mother, Mary. Having Jesus adorn your grave could come off as a bit pompous, but in this case it's as if the interred is saying, "There are more important deaths than mine." If they don't have such a startling statue above their graves, then I disagree.

I didn't give any specific directions to any of these funerary wonders, but the graveyard is small enough that all of the ones mentioned here are easy to find just by driving around the couple of miles of road that twist about its innards. It'll be a nice time. Trust me. I have a skull on the cover of my book.

# Grave of Sarah Winchester
### New Haven, CT

THERE'S ONLY ONE WAY I KNOW to make the extremely rich and famous more so . . . and that's to add crazy.

Sarah Winchester didn't need any more fame or money. She was a member of the Winchester clan, whose rifles adorned just about every holster, fireplace, and bedside in the wild and lawless place that, if the entire western genre is to be believed, was the United States in its early days.

But then, for good measure, she went ahead and added the crazy to her mix. The story goes that after outliving the rest of her immediate family at a relatively young age, she sought guidance from a psychic to see if the Winchesters were cursed and what she should do about it if they were. The psychic, of course, accommodated her. Besides telling her that her bike was in the basement of the Alamo, she advised that in order to keep at bay all the restless spirits of the people killed by Winchester rifles, she must build a house and never stop its construction. Apparently the sound of hammers to ghosts is like crucifixes to vampires.

So in 1884, the widow Sarah moved to San Jose, California, purchased a large farmhouse, and then began the endless work on what today is known as the Winchester Mystery House. By the time of her death in 1922 at the age of 83, the eight-room house had turned into a 160-room yellow and red Victorian mansion with cutting-edge modern amenities and strange-ass stuff, including cabinets that opened into other rooms, windows in the floor, staircases ending at ceilings, and doors opening onto two stories of nothing. All very funhouse and all worth touring.

When I visited that house, the tour guide actually downplayed the whole ghosts of the rifled dead, citing the possibility that Sarah just sucked at designing houses. Either explanation is pretty entertaining, of course, but all things being equal, I'll err on the spooky side every day.

Of course, as cool as all that is, the Winchester Mystery House is still in California, which is the farthest you can get from New England without becoming seaworthy, crossing international borders, or competing for the X Prize. However, in a civilized and lawful land where possession is nine-tenths of the law, New England has her corpse.

Sarah Winchester was actually born in Connecticut and spent the first

half of her life there, up until the demise of her husband, before heading to the West that her family's guns helped win.

At her death, she was brought back and buried in the family plot in New Haven, Connecticut, alongside her husband William and infant daughter Annie, under an approximately 8-foot-tall rough-hewn stone carved with an inset flower-wrapped cross with the surname Winchester carved on the crosspiece.

The grave is located in Evergreen Cemetery on Ella Grasso Boulevard. It's a pretty sizeable cemetery with quite a few large rough-hewn headstones similar to Sarah's, so the Winchester stone can be difficult to find. To locate it, take a left at the crematorium that greets you near the entrance and then follow the outside path for just a little bit. The Winchester plot is right on that path and, besides the stone, also includes a carved basin and a low stone curb that outlines the plot.

The grave is not very deep into the cemetery, so you don't have to go too far, but Evergreen is interesting enough with its plethora of eye-catching statues and fabled grave of Midnight Mary that it won't be the worst thing you've ever done.

Back to Sarah, I guess she showed us how to make oneself a tourist attraction on both U.S. coasts. Maybe the old girl really wasn't that crazy.

# Spider Gates Cemetery
### Leicester, MA

SOMETIMES HAVING A PEACEFUL, secluded location can be more trouble than it's worth. Especially when for no good reason it inspires myths of portals to hell, suicides, occultism, and other spectral fodder that excite paranormal aficionados who love to chase their tales.

Such seems to be the case with the innocuously named Friends Cemetery in Leicester, Massachusetts, a small private Quaker cemetery located within an idyllic and secluded woodland at the southern end of the Kettle Brook Reservoir area of Worcester/Leicester.

Dubbed Spider Gates cemetery by who-knows-who, due to a set of low, black, wrought-iron gates that when you squint your eyes and think creepy thoughts, kind of looks like either a spider or a spider's web, Friends Cemetery has garnered far more than the usual tales of wispy ghosts and shadowy presences that every graveyard must endure.

The stories that circulate around Friends Cemetery are pretty extreme, including the fact that the gates are one of a series of portals to hell, that Satanic rites are regularly held within its stone walls, and that someone committed suicide in a conveniently placed tree near its gates, along with other rumors that seem so random that the place either really must be set at the mouth of Hell, or they are just not worth perpetuating due to their very number. When you tell too many stories about a single place, they have the tendency to cancel each other out.

Unless there's something in the Kettle Brook Reservoir that make locals morbidly imaginative, the tales must've been inspired more by the surrounding wilderness than by its gates. I mean, the cemetery is ordinary enough that were it located on the side of a widely traveled highway, you could give it gates with the devil's own face on them and conjure a glowing vortex in its midst, and it still wouldn't attract the level of rumor that Friends Cemetery currently does.

I visited alone and, other than an ominous creaking of the gates when I entered, there was nothing about them that under ordinary circumstances would make one feel spooked by them or the graveyard itself. No crumbling mausoleums, no works of statuary turned menacing and horrific by exposure, no cryptic epitaphs. Just a few sparse groups of headstones set neat, clean, and even like an enviable set of teeth. Some of them are pretty old, dating back to the 1700s, but they're so well kept and sheltered by the forest that they seem newer.

The only thing even slightly out of the ordinary is a set of four granite posts delineating an open space, the explanation of which is apparently and mundanely that the area was the site of an old meetinghouse.

The cemetery is owned and actively used by a Quaker group known as the Worcester Friends Meeting. According to the group's Web site and a sign posted at the cemetery itself, Friends Cemetery is open to the public during daylight hours, which is either a kind gesture despite the often unfortunate attention that such rumors can attract, or a wise bit of psychology. Officially and ominously restricting entrance would probably only enhance the rumors and succeed in keeping out only the kind of people that would follow rules anyway, while encouraging the kind that wouldn't with even more reason to break them.

The cemetery is located at the end of an unmarked dirt path that some maps designate Earle Street, which is one of the surnames oft-repeated on the tombstones in the cemetery. Earle Street is right off Manville Street, and can be recognized by a yellow metal gate that bars vehicular access. The cemetery can be found less than a third of a mile up the path. Although NO TRESPASSING signs line the surrounding forest, which is a watershed property of the city of Worcester, the path itself and cemetery are open to the law-abiding.

As to the gates, they look like a spider or a spider's web only to someone who really wants them to. In my own Rorschach test, they seem more like sunbursts or wagon wheels or, probably most accurately, abstract pieces of fencing. According to the Worcester Friends Meeting, which I contacted, the gates are merely an art deco representation of the rays of the sun . . . a pleasant, happy image that, all things being equal as the never are, really shouldn't conjure up any ideas of evil.

In the end, Spider Gates Cemetery, despite its cool nickname, is more Quaker than quake-in-your-boots and, as a result, is worth a visit if you dig cemeteries, history, genealogy, or fanciful gates, but you won't get any ghostly encounters to circulate around a campfire unless you make them up yourself.

# Grave of Susanna Jayne
## Marblehead, MA

JUDGING BY THE TOMBSTONES of our colonial-era forefathers, they were much more okay with death than we are today. Our modern tombstones are either plain to the point of muteness or decorated with peaceful images to the point of blandness. It's as if we want our cemetery visitors to think they're anywhere other than above the decaying remains of their loved ones. I guess that's understandable.

As detailed in other places in this book, the early settlers of New England had no problems incorporating death's heads, skeletons, coffins, and other blatant and almost boastful memento mori into their final earthly statements, which apparently went something along the lines of, "Hey, I know you're at my tombstone and all, so you know I'm dead, but I really want the fact emphasized. See you soon."

And when it comes to morbid iconography, one of the most interesting tombstones in the entire region of New England is the one that marks the body of Susanna Jayne in Marblehead, Massachusetts.

Jayne is buried on Old Burial Hill, located at Orne Street. The cemetery is an amazing one for a variety of reasons. Established in 1638, it's one of the oldest cemeteries in the country, and its hilltop setting also gives it a view worth savoring of the older portions of Marblehead and the Atlantic Ocean. It's probably for that reason that such movies as *Hocus Pocus* and *The Good Son* were filmed here, which are both discussed elsewhere in this book. To access the cemetery, you ascend a series of steps, and, due to the various irregularities of the hill, it is naturally sectioned off into sections and levels of tombstones.

Although the graveyard seems small, it boasts the interments of 600 Revolutionary War soldiers, in addition to a cenotaph dedicated to locally born Salem witch trials victim Wilmot Redd. At its highest point, a pair of tall obelisks make the hill pointy. One, the 1848 Fishermen's Monument, memorializes the men who died during an enormous storm in 1846 that killed 65 men, sank 11 ships, and pretty much ended the town's fishing industry. The second is

a tribute to Captain James Mugford and his crew of the schooner *Franklin*, whose exploits during the Revolutionary War made Mugford and his crew heroes to the cause.

Back to Jayne. I'm sure somewhere there is an historical record that reveals the details of her life. However, it's really hard to care about anything but her tombstone.

Carved by Henry Christian Geyer, the tall marker almost demands a knowledge of heraldic terms to describe. The central image is an (extremely) bare-chested skeleton in a wisp of robe that is depicted from the torso up with a crown of laurels on its skull. In one hand it holds an anthropomorphized sun; in the other, what is assumedly a moon. The latter sphere has deteriorated over the years to the point of unrecognizability, so it could be a cantaloupe for all I know. A scythe curves behind its skull, and encircling this image is the frame of a serpent devouring its own tail. Outside the snake, in the top corners of the image, is a pair of cherubic angels. In the bottom corners, a pair of bats. Yes, bats. Above it all, is an hourglass bookended by a pair of bones.

The inscription underneath this unsettling image reads in part,

> *Deposited*
> *Beneath this Stone the Mortal Part*
> *of Mrs. Susanna Jayne, the amiable Wife of*
> *Mr. Peter Jayne, who lived Beloved*
> *and Died Universally Lamented, on*
> *August 8th 1776 in the 45th*
> *Year of her Age.*

It goes on for another seven lines of vague wording about her virtues and place in the afterlife, but in my opinion "Universally Lamented" is epitaph enough.

The symbolism of all that's pretty obvious, I guess, with representations of heaven and the underworld, mortality and time . . . but the image is just cool. The headstone is located near those two aforementioned obelisks and is immediately recognizable because it's one of the few that have been encased in concrete to protect it from breakage.

In the introduction to this section on cemeteries, gravestones, and other memento mori, I mentioned that for most of us, the only thing we're going to leave behind is a tombstone, and for that reason it's almost better to have an interesting one than to be an interesting person. With that highly flawed notion in mind, I'm happy to end this section with the grave of Susanna Jayne. More of us should really follow her lead (or the lead of whoever commissioned that stone for her) and make our final statements on this earth worth some attention.

Bats. Not even Bela Lugosi's grave has bats.

# FIVE

# Classic Monsters

REGARDLESS OF HISTORY, culture, or geographic locality, human beings have in common a few fundamental characteristics. We all love, we all die, . . . and we are all terrified of monsters. New England is no exception, and shares the creatures of its nightmares in common with peoples across the globe, albeit with unique New England twists.

Included in this section of the book are stories of aliens, cryptids, witches, vampires, mummies, demons, ghosts, and other famous monsters, all of whom have found New England to be an adequate place to run amok and wreak their terrors. However, in the character of this work, these stories are not just vague tales recounted with whatever humble stylistic flourish this author can add. Instead, these are vague tales, recounted with whatever humble stylistic flourish this author can add, that are actually connected to physical items and locations, such as monuments, streets, graves, collections . . . and even a few New England monsters themselves.

Sometimes you don't just visit New England . . . you survive it.

## *Aliens*

THE SKIES OF NEW ENGLAND are beautiful when they are not terrifying. New England has been an entry point for extraterrestrials since at least the 1960s. However, instead of leaf peeping, syrup sampling, and colonial history sightseeing, these alien visitors have caused strange sky phenomena, inspired newspaper headlines addled with exclamation points, and, not content with Plymouth Rock refrigerator magnets or moose head key chains, have even gone so far as to abduct some of the local populace as souvenirs of their journeys.

# Hill Abduction, Part I: The Route and the Graves
FRANCONIA NOTCH AND KINGSTON, NH

EVERY STATE STRIVES for some sort of preeminence over its peers. Each one wants to be the location of the first this, the largest that, the oldest these, the original those. Well, congratulations, New Hampshire. You're the location of the first official alien abduction.

On the night of September 19 and on into the early morning of September 20 in 1961, husband and wife Barney and Betty Hill were traveling back from vacation in Montreal to their home in Portsmouth, New Hampshire, when, according to their story, they were followed by a spaceship and eventually accosted, kidnapped, examined, and then released back into the wild by its extraterrestrial crew.

The event has since become the best documented and most famous case of alien abduction in the history of ufology, introducing into mainstream culture such what-was-life-like-before-them terms as *hypnotic regression, missing time,* and *anal probe,* as well as cementing a template for the current mythology of alien visitors both in our fiction and in the abduction claims that have succeeded it. The story of the Hills grew big enough, in fact, that it prompted a best-selling book by John G. Fuller, entitled *The Interrupted Journey*; inspired a television movie called *The UFO Incident,* starring James Earl Jones; and was subjected to debunking by famous intellectual Carl Sagan.

A couple of years ago, on the night of the 47th anniversary of the event, right before New England officially switched over to its renowned autumn outfit, my wife and I got into our car, drove up to northern New Hampshire, and then retraced the route taken by Betty and Barney Hill on that fateful night.

We trekked north to Lancaster, New Hampshire, waited for the appropriate hour of darkness, and then basically turned the car around and drove back home. Technically, we should have started in Montreal, I guess, but the Hills' trip didn't start getting interesting until hereabouts and 2008 was a time of great confusion over what documentation you needed to cross the Canuck border.

I had prepped in advance for the trip by reading *Captured,* an account of the Hill abduction and its aftermath coauthored by Kathleen Marden, the niece of Betty Hill, and Stanton T. Friedman, a nuclear physicist and famous UFO guy. That's in addition to my lifelong preparation of watching every alien abduction movie I could get my hands on, including *Communion, Close Encounters, Fire in the Sky,* and *Altered,* and whatever clips I could find on YouTube of the so far unreleased-to-DVD *The UFO Incident.*

The temperature on the night of our own journey was crisp, bordering on cold, and the sky was perfectly clear for UFO watching. We popped the *X-Files* series soundtrack into the car stereo and took off, our eyes enthusiastically searching the sky, with the occasional glance spared for the darkness of the road in front of us.

According to their accounts, the Hills were driving south on Route 3 when they noticed in the sky an erratic light that seemed to be following them. Eventually, that erratic light grew into a strange ship, which soon landed, trapping the Hills. The ship's inhabitants then escorted the dazed couple into the spacecraft and subjected them to the scientific rituals of some sort of intergalactic catch-and-release program.

The Hills described the physical appearance of the aliens as Irish Nazi Jimmy Durantes. Also as what has become known as classic "grays" with thin, short bodies, an oversize head, and large, dark eyes that even those of us who haven't been abducted can now instantly recognize, thanks to the flypaper that is popular culture. Obviously, that latter description doesn't sound anything like an Irish Nazi Jimmy Durante, but the Hills' story is a little confusing on the appearance of the aliens, as well as on other points. I don't mean for that to sound cynical. It was a rough night for them.

Actually, most of their memories of the night were unearthed a few years later, under hypnosis and further reflection. Their immediate impressions of the night were hazy, disjointed, and included stretches of missing time—everything a long, midnight trip through the mountains of New Hampshire would be even without alien interruption.

Certainly our own more recent trek down that same road seemed, if not as surreal as the Hills' experience, at least somewhere in the same thesaurus entry. But I guess that's more because of what it was intrinsically: a late-night reenactment of an event I don't believe happened in the first place, though I like the story.

During the sixties, the main route for getting from the top of New Hampshire to the bottom was Route 3. It still pretty much is, just with the addition of an interstate highway. As a result, the Hills' approximate route is easy enough to follow, as long as you pay attention to where it merges and unmerges with Interstate 93. And I mean *you* because I didn't and ended up having to retrace my own steps to be able to retrace theirs.

Thanks to the Hills' fuzzy recollections of that night and the various road and zoning changes over the past 50 years, we still might not have followed their course exactly, but we also didn't get abducted, probed, or have our memory erased (that I remember), so I count it as a trade-off.

Even though a lot of the route is highway, much of it is still unlit and was highly spooky at the time of night that we drove it, especially through the mountainous Franconia Notch area. Just as the Hills did 47 years before, we pulled over and got out of our car at various points along the route. Of course, they were checking out in disbelief the pursuing UFO and then being terrified into flight. We were merely taking pictures and spooking ourselves back into our car.

Also like the Hills, we passed by various landmarks, including what used to be the rock formation known as the Old Man of the Mountain. Back in the Hills' day, he still had a face. These days, he's nothing but landslide remnants and an awkward New Hampshire marketing icon. When we drove past it, we could detect the smooth black outline of its decapitated stump against the stars. We also passed by the 75-year-old Jack O'Lantern Resort in Woodstock, with its pumpkin face sign that the Hills probably would also have passed back then.

As to the actual touchdown point of the encounter, the spot is basically unknown, even to the now-deceased participants. Betty claimed to be able to find it later in life, but by then she was so immersed in UFO culture and her status within it that even UFO believers were starting to doubt some of her assertions.

Finally, we made it home . . . completely uninterrupted, I'm loath to add. I basically spent the whole trip forgetting to turn off my high-beams for passing cars, braking for phantom moose, and wondering if anybody else on the road was saying, Large Marge–style, "On this very night, 47 years ago, on this very stretch of road . . ." For the record, I also didn't see anything I could have even forced myself to mistake for a UFO, but then again, I probably would've mistaken an actual UFO for not being one, I'm so skeptical in general.

In the end, for us, it was only a three-hour tour. For the Hills, it lasted until their dying days. Barney passed away at the young age of 46 due to a cerebral hemorrhage, eight years after the incident. Betty died in 2004, after living a long life fully enmeshed and celebrated in UFO culture. They're both buried at the back of Greenwood Cemetery off North Road in Kingston, New

Hampshire. Below each of the names on their cemetery plaques is stated, "of The Interrupted Journey." Would that we all had such an interesting journey . . . minus the anal probes.

# Hill Abduction, Part II:
# The Bathroom Shrine
# and the Artifacts
## LINCOLN AND DURHAM, NH

IN THE LAST ENTRY, I recounted the semireenactment on the part of my wife and I of the night that Barney and Betty Hill found themselves on the wrong end of an alien abduction claim. I say semireenactment, of course, because our retracing of their route left out the bits about being hijacked by aliens and having our noses lit up by an extraterrestrial game of Operation. Not by choice, mind you. In the missing time since then, we've come across other Hill-related oddities worth visiting in New Hampshire, including a homemade alien abduction exhibit in a gas station bathroom and the official university-held collection of original artifacts and documentation from the Hill incident.

I'm going to start with the former because, well, you stopped reading the sentence at that point. But "homemade alien abduction exhibit in a gas station bathroom" is exactly what it is. The strange rest stop can be found in the town of Lincoln, at the Franconia Notch Irving Express gas station located right off exit 33 on I-93/Route 3, the same route down which the Hills traversed on that dark night of decades past.

Upon pulling up to a pump, the first inkling you get that this gas station is more than mere pit stop is the large 8-foot-square painting of a spindly, big-headed alien standing in the middle of a dark forest road, which is hanging beside the ice freezer where any other gas station would have a vinyl banner hawking beer, cigarettes, and stale snack cakes. Above the painting are the words, "First Close Encounter of the Third Kind, Betty and Barney Hill, Sept. 19th, 1961."

After I pretended to fill up my gas tank, all the while merely checking out the painting, I went inside to see the inevitable alien-themed wares for sale.

The gas station had some, of course, although not as many as I thought an 8-foot-square painting of an extraterrestrial would presage. Clustered around the register counter were various trinkets in alien form, including Day-Glo inflatables and key chains, as well as a few copies of the Marden and Friedman book *Captured,* which I mentioned in the previous entry.

As I started to leave the station, trying to weigh whether the outside painting by itself was enough to merit more than a passing mention in this article, my bladder made a better decision than my brain. When I walked into that gas station's single unisex bathroom, I felt like Ali Baba must have after uttering the phrase, "Open, Sesame."

The walls inside this relatively spacious bathroom were plastered all over with articles about the Hills and other alien incidents, facsimiles of official documentation, drawings of extraterrestrials, photographs, spreadsheets (yup, spreadsheets) regarding alien encounters, and, most oddly (if possible), images from random science fiction television shows and movies. It looked like one of those rooms they have in police detective movies, where evidence and assorted paper slips are tacked everywhere on boards while

the protagonist tries to fit them together to solve some crime "before it happens again." That bathroom might make you believe.

At the very least, it'll make you leave with a big grin of satisfaction, nodding to the cashier as if you've just been indoctrinated into some private and rare mystery before buying a Twix, a Coke Zero, and an alien key chain, and getting into your car and driving off into the sunset. Or at least, that's how my time at the gas station ended, minus the sunset. It was noon, and I was headed south.

Then, in the spring of 2009, the Betty and Barney Hill archive, which had been donated to the University of New Hampshire in Durham, went on temporary public display at the Milne Special Collection and Archives Department of the UNH library. The archive includes letters and personal journals from the Hills, audiotapes and transcripts of their hypnosis sessions, essays, newspaper clippings, reports, photographs, artwork, and even artifacts from that surreal night.

Because I couldn't make it to see the display during the regularly operating Milne Special Collection hours, I took the rare step of contacting them to see if it was possible to view the exhibit after hours and the even rarer step of being honest about who I was instead of lying about being a *Time* magazine reporter. For some reason, they agreed.

The public exhibit was located in a hallway on an upper floor of the library, where the Milne Special Collection and Archives Department is housed, and included one of Betty's handwritten journals, a box of her notes on extraterrestrial sightings, a few pieces of artwork, including a papier-mâché bust and painting of an alien, some photographs of the couple, and other assorted bits.

The piece I was the most interested in from the start, even before arriving, was the purple dress Betty wore the night of her abduction, for that reason and because she claimed to have found some unidentifiable pink, powdery substance on it that apparently defied scientific analysis. Also because I'm into women's fashions of the 1960s.

Immediately apparent is the missing swatch on the dress that had been removed for analysis, and the discolored patches from the mystery substance were evident as well. The dress should have been the highlight for me, but then we were allowed to see the files containing most of the original materials from the archive. The first items I pulled out were the original stained pencil drawings that Betty and Barney had sketched of the spaceship that had accosted them and the famous star map that Betty claimed was shown to her by one of the alien crew. I'd seen these rude drawings reproduced in books since I was a child, and here were the originals, right in my very own white-linen-gloved hands. Oh, the gloves weren't mine. The curator gave them to me to wear to protect the delicate photos from the horrible oils that my hands excrete. She could tell I was that type, I guess.

Next were the hypnosis transcripts. They had the original tapes, and it would have been swell to hear them, but they were off being digitized or some such other more worthwhile purpose than my excreting oils on them, or they were there and I was too chicken to push my luck and ask to hear them, I can't remember. Still, the transcripts were the next best thing, and I got to read the dramatic memories of the Hills' emotional abduction experience vividly surfacing/being falsely created right in the moment.

After that, we read through a few more letters and journal entries and viewed a few more photos before taking our leave, grateful to the UNH library for the great opportunity and cautiously watching the skies on our drive home.

# Incident at Exeter
## EXETER, NH

AT SOME POINT, I'd like to get my hands on the 50-year-old intergalactic travel brochure that blurbed, "When in the Milky Way, visit New Hampshire." You see, the thing about living in that state in the 1960s, man, is that you had to put up with all the extraterrestrials.

The 1961 alien abduction of Betty and Barney Hill in the White Mountains of New Hampshire wasn't the only high-profile UFO event that occurred in that state in that decade. On a September night in 1965, on a dark road just outside the town of Exeter, an 18-year-old local hitchhiker by the name of Norman Muscarello witnessed some intensely bright, low-lying aerial lights unearthly enough to panic him into going to the police.

And while that's usually the point in every tabloid-published UFO story where the account dies with a resounding "wacko," in this particular case it's where the story gets interesting . . . and borderline credible . . . or as close as these types of accounts get to that famed wonderland, at least.

Muscarello was able to convince the local authorities to accompany him back to the spot that night. Two officers, David Hunt and Eugene Bertrand, returned to the location on Route 150 between Exeter and Kensington, where the cosmic jacklighting occurred, and actually witnessed the phenomenon at close range themselves. Meanwhile, other corroborating reports of strange sky sightings came in to the police station.

And that's why the Incident at Exeter started making at least national headlines (possibly international . . . it's hard for me to gauge the whole world sometimes), finding itself in various media reports, air force files, and a snug little niche in the overall UFO mythology.

Beside alien visitors, the time of year, the decade, and the national response, the other thing that the Hill abduction and the Muscarello experience had in common was investigative reporter and columnist John G. Fuller. In 1966, he published best-selling nonfiction works about each of these incidents (*The Interrupted Journey* and *The Incident at Exeter*, respectively), further ensuring that these stories would stay afloat amidst the flotsam and jetsam on the surface that is popular culture.

Now, the fine print on this story is that there's an air force base in nearby Portsmouth, and according to the official air force explanation, some sort of military air activity was going on at the time. However, even if the air force didn't admit to any such thing, it's a reasonable assumption that strange lights are still an FDA-approved side effect of air force bases. And while that's enough of an explanation for a lot of people, the story still just won't die no matter how many attempted murderers it has had.

In fact, in 2009, the town of Exeter celebrated its first festival commemorating the 44-year-old event.

These days, the relevant area of Route 150, also known as Amesbury Road, where Muscarello witnessed the UFO activity is mostly taken up by an equestrian center, the white fences of which nicely delineate the fields that made him famous.

In the end, the cops never caught the aliens. Some say they still roam those horse pastures, awaiting just the right shade of night and just the right errant hitchhiker . . . unaware as they apparently are that the practice of thumbing a ride stopped being cool by the end of the 1970s.

# Cryptids

SOME MONSTERS DON'T EXIST in a different way than most monsters don't exist. We call these creatures *cryptids,* and there are
those who say that one day science will officially recognize these animals, putting such celebrity cryptids as yetis, sea serpents, and chu-
pacabras on the auspicious rosters that include blue-footed boobies,
stinkpot turtles, and schnoodles. And while New England isn't
exactly world renowned for its cryptids the way some locations are, it
does have a few more-than-notable offerings for the field.

# International Cryptozoology Museum
## PORTLAND, ME

IF YOU PUT TOO MUCH STOCK in the name of the International Cryptozoology
Museum in Portland, Maine, you're going to be a little disappointed on
your visit. I mean, sure, the ICM is a collection of cryptozoological objects
from around the world, but the grandiose name falls short of the reality. However, if you realize ahead of time what the ICM really is, a humble personal
collection of some pretty cool stuff, you're going to have a blast.

Of course, first you're going to have to get over the irony that you're
somehow about to see artifacts related to creatures that don't exist . . . making
for possibly a very empty museum.

To review, cryptozoology is the study of creatures that either don't exist
(or, depending on your stance, haven't been discovered by science yet) or
don't exist in modern times (or have been mistakenly thought to be extinct by
science). The ICM is the project of Loren Coleman, one of the foremost
activists in cryptozoology. He has published numerous works on the subject,
consulted on various films and television shows involving cryptozoology, and
contributed his own investigations to the field.

He also collects some pretty cool stuff. I know that's the second time I've
used the phrase, but it's the best umbrella description I can conjure for the
contents of the ICM.

For years, the ICM was run out of Coleman's house in Portland. How-

ever, in November 2009, he debuted his collection in a new public space in the downtown area. Located at 661 Congress Street, the ICM shares its space with the Green Hand, a bookstore run by Michelle Souliere, who is also the editor of the "Strange Maine" blog.

Upon entering, you'll find yourself in the bookshop portion of the space . . . and in the shadow of an 8-foot-tall, 400-pound Bigfoot. Called the Crookston Bigfoot after the town of Crookston, Minnesota, where it was first displayed, this musk-ox-fur-covered replica was created in 1990 by a Wisconsin taxidermist who wanted to do something more challenging than stuffing ducks and moose.

If you can tear yourself away from this monster, at the back of the bookstore is the entrance to the actual museum, which as of the writing of this piece, cost a mere five dollars to get in. Unless he's out in the field, Coleman is usually on hand to tour you through his collection. He happened to be there upon my visit. I'm not sure what my personal vision of an intrepid monster hunter is, but Coleman, who is in his sixties, was short (I think . . . he was standing next to a Bigfoot), white haired and bearded, refreshingly amiable, and, like all collectors, bad at hiding the pride he feels in his modern-day cabinet of curiosities.

The museum space is tiny, a mere room, but Coleman has crammed every inch of it with as much of his collection as physically possible. The museum contains a few movie props, including a giant pterodactyl from the short-lived television show *FreakyLinks*, a police coat from the 2002 film *The Mothman Prophecies* (for which Coleman was a consultant), and a Feejee Mermaid prop used in a television movie about the life of P. T. Barnum (see the Feejee Mermaids entry on page 212).

On the tour, Coleman made sure to point out his special appearance as a character in one of the issues of the comic book *Swamp Thing*; a small display on the Dover Demon (which Coleman introduced to the world), a lake monster statue; and various other artifacts, models, and stuffed specimens of a range of beasties—real, cryptid, and whimsical (like the jackalope and the fur-bearing trout).

Mostly, the museum has a lot of toys. After all, kids love cryptozoology, even if they don't know the term for it. Some of the toys on display at the ICM are so recent you could buy them off a Toys Я Us shelf right now. Others are awesomely vintage, including a foot-tall robot Bigfoot from the 1970 series *The Six Million Dollar Man*.

You expect people with fringe ideas to be annoyingly evangelical, but Coleman was more humorous than anything. For instance, in discussing a "life-size" wooden Bigfoot cutout, he took pains to emphasize that the current scientific hypothesis on the Bigfoot is that it is not, in fact, flat, and he also wanted to make clear that he was never a porn star . . . despite the shirt that the artist gave him in his *Swamp Thing* cameo.

Other times, it's hard to tell when he's being funny, for instance when he discusses whether Bigfoots have beards and when he shows you a collection of actual Bigfoot footprint casts right beside a collection of obvious hoaxes of Bigfoot footprint casts.

However, one of the things he was serious about, and the main theme of the ICM in general, is that a lot of scientifically (and Animal Planet–) verified animals at one time were just scoffed-at stories, including gorillas and okapi, whereas others were mistakenly labeled as extinct, such as the coelacanth, which, tellingly, is the symbol of the ICM. Of course, that was probably a much more valid point half a century or more ago, before the advent of satellite tracking, the modern-day transportation network, and content-hungry 24-hour science and nature cable channels.

In the end, whether you believe cryptozoology is a legitimate field or just a waste of a suffix (my spell checker sure doesn't think it's legitimate), what Coleman has amassed at his ICM is still some pretty cool stuff.

# Lake Champlain Monster
### BURLINGTON, VT

L AKE CHAMPLAIN is the defining feature of Burlington, Vermont, although the body of water is large enough that it's also the defining feature of quite a few other places, as well. While not quite the mini-ocean of one of the Great Lakes, it's still pretty big . . . large enough, in fact, to be shared by two states and Canada, as well as to impeccably hide a giant lake monster within its placid depths.

Naturally, the people around Lake Champlain call their hydrous denizen "Champ," and it's most often depicted as being the usual water-dinosaur-looking creature with a serpentine neck, small head, long tail, humped back, and funny little flippers for feet. "Plesiosaur" is the currently held theory for the identity of the beast. And by theory, I mean absolute guess-in-vacuum.

At some point in the history of towns on large lakes, somebody realized how lucrative to the local economy it could be to claim to have a lake monster. As a result, there's a long tradition of reports of reports of reports of lake-monster sightings in the world. The first verifiable report of a Champ sighting was back in the 1800s, and you usually only need one to get the ball avalanching. P. T. Barnum once offered a reward for the capture of Champ, dead or alive or in any possible third stage of being.

Perhaps more important to the legend of Champ than the "eyewitness" reports, though, is that it has indeed been captured, in one iconic, blurry photo. The picture was taken by Sandra Mansi in 1977 and shows a remarkably driftwoodlike object with no sense of scale protruding from the lake's surface. And that's pretty much the formula you need for a lake monster: a history of sightings longer than the life span of any possible biological entity and a controvertible photo. Oh, and a lake, I guess.

DED'CATED TO CHAMP

BELUA AQUATICA CHAMPLAINIENSIS
AND THOSE PEOPLE IN VERMONT
WHO HAVE SIGHTED CHAMP
AND ARE IN SEARCH OF CHAMP

ROCK of AGES                    JUNE 29, 1984

If one were really looking for Champ, Burlington is probably the last place one would check. Standing on the Burlington shore and looking out at the lake, it's difficult to imagine a monster rearing its terrifying head in all that crammed picturesqueness. At least, any self-respecting one. Mysterious water monsters go best with dank weed-strewn lagoons, murky pools, and isolated stretches of storm-colored water, not the layered mountains, bright sailboats, and charming lighthouse-ornamented quay of Burlington.

However, if you're a lake monster fan, there's still a giant reason to go to Burlington, or at least a 4-foot-square one. At the end of King Street, which leads right down to the harbor, is Perkins Pier. Here you'll find a small, tombstonelike granite slab dedicated to Champ and "those people in Vermont who have sighted Champ and are in search of Champ." That's right. A Champ memorial.

It's not the most memorable memorial you'll come across in your life, but how often are you going to see a piece of stone dedicated to a figment, hoaxers, the gullible, the bad-sighted, the lovers, the dreamers, and me. Besides a cartoony depiction of the creature, it bears the monster's pseudoscientific name *Belua aquatica champlainiensis*. Scientists get bored just like the rest of us. Near the monument on this parklike pier are a few benches, where you can sit, stare out at the water, and lazily search for your own driftwood dinosaur.

This lonely stone isn't the only way that the city of Burlington has embraced its monster. In fact, it has firmly wrapped both its arms and legs around Champ's sinuous neck for what it hopes to be a grand ride. Champ has been labeled as an officially protected species by the government of Vermont (politicians also get bored), and businesses often incorporate Champ into their trademarks and decorations. The most notable example of this being Burlington's Minor League baseball team, the Vermont Lake Monsters, which makes for a great symbol to throw on a baseball cap.

Incidentally, I hope you understand the restraint I've exercised in this entry by not once mentioning Loch Ness. Well, at least not twice.

# Feejee Mermaids
### GRAFTON, VT; PORTLAND, ME;
### CAMBRIDGE, MA; BRIDGEPORT, CT

THE FEEJEE MERMAID is not a species native to New England, although it does pop up from time to time, mostly in museums. However, even then it's an elusive creature often confined to the museum's basement storage spaces.

Feejee Mermaids are taxidermist-created chimeras whereby the back half of a fish is Frankenstein'd onto the front half of a mammal, normally a monkey, and then preserved. The result is usually quite harrowing and monstrous. These artifacts originated in the islands of the Far East for, it is assumed, artistic reasons. Before the inventions of printed T-shirts, key chains, and refrigerator magnets, sailors often brought them back as souvenirs and examples of the exotic wonders that were only accessible to the most adventurous of human stock. On this half of the world, the faux creatures usually ended up in sideshows or the curio cabinets of private collectors, and then eventually in the museums that those private collections became.

Feejee Mermaids were popularized in the 1800s by P. T. Barnum, who also coined the term for them. The specimen that Barnum is renowned for exhibiting was loaned to him by Moses Kimball, a Boston-area counterpart of Barnum's. That originally named Feejee Mermaid was touted with all the public relations stunts and bamboozlement for which Barnum is infamous.

Of course, in modern times, where our huckterism is confined to television ads and political speeches, our auspicious museums don't quite know what to do with their Feejee Mermaids if they happen to have been bequeathed one. Not being real creatures, they don't belong in the natural history section. To include them in an anthropology exhibit stretches that science to the point of meaninglessness. And, as an art form, Feejee Mermaids haven't quite yet staked out a genre. In addition, because these artifacts usually have a vague, mysterious past, it's difficult to determine whether one has a legitimate antique specimen or one of more recent vintage, as somebody somewhere is always apparently making these. It's easy to fake a fake.

Because Barnum is so tied to these creatures, the Barnum Museum in Bridgeport, Connecticut, has one on display. Actually, the one they have is a papier-mâché reproduction of Barnum's original Feejee Mermaid that was created for the purposes of an HBO special about him. As a result, it's not exactly the most exotic thing, although it is interesting looking. Incidentally, no one knows what happened to his original. It could have burned in the fire that took out his American Museum, or it could have ended up back with Kimball and then burned in the fire that took out his museum. Fires hate museums most of all.

The Peabody Museum at Harvard University in Cambridge, Massachusetts, has an authentic one that traces its lineage all the way back to Moses Kimball. When compared to pictures of Barnum's creature, it becomes apparent that Kimball had more than one. The Peabody Museum

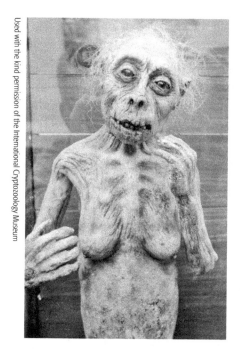

rarely displays their grisly little treasure, though, choosing instead to keep it in storage. However, for the past few years, they've loaned it out to various temporary and traveling exhibitions. I personally caught it at the Mythical Creatures exhibit at the Boston Museum of Science in early 2009. Decrepit, creepy, and made of actual animal parts, it's exactly what you want to see when you go see a Feejee Mermaid.

Even though he doesn't claim Feejee Mermaids are real as he does with other not-real creatures, Lauren Coleman's International Cryptozoology Museum (see page 207) has a few specimens on display. All are reproductions, but a couple of them are still reproductions of note. For instance, the museum boasts a 3.5-foot-tall Feejee Mermaid that was created, like the one owned by the Barnum Museum, as a movie prop, this time for a 1999 A&E movie about Barnum. You apparently can't make a movie about Barnum without a Feejee Mermaid. Another interesting specimen on display is a terrifyingly realistic-looking piece that is the product of artist Juan Cabana, who has made his name creating terrifyingly realistic-looking mer-creatures.

My most intimate experience with a Feejee Mermaid in New England occurred at the Nature Museum in Grafton, Vermont. Located at 186 Townshend Road, this small natural history museum can be found in a converted house, and is dedicated to Vermont flora, fauna, and geology. It's mostly geared toward children, but does contain numerous preserved animal specimens and other exhibits of interest, no matter what your age. From all appearances, you'd never know that it had a Feejee Mermaid in its basement.

At the time of my visit, the museum's Feejee Mermaid was not on display for the public. Betsy Stacey, the curator, was kind enough to let me see it, though. According to the little bit of documentation that the museum has for it, this Feejee Mermaid was acquired a little less than a decade ago from the

Odd Fellows Hall in Brattleboro, Vermont. Included in that documentation is a picture of the creature hanging unceremoniously on a wall of the hall above a large trophy fish.

Like the specimen of the Peabody Museum and the Juan Cabana piece at the International Cryptozoology Museum, the mermaid at the Nature Museum is about a foot long, fragile looking, and eerie to a satisfactory degree. The bottom half is the requisite fish tail, and the top half contains unidentified animal parts arranged under some sort of dark plaster. Beneath its mustachioed face could easily be the delicate skull of a small monkey. The tips of its arms bear webbed fingers with definite animal claws, and its tiny sharp white teeth could feasibly have been of animal origin, as well.

Betsy is considering displaying it just as a curiosity. However, if by the time you're reading this book, she hasn't put it on public display, I'm sure she'd still be willing to show it off to interested parties.

And who isn't one, when it comes to Feejee Mermaids?

# Dover Demon
## DOVER, MA

AT NIGHT, IN A CAR, on dark roads lined in vague silhouettes, every creature encountered is a shambling shadow-warped monstrosity with two evil points of reflection for eyes. As a result, I've mistaken the identities of my share of animals under those circumstances, unable to quite grasp what a particular creature is in the brief seconds of headlight shine and my own blinding surprise. But I can honestly say that I have never once mistaken anything—animal, vegetable, or mineral—in the day or in the night—for something unknown to science.

And the witnesses of the Dover Demon will say the same thing. They've also never mistaken any animal for something unknown to science on a dark road after nightfall. But they will tell you that they have unmistakably seen something unknown to science on a dark road after nightfall. Something goat size and hairless, with a bulbous head, tiny glowing eyes, and four thin limbs with long digits, scrabbling about a random stretch of Dover, Massachusetts.

In the late 1970s, four teenagers in three separate instances claimed to have seen such a mysterious creature as the one described above. And while it's easy to write off 127 percent of what any given teenager has to say, this particular story, despite its humble beginnings, has since traveled the world and is still being told three decades later.

It all started when 17-year-old William Bartlett was driving home on April 21, 1977. Somewhere around 10:00 PM, he spotted a hairless, strangely limbed and craniumed beast clambering on all fours along a stone wall near the road, like some lost alien pet. The creature made such an impression on him that as soon as he got home, he told his parents and drew an image that has since become the most famous piece of the Dover Demon story . . . and the most famous work of a man who since has made a living in the art world.

Of course, a few things besides his age cast doubt on his story. The length of time he saw it (about 15 seconds), the fact that he had been smoking marijuana about an hour before (it's the best PSA that's never been made: You'll never be a credible witness to a monster if you smoke pot). Finally, the fact that it was hairless, which makes me realize for the fourth time in my life that the world really needs a photographic database of every furred mammal in a shaven state.

Still, the story conflagrated due to the actions of Loren Coleman, owner of the International Cryptozoology Museum already mentioned twice in this section of the book. When Coleman found out by chance about the story, only a week after it happened, he put together a team of investigators who documented the locations, testimony, and other factors . . . uncovering three more witnesses in the process. It was this quick action to collect fresh details that gave the story legs sturdy enough to walk on for the past few decades. Well, that, and the hugely marketable name "Dover Demon," which has been attributed to Coleman himself.

The second witness that the investigators found was 15-year-old John Baxter, who claimed to have seen a similar creature running on two legs on a nearby road on the same night as Bartlett. The other two witnesses were 15-year-old Abby Brabham and 18-year-old William Taintor, who saw a creature cross the street on the night of April 22. All three sightings were apparently within a mile or so of one another, and apparently all the eyewitnesses corroborated enough in their facts to keep the investigators' interest.

The site of the first sighting is on Farm Street, a picturesque little backwoods residential road outside town. Low stone fences still line the street there, and it seems a place that one could very well have a mysterious encounter late at night. The exact location of the sighting is on the section of Farm Street near where Smith Street branches off and across from addresses 114 and 116. One the other side of the stone fence is a field over which the creature was supposed to have dashed off into the night for his two other rendezvous. Those other two encounters happened close to Farm Street, with the Baxter sighting occurring on Miller Hill Road, and the Brabham/Taintor one on Springdale Avenue.

The creature was never seen since . . . except for on T-shirts, merchandise, and Web sites. The local historical society in Dover has embraced it, locals have embraced it, cryptid aficionados have embraced it. Heck, I've even embraced it. Although *embrace* is a much different verb than *believe.*

## Witches

JUST AS EVERY TOWN has its official haunted house to test the mettle of neighborhood kids and nourish stories to full blossom in the cozy heat of living room fireplaces on dark autumn nights, every town has its witch legend. New England, above any other area in the United States, is just Black Sabbathy with them. Each of these tales of religious fervor and dark demonic pacts have left for posterity a string of curses and faint cackles that can be traced to gravestones and monuments across New England, all of which can be found with the right direction and a good sturdy broomstick for a compass point.

## Goody Cole
### HAMPTON, NH

ONE OF THESE DAYS I'm going to stumble upon the true-life story of an executed witch that not only doesn't involve a years-too-late postmortem pardon, but which further evidence has revealed that, indeed, the condemned was a nefarious, spell-casting consort of the devil. Until then, I'll just have to be entertained by variations on the other theme, and the case of Goody Cole is definitely one of those.

Although the state of Massachusetts pretty much ran the Monopoly board when it comes to witches, New Hampshire has a pretty famous one of it its own to proudly claim . . . who it horribly mistreated and (basically) killed.

The year was 1656, and the town was Hampton, New Hampshire, located on the short stretch of ocean coast that the state dares to claim from the other coastal New England states. For any in the wide range of reasons that a person can hate their neighbor, Goodwife Eunice Cole was accused of the easy-to-launch crime of witchcraft.

Goody Cole was arrested, tried, and thrown in a Boston jail for 15 years. After she was released, impoverished, widowed, and still mistreated by superstitious neighbors, Cole eventually died alone and miserable in the corner of a dilapidated shack. Upon discovering her body, the townspeople drove a wooden stake through her heart and buried her in an undisclosed shallow grave. Indignities never cease.

The centuries passed, the witch fad faded into folklore, and then, in 1938 at the town tercentenary celebration, Hampton found itself in need of a publicity stunt. They found one, and it worked. The public exoneration of Goody Cole 300 years after her maltreatment became an international story. The town burned reproductions of her trial papers, mixed them with dirt purportedly from her undiscovered grave, and then sealed it all in a can, to be buried under a proposed monument that was never really built.

When you visit the Tuck Museum in Hampton these days, you can see on a shelf in a corner a display with a homemade Goody Cole doll and the above-mentioned metal canister. In the back of the museum, a substantial collection of magazine and newspaper articles on Cole's story and her eventual acquittal attests to how big the story became.

Big enough, in fact, to merit a rock.

In the 1960s, locals placed a 4.5-foot-tall rock on the grounds of the Tuck Museum to honor Goody Cole. The rock is flat in the back, bulbous in the front, and, strangely, has no plaque or any other distinguishing feature that could lead one to realize that the rock honors anyone, much less an almost 400-year-old pardoned witch. Beside her stone is another, this one encased in an iron-barred enclosure. Similarly unlabeled, this rock has long been touted (and disproved) to mark the grave of a Viking named Thorvald.

I'm not sure how much these more recent events comfort Goody Cole in whatever afterlife is reserved for falsely accused witches, but I hope she at least takes consolation in the fact that her legend makes Halloween in New Hampshire a lot more fun.

# Grave of the Witch
### York, ME

SAMUEL NASSON didn't intend to turn his wife Mary into a witch. In fact, he was trying to do the opposite—honor her in perpetuity, and he went to his grave thinking that was what he had done. But the people must have a witch.

The Old Burying Yard of York, Maine, at the intersection of York Street/Route 1 and Lindsay Road, dates back to the 17th century. It's a small, sparsely tombstoned cemetery surrounded by a low stone wall that sits peacefully in a shady spot among the historic buildings of the Old York area of town.

However, inside that graveyard is the tombstone of a witch. And that's kind of the whole story. Seriously. I mean, there are the usual briefly worded anecdotes about her being "good with herbs" or some such that are present in every witch legend in New England and another about crows always gathering around her grave, but that's all. Now, that said, it's not all that surprising that the legend exists.

Mary Nasson died on August 18, 1774. Her husband, Samuel, had carved on the crown of the gravestone an image of her. It depicts Mary, or at least her upper half, as a loosely robed woman with bugged eyes, a thin nose, a slightly upturned mouth, and a humped hairdo that looks like two skeins of yarn. Think Gary Oldman as the ancient-looking Count Dracula from Francis Ford Coppola's movie version of the Bram Stoker tale.

There's actually nothing incidentally evil in the image's expression, nor has natural wear unpleasantly distorted her face in any way. In addition, the flowing script of her epitaph does not yield any opportunities to distort a nice sentiment into an ominous one. It merely states that she was a loving mother and wife, and that her husband looks forward to when his dust can "mingle" with hers.

But the people must have a witch, and a unique carving of a woman on a gravestone will do nicely for that, thank you.

On her grave is a granite slab, which the legend weaves into the witch's story as an attempt to keep her from rising from the grave. However, these types of stones are pretty common in old New England. They're called wolf stones in Europe, and were used to keep wolves from disturbing graves. Here they used them to keep free-range pigs and cattle away.

Other graves in the Old Burying Ground probably had them as well, but over time they disappeared, probably recycled for building materials. Some have suggested that they might have been used in the coping of the cemetery wall itself.

Mary's grave is supposed to have a footstone, as well. Older pictures depict it as slightly smaller than the headstone, with the head, halo, and wings of an angel carved into it. When I visited, that part was missing, gone wherever old gravestones go. The fabled crows were also missing, even though I have seen crows in just about every cemetery I've ever visited.

Surprisingly, the information sign on the wall of the cemetery actually addresses, amid the usual paragraphs of historical facts, the legend of the witch's grave. Of course, it merely states the myth, including the bit about the stone keeping her from rising, and then goes on to explain the truth. Still, I like it when a myth becomes an officially recognized version.

An easy way to find the grave of Mary Nasson is to park in the lot by the pair of burgundy-colored historical buildings on Lindsay Road. As soon as

you cross the street to the graveyard, you'll see the information sign on the wall and then Mary's stone inside. Like I said, it's a small cemetery and hers is the only one with a horizontal slab of rock on it.

These days, many often opt to etch photo-realistic images of their dead loved ones on the polished surfaces of their tombstones. To those well-meaning souls I gently suggest, let the grave of Mary Nasson be a warning.

# Witches of Salem
### SALEM, MA

YOU KNOW THAT BIT OF AWKWARDNESS you feel when you're pretty sure no introductions are necessary between two people, yet it's still your social responsibility to assume otherwise and make a half-hearted attempt? Well . . . meet Salem, Massachusetts.

If the witch-fest that is contemporary Salem is any indication, the moral of the witch trials of 1692 is that tragedy births festivity. This is especially true if you visit Salem in October. Interest in cauldron-hunched hags seems more excusable in that month, and it is also, as a result, the time of year when Salem celebrates its monthlong Haunted Happenings, a Halloween-dyed celebration when special events are scheduled, stores and attractions stay open longer, street vendors proliferate, and the usual skim of witchiness that always overlays the town is given a second coat.

My first stop in Salem is always the Salem Witch Museum across from the Salem Common on Washington Square North. Not to go into it, though. Just to hang out around it. With its reddish medieval-looking exterior, towering statue of town founder Roger Conant, and autumn decorations, it's Salem on a postcard, and if you kill some time there and then skip the rest of the town, you can still pretty much say you did Salem.

The one time I actually did go into the Witch Museum, I found it rather misnamed. The museum's a one-room show involved an encircling diorama of life-size figures in scenes that are sequentially lighted and narrated to tell the story of the Salem witch trials. It's a decent little show, but with such a great façade and all-encompassing name, it's a bit of a letdown.

Salem is a harbor town, and if it didn't have its witches, it would probably put more of its eggs in its maritime history basket. Derby Street parallels Salem Harbor, and a pleasant walk along the waterfront area will take you to what is supposed to be the oldest candy company in the country, Ye Olde Pepper Companie, and the birthplace of Nathaniel Hawthorne, as well as the house that inspired his *The House of the Seven Gables.*

Once you have some hard candy to chip your teeth on and the smell of dead sea things in your nose, you can backtrack along the painted red line of the Salem Heritage Trail toward the epicenter of Salem's Haunted Happenings shenanigans to the Witch Trial Memorial and the Burying Point cemetery located on Charter Street. The memorial is an open space surrounded by a low wall, with inset stone ledges for benches around the perimeter and some barely visible witch trial victim quotes engraved on the paving stones of the threshold of the enclosure. It's a subtle memorial that makes you forget that you're at a memorial . . . which is, well, funny.

Created in 1637, the Burying Point cemetery beside the memorial is pretty much as old as American cemeteries get. In it are buried historical notables such as a *Mayflower* passenger and John Hathorne, one of the villains of the witch trial hysteria. The cemetery is small, open, and filled with those thin skull-inscribed tombstones popular in those times.

I've been to more cemeteries than is probably proper, but this is definitely one of the stranger cemetery experiences I've had. Normally, I feel half out of place at the graveyards I visit, which I guess I should clarify, I go to for aesthetic, historic, or cultural reasons. Maybe one or two morbid ones, as well. Regardless, I still often feel as if, if I'm not visiting a dead relative, I

SALEM WITCH MUSEUM

don't really belong there. However, at the Burying Point during Haunted Happenings, it's like a party, which I guess often still implies a place where I don't belong, but in this case everybody's welcome to mingle among the gravestones while eating carnival-type foodstuffs and treading festively above the dead. This convivial atmosphere is due to the fact that in October it's hemmed in by Salem's Haunted Neighborhood, an area that features haunted house attractions, museums, and vendors. As a result, funhouse screams, ware hawking, and teenagers loudly overreacting to one another are the sound-track for your cemetery stroll.

Gift shops and stores are everywhere in Salem. One of the better places for shopping is the Essex Street Pedestrian Mall, which, in addition to stores, has various vendors lining the streets during Haunted Happenings.

Scattered throughout Salem are other attractions and tours of varying worth and interest, all of which at the very least give you something to do while you're walking around town eating a plate of fried dough and wearing a conical hat. Some of the more popular include the Witch House, the Peabody Essex Museum, the Salem Wax Museum, Count Orlok's Nightmare Gallery (see "Famous Monsters"), and the New England Pirate Museum. You can even spend some time at Gallows Hill Park, named for the hanging spot of the Salem witch trials, the actual location of which is, surprisingly, unknown.

Of course, the truth is, there are much better ways of finding out the actual story of the witch trials than by going to Salem or any of its attractions. But that observation is pretty irrelevant to what Salem's all about these days. That's way okay by me. Personally, I dig it when towns form identities beyond sports teams and generic historical worth.

# Salem Village Witchcraft Victims Memorial
### DANVERS, MA

OFTEN LOST IN ALL THE BROOMSTICK BLUSTER that goes on in Salem, Massachusetts, is the fact that the witch hysteria actually started in the neigh-boring town of Danvers, where most of the participants lived. Back then, it was called Salem Village, and it was in the town meetinghouse there that the often-dramatized examinations first started taking place. Later, the more official trials, executions, and municipal goings-on occurred in late-to-the-party Salem.

However, while its neighbor gets worldwide fame, festivals, witch-embossed taxicabs, and a copyright on Halloween, pretty much all Danvers

has to pull in those same tourists are a few historic houses where some of the victims lived, a couple of informational signs, and a memorial. The Salem Village Witchcraft Victims Memorial. That's the name, although I don't think any of the victims actually died of witchcraft.

Installed in 1992 in front of a baseball field at 176 Hobart Street, the memorial sits directly across from the original site of the aforementioned meetinghouse, which is currently a residential property where lives a family who, I'm sure, is tired of visitors across the street staring at their house as they mow their lawn and refresh themselves on their Slip 'n Slide.

The monument is a large, severe, granite construct made up of two separate pieces. In the front, a dedication-carved square block is topped by a granite slant-top box and book in which is engraved the phrase, "The Book of Life," and on either side of which are hand-forged metal chains and manacles. Behind that is a series of five vertical and continuous granite slabs incised with the names of all 25 victims, along with some of their more inscribable quotes maintaining their innocence. Topping all that is the image of a 17th-century cleric, the symbol of the group that arranged for the creation of the memorial.

Although the memorial was constructed to have various redemptive and inspiring meanings, the whole thing is reminiscent to me of a giant pulpit from which I can imagine magistrates and clergymen judging and condemning witches, and from which we now in turn can judge and condemn the magistrates and clergymen. Way to become villains and laughingstocks of history, guys.

# Cursed Memorial of Colonel Buck

### BUCKSPORT, ME

I'M NOT A BIG FAN of this little Maine folk legend. Pretty much the only reason I'm including it in this book is so that I can state that opinion.

It starts out promisingly, if unsurprisingly, enough. During the early years of Bucksport, Maine, its founder, Colonel Jonathan Buck, had a witch executed. Before she died at the bad end of a hangman's noose, she cursed Buck to always bear the mark of that deed. You've seen this movie, I know. But I doubt any movie has ended quite as this story does.

For you see, that prophesied mark is apparently a water stain in the shape of a pointed stocking that appeared on a monument honoring him 75 years after his death. Some witches are just bad at curses, I guess.

Of course, there are variations that make it a better and slightly more sensible tale. In one version, instead of hanging her, he had her burned, and her leg fell off and rolled out of the fire to Buck's feet. In another, she wasn't a witch, just pregnant with his child in a socially unacceptable situation; the burned-at-the-stake-as-a-witch bit was just an easy way out for Buck. In yet another version, her already born and deformed son grabbed the leg when it fell off and ran away with the relic, never to be seen again.

Regardless of the embellishments, what we're actually left with these days is a water stain on a granite obelisk in a hilltop graveyard on Main Street in downtown Bucksport, which hangs just below the founder's name like a stocking hung by the chimney with care.

Of course, the requisite "impossible to expunge from the stone" caveat comes into play here, but something tells me that the town board of selectmen has never tried too hard to remove it. The nearby sign explaining the legend for all the tourists that it draws to their town tells me that they probably won't ever. A wrought-iron gate around the monument precludes anyone else from trying, as well.

Also, far from this being a random rumor that I've seized upon to pad out the content of this book, the town of Bucksport itself has invested quite a bit into the myth, including signs, postcards, and a whole page on the town's official Web site.

Now, the Buck Memorial myth does have some age to it (it's been in circulation for at least 100 years), so in these days where a silly piece of false information can be circulated internationally to a vast audience in seconds, it does have that going for it. But the negatives still outweigh the positives. For instance, water stains suck in bathtubs and ceilings, but I'm not sure how effective they are as curses. Also, it doesn't take much to see that the monument is just dappled with similar stains.

I'm all for passing along good stories regardless of their veracity, but when it's based on something as sheer as this, I say start over. I put this myth about three notches below images of Christ on toast and Mary in tree trunks.

Anyway, I hope this entry doesn't count as me perpetuating the myth, because otherwise, I'm not a big fan of myself, either.

# Witch Rock

## ROCHESTER, MA

THERE IS A HAUNTED ROCK in Rochester, Massachusetts. Which rock? Witch Rock.

The story of Witch Rock follows the same general pattern as just about every other story of its ilk. It begins with the perennially frightened Native Americans shunning the area due to the rarely elaborated-upon evil spirits, and then switches gears to the European settlers who were equally terrified of it but had a much more codified spiritual framework from which to pull their fear-provoking spooks. In contemporary times, of course, we just painted the silhouette of a broomstick-straddling witch on it and drunkenly dare one another to visit it in the middle of the night.

There's not a whole lot of information floating around about this haunt, mostly just people saying, "There's a rock in Rochester, Massachusetts, with a witch painted on it called Witch Rock," and moving on to more easily elaborated topics. Basically that is what I'm doing here, except I'm bloating it into 450 words. Information is also vague on just exactly how the rock is haunted. Alternatively cited are sounds of laughter, creepy voices, or full-bodied specters, all of which are said to seep from the various nooks and crannies that can be found all over the rock.

Located on a corner lot at the intersection of New Bedford and Vaughan Hill roads, Witch Rock is hulking and completely hard to miss. It's more a giant boulder than a rock, standing about 12 feet tall and about 15 feet wide. I can substantiate that the rock does have many nooks and crannies from which sounds of laughter, creepy voices, or full-bodied specters could seep. In addition, a large tree grows right up against the rock, which shades the black witch painted on its flattest face and probably prevents its fading from sun and rain.

The best part about Witch Rock is that the giant boulder is literally sitting in somebody's front yard. Heck, it's absolutely dominating it. When I visited, I knocked on the door of the house to talk to its residents about what it's like to have a haunted rock ruling one's property, but nobody answered, meaning I missed the chance to add colorful anecdotes about annoying teenagers with spray paint cans and even more annoying writers with book deadlines.

Still, Witch Rock has a silhouette of a witch painted on it, so it has that much going for it over the many other generic rocks connected to random legends. In addition, although I'm not sure how much having a giant haunted thing sitting firmly on one's real estate adds to the resale value of a house, it's for sure a much cooler lawn ornament than a ceramic gnome or plastic flamingo.

## Vampires

IN RECENT DECADES, the vampire has been so badly used in our horror stories that just about all terror has been exsanguinated from it. Once the personification of evil and a nefarious seducer of the innocent, these days he's pretty much a lackluster fiend, effeminate and clichéd. For this reason, it does the monster aficionado good to go back to a time when vampires were not only terrifying in our stories, but when people were actually scared of them in real life.

To get there you have to go back pre–Christopher Lee, back pre–Bela Lugosi . . . heck, even back pre–Bram Stoker. In fact, all the way back to a time when it was a medically recommended course of action to dig up loved ones and mutilate their corpse to keep them from rising and destroying others in your family. As extreme as that sounds, this happened pretty regularly in New England in the 17th through 19th centuries. The true stories of New England vampires all seem to follow almost the exact same template, so I've only included here as examples a couple of the more famous cases.

## Grave of Mercy Brown
### EXETER, RI

SOME PEOPLE GET NICKNAMES, some people get titles, but a lucky few on this planet actually get subtitles—pithy descriptions of the most notable part of their lives tacked onto the end of their names. For instance, Lon Chaney is "the Man of a Thousand Faces" and Helen of Troy is "the Face that Launched a Thousand Ships." The name of the subject of this entry,

Mercy Brown, is almost always followed by the phrase, "New England's Last Vampire."

Mercy Lena Brown, a 19-year-old resident of Exeter, Rhode Island, received her subtitle posthumously in the year 1892. The case of Mercy Brown was the last known instance in Rhode Island and probably the rest of the United States, of a large group of otherwise sensible folk exhuming, mutilating, immolating, and cannibalizing a corpse to cure the dreaded scourge of . . . vampirism. Today we know Mercy's condition as tuberculosis . . . because we are on much more friendly terms with it.

You see, for a few centuries in our history, this nation and its previous evolutionary forms wanted to be medieval Europe. We ran ourselves frothy ferreting out witches, staking vampires, bustin' ghosts, and pretty much setting the stage for the American horror genre.

This happened all over New England, but tiny Rhode Island seems to have featured a disproportionate number of cases of tubercular vampires—Sarah Tillinghast, Ruth Ellen Rose, Abigail Staples, Nancy Young, all young women with macabre little postscripts to their lives. You can actually still visit some of their graves in the historical cemeteries of the state. None are as famous as Mercy Brown, though, due to the media documentation and the fact that she is the most recent.

In her particular story, a farmer named George Brown had a problem. His family was dropping like dead people around him—first his wife Mary, then his daughter Mary, and then his daughter Mercy. Nothing worked to stop this series of deaths, and, as usual, when the landish doesn't work, you turn to the outlandish. When his son Edwin verged on death himself with the same symptoms, George and the villagers grabbed their pitchforks and torches and went on a monster hunt. All right, well, nothing that dramatic. Still, there was talk, and with a whole family's succumbing to a mysterious blood-coughing illness that could, for all they knew, be contagious and/or transmitted by fangs in the neck, something had to be done.

After exhuming the bodies of the two Marys and finding nothing but bones, they turned to Mercy's body. Here the accounts diverge a bit. Some say she was exhumed from the ground. Others say that because she died in the month of January, corpse planting would have been out of season due to frozen ground, and she would have been kept in a nearby crypt until the thaw. Either way, the body was . . . uh . . . accessed.

Now, not everybody thought Mercy was a vampire, but when people saw her body, it was supposedly in a physical condition and position not assumed by the long-dead, even in winter. As a result, they thought it wouldn't hurt to treat her like a vampire "just in case." In this case, "just in case" meant that the villagers cut out Mercy's heart, burned it, and then had Edwin, the ailing son, drink the ashes.

The attempted cure didn't work . . . he still died, although he was the last in the family to do so (not ever, but from TB), and the blandly named Brown family didn't seem to be cursed anymore.

Mercy's grave exists to this day in Chestnut Hill Cemetery, a small graveyard behind an unassuming Baptist church off Ten Rod Road, just a couple of miles from I-95. A path goes directly through the center of the cemetery, about halfway down which and on the left is the Brown family plot, beneath an evergreen tree. Mercy's grave is reinforced with a metal band connected to a post imbedded in the ground to protect it from being stolen. You don't need McGruff the Crime Dog to tell you that people will steal vampire headstones.

Directly across the cemetery from the Brown plot is a small, triangular stone building that looks like a toolshed but is referred to as a crypt by everyone who talks about these types of topics. It was in that building that those who say her body wasn't buried say her body was stored until the ground stopped being unshovelable tundra. The structure doesn't look over 100 years old, but then again, nothing in the cemetery really does . . . not even its vampire.

# Ray Family Plot
## Jewett City, CT

THE SKELETONS IN THE CLOSETS of some families are vampires. That's right. The thing about vampirism that they don't always tell you in books and movies is that it can run in the family. In 1854, the Ray family of Jewett City, Connecticut, found this out the hard way . . . and by hard way, I mean by having to dig up and immolate the rotting bodies of their beloved relations.

In the first half of the 19th century, Henry and Lucy Ray had a comfortably sized family of five children who all grew up and made it past the many natural perils and hardships of childhood that were present in colonial America. Unfortunately, they were not immune to unnatural ones.

During the late 1840s to early 1850s, Henry and two of his adult sons, Lemuel and Elisha, died of a peculiar wasting disease. Then, in 1854, a third son, Henry Nelson Ray, was also struck by this strange illness, then resistant to all known cures. Tuberculosis, thy maiden name is vampirism.

Back then, the common medical lexicon featured an entry on vampires more prominently than its end-of-the-alphabet name would suggest, so the family decided to go Van Helsing on the buried remains of their siblings and sons.

Seeking to end the death streak once and for all, the surviving Rays exhumed the bodies of Lemuel and Elisha, and burned them right there in the graveyard. Folks were hardier back then and could do grotesque stuff like that. For some reason, they left the body of the patriarchal Henry alone. I guess it's easier to incinerate brothers than fathers.

The macabre family reunion made the newspapers of the day, and, as a result, in modern times, although it sounds like the name of a sports team, we know the Ray family as the Jewett City Vampires.

This team had other members, too. Nearby, in the greater town of Griswold, of which Jewett City is a borough, the chance play of some children led to the discovery of more than two dozen graves that were traced to the 1700s and 1800s. Turns out, the children had stumbled upon what was at one time the private burial spot for a family named Walton. After an investigation, it was discovered that one set of male remains, labeled "JB-55" on the coffin, had been disturbed centuries ago, his femurs and skull Jolly Roger'd carefully atop his rib cage and the tell-tale lesions from a tuberculosis-like condition present on his bones . . . evidence that the Rays weren't the only ones in the area fighting vampires in their spare time.

Although accounts diverge on where all those Waltons ended up after their archeological analysis, the Ray family plot can still be found toward the northern end of the small graveyard known as Jewett City Cemetery, which is located at the terminus of Anthony Street in Jewett City.

A line of headstones all bearing the three-letter surname now mark both the final resting places of most of the family as well as the site of the bonfire of the vampires. You can follow the timeline of events by the years incised into the gravestones.

Henry Nelson Ray's stone is absent from the family plot, but there is one with his name incised on it at the other side of the cemetery, with the death date of 1854 . . . so apparently the drastic action didn't quite work. As a result, his death has ruined my planned ending of this entry. I was hoping to be able to suggest the idea that an undead Henry Nelson Ray may now roam Connecticut, taking advantage of the fact that these days we diagnose vampirism as tuberculosis. Ha. I still used it.

## *Mummies*

I ONCE READ AN ARTICLE where a museum curator was quoted as saying, "In museums, there are only a few blockbuster attractions—a Monet, a mummy, or dinosaurs." I don't know about Monet, and dinosaurs will certainly draw me off the well-formed posterior indentation in my couch, but the Holy Father of that trinity certainly has to be the ancient desiccated corpse that we affectionately call Mummy.

Now, New England might not necessarily be New Egypt, but it certainly has its share of mummies. Some can be found in prestigious museums, others in more humble collections. Others still can be found in completely surprising locations. Regardless of where they are, the embalmed remains of humans long past their expiration date is a topic the fascinating aspects of which have outseesawed its morbid ones. A mummy exhibit is the only time other than a funeral that you'll take your child to see a dead human. And there are plenty of places to do just that in New England.

## P. T. Barnum's Pa-Ib
### BRIDGEPORT, CT

E GYPTIAN MUMMIES are invaluable cultural artifacts worth scholarly study and dignified display at our most prestigious and elegant museums. Of course, that doesn't forestall the fact that sometimes you just want pull them out and gawk at them like a slack-jawed rube.

Fortunately for us, such people as P. T. Barnum sprang up to fill that evolutionary niche. In the 1800s, Barnum got his huckster hands on an old desiccated corpse in a painted sarcophagus and paraded it around as real,
honest-to-God, 2,500-year-old Egyptian mummy named Pa-Ib.

Mummies are made to last, and this one actually outlasted both Barnum
and most of his unique and uniquely marketed exhibits, many of which per-
ished in various fires that seemed to afflict the showman's properties
throughout the years. In 1892, less than a year after his death, Barnum's wife
donated Pa-Ib to the Barnum Museum. It gives one a sense of perspective to
realize that some people actually don't have a use for mummies in their living
room.

Located in Bridgeport, Connecticut, the uniquely designed and exotic-
looking Barnum Museum is home to less of Barnum's life than you'd think
something called the Barnum Museum would be. It's worth visiting for a few
reasons besides the building itself, including a preserved elephant and a
replica Feejee Mermaid, discussed earlier. However, sharing the third floor
of the Barnum Museum with a giant, 1,000-square-foot miniature replica
circus, lays Pa-Ib, the undeniable star of this particular show.

Barnum's mummy is displayed by itself in a vertical glass case set on the floor in a side room, in front of a large, ornate fireplace. The lid to the human-shaped and -sized sarcophagus is open, allowing you to see the full length of the shriveled Cracker Jack prize inside. I'd describe it to you, but I'm betting that you've seen enough of these arcane embalmed corpses that I don't even have to. The world is a strange place.

The only other item sharing space in the room with Pa-Ib, when I visited, was a craft table for kids to do something (I assume) mummy-related. I can't remember exactly what, because it's hard to focus your attention on anything else when you've got an ancient Egyptian corpse lying at your feet.

In 2006, radiology experts performed a CT scan of the mummy to figure out if it was legitimate or just #367 on Barnum's long lists of boondoggles and hornswoggles. In addition to identifying its gender as more than likely female (even a 50-50 bet needs to be hedged sometimes), they scientifically verified that what Barnum promoted as a real, honest-to-God, 2,500-year-old Egyptian mummy was . . . a real, honest-to-God, 2,500-year-old Egyptian mummy. Something tells me that no one would have been more surprised by that than Barnum, himself.

# Grave of the Mummy
## Middlebury, VT

THIS IS THE STORY of the Christian burial of a pagan mummy prince. Despite all of the cool words in that sentence, the story's actually pretty mundane. However, it does yield a rather astonishing artifact at its conclusion. So skip to there, I guess.

Henry Sheldon was an eccentric collector of eccentric items in the town of Middlebury, Vermont, in the late 1800s. His collection included such things as a stuffed house cat, an object fraudulently touted as a petrified Indian boy, and a cigar holder made from a chicken leg. Not exactly museum-quality pieces, but that didn't stop him from opening a museum right in his own house.

Of course, any collector worth his glass display cases and log books needs a genuine Egyptian mummy in his collection. So Sheldon bought himself one.

According to the story, he ordered the mummified remains of a two-year-old Egyptian prince named Amum-Her-Khepesh-Ef. When his purchase finally arrived, Sheldon was dismayed to find the body so badly preserved that he didn't even bother to put in on display, merely shoving it into the attic of his museum. I'm sure Vermont treats visiting royalty much better these days.

When Sheldon died, his collection lived on as the Henry Sheldon Museum in his house on 1 Park Street, which currently focuses mostly on more sedate historical artifacts from Vermont history. In the mid-20th century, though, one of its curators, George Mead, discovered the mummy in the attic during what was surely one of the most memorable moments in his life and decided to give it a better afterlife. Not having a pyramid handy, he had the bundle of decaying rags cremated and buried in his own family plot in town.

Judging from all the mummy monster movies I've seen, Mead's choice was a brave act, although I'm sure he was protected by the fact that the mummy was just a toddler and the good chance that Mead was degrees less silly than I. Still, if real life is the horror story that I believe it is, that mummy might still one day gather its ashes and rise from the grave, seeking retribution for the many desecrations it experienced throughout its afterlife.

The grave can still be found in West Cemetery, a small graveyard on Route 30 directly across from the Middlebury College Museum of Art. The tombstone is located about halfway into the cemetery on the left.

The marker is a basic, rectangle slate headstone, easily missed by even those with the pointiest of eyeball, but it features an epitaph few could claim for their own. It says:

> *Ashes of Amum-Her-Khepesh-Ef*
> *Aged Two Years*
> *Son of Sen Woset 3rd*
> *King of Egypt and his wife*
> *Hathor-Hotpe*

Overall, it's a suspiciously specific and auspicious lineage for an artifact that was delivered so haphazardly to Sheldon half a century earlier. The headstone also features at its top a cross, an ankh, and a bird, so eternity is probably going to be pretty confusing for this kid.

# Boston Museum of Fine Arts Funerary Exhibit

## BOSTON, MA

THESE DAYS, a trip to Egypt to see its renowned funerary wonders is almost unnecessary. Every museum, wherever you are, seems to have some bit of Egyptalia in it to sate our fascination with history's most famous death rituals. The Museum of Fine Arts in Boston, Massachusetts, touts its collection as one of the finest in the world. After seeing its Egyptian Funerary Arts exhibit, I'm apt to believe this.

The museum is located at 465 Huntington Avenue, right in downtown Boston. It houses exquisite works of art in just about every genre from cultures across both the world and time. But its mummy exhibit is the anchor store to its mall.

Just about all of the 45,000 items in the Museum of Fine Arts Egyptian collection were gleaned from a single joint archeological dig between the museum itself and Harvard University that was conducted over the course of four decades in the first half of the 20th century. The dig was located at the Old Kingdom Giza Necropolis, which dates back 4,500 years and contains thousands of tombs with wonderful creamy centers full of the treasures of the Egyptian dead. As a result, there's almost a direct line between these desert tombs of Egypt and your Saturday afternoon jaunt to the museum.

The dimly lit and darkly painted exhibit hall of the permanent Funerary Arts exhibit is purposefully set up to make it seem as if you're entering a tomb. Nothing hurts the mystique of decorated coffins that have survived millenniums of darkness like bright fluorescent lights and gaudy wallpaper.

On display are all kinds of sarcophagi, caskets, funeral items, and, of course, mummies. The mummy specimens are of various styles and are exhibited in various manners. For instance, one display is a pair of exposed portrait mummies from the later-era Roman period of Egyptian history. These mummies have actual paintings of their face fastened to the head of their wrapped body, like dollar-store Halloween masks.

Elsewhere in the exhibit, another mummy remains sealed inside its casket, which shows off a level of workmanship and detail that puts our silk-lined oak boxes to shame. Various empty caskets and sarcophagi are on display as well, including the massive black stone lid of the impressive sar-cophagus of Kheper-Re, an Egyptian general, which is set on end in an alcove near the entrance to the exhibit.

The centerpiece of the entire exhibit may be the mummy and caskets of Nes-mut-aat-neru, the wife of a high-ranking priest. Her linen-wrapped mummy is set beside a row of her caskets, each of different design and each fitting inside another like Russian nested dolls until finally they all fit into a large wooden box topped by a statue of Anubis, the jackal-headed God of the dead.

Besides human mummies, the museum also has a collection of animal mummies, including the auspiciously mummified remains of a ram, a cat, and a baby alligator, as well as a small, empty coffin that at one time housed a mummified falcon. Your goldfish was flushed down the toilet.

Interspersed among these ancient dead are all the wonders they took with them. Alabaster animal-headed canopic jars that held the organs of the embalmed, jewelry, statues, and shawabati, carved figures created to serve the individual in the afterlife.

All in all, the Boston Museum of Fine Arts has everything one needs to make a Boris Karloff or Christopher Lee film. The only thing missing is a short, well-groomed Egyptian man in a red fez ominously droning on about a curse. I put that in the suggestion box before I left.

# Hands of the Mummy
## WOLFEBORO, NH

IF YOU CAN'T GET YOUR HANDS ON A MUMMY, you might as well get a mummy's hands. And, you know what? I really can't call that settling.

By profession, Henry Libby was a dentist; by passion, though, he was a collector. And this was back in the day when collecting wasn't a cheesy occupation. You'll find no limited edition, individually numbered, mass-marketed, officially licensed silliness in his collection, only authentic nat-ural, anthropological, and historical wonders worth studying for science, cataloging for posterity, and displaying under glass for the general public.

After decades of collecting, in 1912 Libby designed and built a museum to house and display his burgeoning collection. Now, a century later, you can still see that eccentric and personality-driven collection in its natural habitat. And everything I own will be pawned off by my kids for spending cash when I die.

The Libby Museum is only open seasonally (the pleasant ones) and can be found on Route 109 right across the street from Lake Winnipesauke and about 3 miles north of the downtown tourist town of Wolfeboro, New Hampshire. When I visited the museum, the admission fee was embarrassingly low, just a couple of bucks.

The Libby Museum is a small, plain-looking building, with most all of its collection displayed in a single large room (Lobachevskian geometry allows one to fit a large room into a small building). You can scan the room in mere seconds, but you could delve for hours.

Regardless of its size, the place is chock full of dead bodies . . . all taxidermed, of course. The sawdust-stuffed menagerie includes a 7-foot-long alligator, a flying fish, a tarantula, a bear, a bobcat, and all sorts of creatures that will continue to stare glassy-eyed in your dreams and nightmares from the moment of your visit to the last gasping images you see before your death.

Also in the collection are exhibits of more cultural worth, including Abenaki Indian artifacts, colonial-era weapons, weird hairballs, a necklace made of monkey teeth, and something that should be given its own spotlit, revolving display case but which in reality is grouped humbly together with a bunch of other random paraphernalia—a genuine pair of Egyptian mummy hands.

Not much information adorns the small card that labels the mummy hands as mummy hands, but who cares about reading when you can stare in awe at the pair of severed body parts that society, under rare circumstances such as this one, lets you gawk at unashamedly.

The hands have a pleasingly aesthetic ratio of tattered winding cloth to mummified skin, with a pair of rings completing the ensemble and making the dead flesh ready for its close-up. Hardly gruesome, the hands look almost like a prop that one could buy in most any seasonal Halloween store . . . which, instead of making me at all disappointed with the ancient artifacts, actually makes me proud of the Halloween industry.

In the end, if in my entire life all I am able to accomplish is to come into the ownership of a mummified body part, I'd be able to make a pretty strong case before the lords of the afterlife that my life was a worthy one.

# Mummy of
# Massachusetts General Hospital
### BOSTON, MA

A MEDEVAC HELICOPTER swooped determinedly down from the sky, ambulances screamed pedestrians out of the way, men and women in sterile-looking attire rushed this way and that . . . in all, a chaos of knowledgeable people were doing vital, life-saving acts of humanity in a bustling multi-building warren filled with miracles and miracle workers of medical science. And I was there to gawk at a person that had been dead for 2,500 years. I am just not important.

Massachusetts General Hospital (MGH) at 55 Fruit Street in Boston, Massachusetts, has been around as an entity since 1811. That's long enough to be an historical landmark . . . and MGH's oldest building, the 1823 Bulfinch Building, certainly is one.

However, standing in front of the Bulfinch Building, one will see a cupola of sorts crowning it. Inside the arc of that half-sphere is a single room . . . a room that out-historics the Bullfinch Building itself.

The Ether Dome at MGH is an old operating theater where, in one of the biggest game-changing moments in medical science and the biggest blow to the whiskey industry outside of Prohibition, ether gas was first used as an anesthetic to enable painless surgery. It occurred on October 16, 1846, and it meant that no longer would people have to bite belts to deal with pain, no longer would surgeons be glorified (if well-meaning) butchers, and no longer would operating rooms have to be built on top floors to dampen the mind-searing screams from the rest of the hospital.

The Ether Dome closed as an operating room in 1868 after more than 8,000 operations. Since then, the room has been used as a storage area, a dining hall, a dormitory, and, these days, a lecture hall and classroom. It has also since been sanctified into both a monument and a museum.

But I wasn't there to see the historic Bulfinch Building at MGH. I wasn't

even there to see the historic Ether
Dome inside the Bulfinch Building. I
was there to see a historic artifact inside
the historic Ether Dome inside the historic Bulfinch Building—Padihershef the
mummy.

That's right, 90 percent of museums
don't have their own Egyptian mummy,
but a state-of-the art hospital in Boston
does.

The embalmed corpse of Padihershef, a stone artisan in Thebes, was given
to MGH in 1823 by a Dutch merchant
named Jacob Van Lennep. The gift was
the first fully intact mummy burial
ensemble to ever come to America and
only the second fully intact mummy to
successfully cross the Atlantic.

Originally, MGH used Padihershef
as a fund-raising tool, putting it on dis-
play and then touring it around various cities to a populace that had never
seen an Egyptian mummy before. After a while, the mummy was placed in
the operating theater that was eventually to become the Ether Dome, where
it presided, mute and ancient, over the landmark surgery. Over the years, it
has also been loaned out to various museums, examined, x-rayed, and had
its hieroglyphics translated.

To visit Padihershef and the Ether Dome in general, you have to time it
right to ensure that no classes are in session. The reception desk inside the
main entrance at MGH will direct you to the elevator that will take you to the
appropriate floor.

Inside, the room looks like the classic operating theater. A space at the
bottom features a lectern, and the rows of curving theater seats that face the
space extend all the way to the ceiling. At the center of the ceiling are the
cupola windows that flood the room with natural sunlight during the day.

Most of the interesting artifacts on display at the Ether Dome are also in
that main space, against the walls behind the lectern. These include a pair of

glass-topped table displays of antique surgery/amputation kits, a human skeleton, a marble statue of Apollo that was also present for the famous surgery, and a giant 10- by 7-foot painting of the event that used contemporary MGH doctors as models for their historical counterparts during the surgery.

Flanking this enormous mural of a painting is a pair of upright cases. On one side is the coffin lid that had been Padihershef's sky for most of his two and a half millennia since his death, its hieroglyphics still bright. On the other, meet Padihershef. He's framed in the bottom half of his coffin, a lattice of beads draped down his front, with his blackened face and skull exposed . . . so you can get a really good look at him, if staring deep into the sunken eye sockets of a mummy is your thing.

A side door leads to a short corridor that wraps around the back of the theater seating and gives access to the top row and the hallway on the other side of the room, in case you are late to the lecture or are just passing through. In that hallway are displayed a few more artifacts, such as an original surgical operation chair, period clothing, and images from the era. In one, you can see Padihershef, silently doing his mummy thing while surgeons operate on a patient, completely at ease with their embalmed witness.

Entering a giant hospital like MGH when you're not in need of medical attention can be a daunting proposition, probably only slightly less daunting than being the first to enter an ancient Egyptian tomb. But the payoff is worth it. Seeing an exposed Egyptian mummy at a museum is pretty cool . . . but seeing the same in the middle of a busy hospital is a story worth telling. Better than I did, hopefully.

## Demons

WHEN THE ORIGINAL EUROPEAN SETTLERS came to the New World, they brought with them a religion whose main tenets included a loving God, a moral life . . . and legions of horrible hellspawn in invisible warfare around us. It is not at all comforting to be a Christian.

Of course, New England was one of the original entry points on the continent for this religion, and when you add to that spiritual melee the evil spirits believed in by Native Americans of the region, you end up with a whole pandemonium of dark entities crawling about the New England landscape. And these monsters don't suck your blood, strangle your throat, or tear you with their teeth . . . they head right for the soft spots of your eternal soul. It is not at all comforting to be a New Englander.

# Devil's Footprint
### MANCHESTER, ME

FOR MILLENNIA, the devil has traipsed his way all over this planet of ours, leaving nothing in his wake but evil deeds and rock 'n' roll songs, but for some reason he left a single footprint in a medium-size rock in Manchester, Maine.

Because this is a story about the devil, it, of course, involves somebody's soul. In this little myth, a crew of construction workers from some vague time period were engaged in building a road when they came upon a boulder that proved to be immovable by natural means. One of the construction workers climbed onto the rock and swore he'd sell his soul to the devil if that rock could be moved.

Sometimes souls are a bargain, and the next day, the rock had been moved and the melodramatic construction worker had disappeared. All that was left as evidence of the deal were some strange indentations in the rock. Apparently, that rock is now part of a cemetery wall, and it is semifamous for holding the devil's footprint.

The North Manchester Meeting House is located on 144 Scribner Hill Road. Built in 1793 and still serving as a church, the building abuts the above-mentioned cemetery. The fossilized footprint can be found in a rock on the corner of the wall right beside the meetinghouse, with the impressions facing the meetinghouse.

The stone actually has two imprints, a triangular one that I assume is supposed to be the mark of a cloven hoof and another that looks vaguely like a set of human footprints merged together. The arrangement of the indentations has also catalyzed another story about a man's being chased by Satan across the rocks. Although usually an exercise in matrixing, vandals have made the task of seeing the mark easier by politely adding graffiti to the rock, including spray-painting the footprints in the devil's favorite color.

The fact that devil's footprint can be found on a cemetery fence has naturally, or unnaturally, given rise to rumors of ghosts in that cemetery, not that any graveyard in New England needs that kind of help. If there are dead people in the ground, people will claim to catch spirits in their cameras.

Unlike some of the entries in this book, the devil's footprint is a far cry from a tourist destination. No signs point out the rock, no pamphlets are printed that tell its story. For most people who frequent the area, this is just a rock. Actually, for most people who frequent the area it isn't even that, it's just a fence.

Now, this particular indentation isn't the only fabled devil's footprint in New England. Satan has apparently paced long and hard in the northeastern United States. For instance, he's kicked up his heels in at least two Massachusetts towns: His hooves have punctured a boulder in Norton and treated a bit of exposed bedrock near the First Church of Ipswich in Ipswich like his own personal Grauman's Chinese Theatre. Each print comes complete with its own legend of how the devil came to make it, of course, and, also of course, none of the stories contains anything you wouldn't expect to be in a story about Satan. I guess the real surprise would come if somebody took the time to map out all the tracks and see where they lead.

Back in Maine, I didn't stay long at the devil's footprint. Not because I was spooked by the idea of the diabolic mark, or because I believed the graveyard to be haunted. I was just embarrassed. I didn't want anybody to stumble upon my photographing and contemplating a pockmark. I might as well have been studying a sidewalk crack or analyzing a street pothole.

Sometimes I think I'd sell my own soul for a supernatural myth that doesn't seem ludicrous in the light of, well, anything.

# Demon Murder Trial Sites
### BROOKFIELD AND DANBURY, CT

IN OUR STORIES, we love to put the devil in court. Often as a lawyer. And while that might say a lot about our general opinions concerning lawyers, it's more likely because the devil's Christian name, Satan, literally means "the prosecution" or "the accuser." Of course, there are probably a couple other reasons why our storytellers like to do such. Perhaps it's because the devil usually stands for the opposite of the justice and fairness that our court system is supposed to represent. Maybe it's because he is the patron saint of sneakiness and greed that other parts of our court system have also come to represent. Either way, we seem to think he'd be right at home in a courtroom. In 1981, the state of Connecticut found that idea tested in real life.

The crime at the center of the trial was a simple one. In February of that year, 19-year-old Arne Johnson stabbed his landlord Alan Bono to death after a day of drinking, partying, and general white trashery that ended at Bono's apartment at a dog kennel that he ran in Brookfield, Connecticut. It was the first murder ever recorded in the town, and Johnson was put on trial for first-degree manslaughter.

Then things got famous.

At the Connecticut Superior Court in Danbury a few days before Halloween, Johnson's lawyer, Martin Minella, entered a Flip Wilson defense of not guilty by reason of demon possession. I'm sure he had to repeat it multiple times before it sank in.

You see, it turns out that a year or so earlier, the 11-year-old brother of Johnson's fiancée, who was also on-scene for the Bono murder, was treated for demon possession by various priests as well as none other than Ed and Lorraine Warren, the husband-and-wife demonologist and paranormal investigative team that seems to pop up in any modern-day story involving the East Coast and demons, especially in their home state of Connecticut (this is actually the first of three mentions of them in this book). Johnson was involved in the exorcism and, since possession is apparently a transmissible disease, unknowingly caught it, which then manifested itself in the single, giant symptom of spontaneous murder . . . coincidentally involving arguments and alcohol.

With support from the Warrens, Minella was prepared to subpoena priests, God, and Satan himself to prove that not only did demons exist, but they physically manipulated his client into committing murder. Suddenly, the entire supernatural world found itself teetering on the possible precedent that could be set in that New England court system, which found itself in the position to indirectly substantiate in the court's blindfolded eyes the existence of the devil. And Ed and Lorraine Warren got a brand-new chance for an international media blitz.

Two seconds later, though, the judge threw out the defense, and the lawyer had to fall back on the more conventional tack of self-defense. Johnson was ruled guilty of manslaughter and served a five-year prison term.

The Connecticut Superior Court where this occurred is found at 146 White Street in Danbury, and the location of the original crime is the still-standing kennel on Federal Road in Brookfield that these days is called Marta's Vineyard.

Of course, every story has been dramatized into a movie to the point that I'm tired of mentioning the fact, but this story spawned a made-for-television flick with a confluence of cast and topic that make it worth bringing up for a chuckle. *The Demon Murder Case* (1983) starred Kevin Bacon as the possessed murderer, Cloris Leachman as a psychic, Harvey Fierstein as the voice of the devil, and Andy Griffith as a demonologist. And that's my conclusion to this entry, "Andy Griffith as a demonologist."

# Moodus Noises
## Moodus, CT

THE SMALL VILLAGE OF MOODUS, CONNECTICUT, has had its own official soundtrack since before colonial times. In fact, the name of the town is derived from the Native American term for the area, Machimoodus, which means either "Place of Bad Noises" or "Place of Noises," depending on which Google result you select.

Moodus is located within the town of East Haddam, Connecticut, and encompasses a mere 3 square miles of area. As a result, it has a population of just over 1,300 people, and while on the surface that might seem to make for a pretty sleepy little town, below ground it's a different story.

Moodus is known for what has been dubbed the "Moodus Noises," strange rumblings, thunderings, and crashings that often sound like the proverbial trees that nobody sees falling in forests. The noises seem to originate somewhere in the vicinity of the Mount Tom area of Moodus, located in what is now Machimoodus State Park.

Back in the day, Native Americans attributed the noises to a god named Hobbamock or, more generically, evil spirits. Of course, in our stories, Native Americans attribute enough phenomena to evil spirits that I'm pretty sure it was a fundamental translation error on the part of the colonials for a term that merely meant "nature" or "we don't know what that is." However, when the Europeans came in, they transmogrified those evil spirits into European devils . . . and witches, as those were all the rage in the colonies as well.

In addition, a giant carbuncle sometimes figures into the legend. The hypogeal cavern from which the noises were often said to originate was apparently somehow lighted by one, and at one point in the history of the village, an eccentric Englishman by the name of Dr. Steele was supposed to have set up shop on nearby Mount Tom to extract the giant carbuncle to stop the noises.

Of course, minus the carbuncle, the legends put me in a bind regarding the organization of this book, since I didn't know whether to categorize the Moodus Noises in the section on demons or the section on witches. As you can see, I chose the former, basically because I more associate demons with subterranean high jinks.

However, truth be told (just this once), science has already pretty much made the decision a moot one for me. The Moodus Noises are earthquakes—microearthquakes, in fact, which are quakes at the far lower end of the Richter scale. Of course, microearthquakes happen just about everywhere and for a bunch of different reasons, so why the Moodus ones got all gussied up in myth, I don't know.

These days, you can still hear the Moodus Noises, although it's hard to differentiate them from the general postindustrial cacophony of modern life . . . quarry blasting, construction machines, airplane engines, subwoofers. It's enough to make those demons down below bang on their roofs with witch's broomsticks and yell at us to knock it off or they'll call the landlord . . . of the flies.

# Moulton Mansion and Cenotaph
### HAMPTON, NH

I'M NOT SURE AT WHAT POINT IN THE HISTORY of Christian culture they decided that the devil works according to best business practices, but if all of the stories are to be believed, he's signed more contracts in his day than a few leagues worth of professional athletes. And the interesting thing about those contracts is that he always keeps his end of the bargain. It's the human parties in those business deals who seem to be constantly reneging. We really do suck.

From Faust in the laboratory to Daniel Webster in the courtroom to Robert Johnson at the crossroads, it's a bull market for souls. We all have things we want more than our souls, apparently. In New Hampshire, the resident soul-trader was General Jonathan Moulton.

Moulton was a veteran of various colonial wars, including the Revolutionary, and a wealthy man in the seacoast town of Hampton, New Hampshire. Apparently, though, that gain was ill-gotten. At some point he wanted to sell his soul for riches, and clop, clop, knock, knock, the devil was there to take him up on the offer. Any man who makes a deal with the devil has an empty soul. Moulton apparently also had empty soles. The story goes that the terms of his contract were that in exchange for his soul, the devil would be required to fill his boots with gold once a month.

Well, Moulton of course started to get greedy. To trick the prince of darkness, he cut out the bottoms of his boots and fixed them to a hole in the floor of his house. To fulfill the terms of the bargain, the devil now had to fill up the entire cellar with gold, to fill the boots.

Obviously, Satan hated being tricked, so he burned down Moulton's house. Fire is the devil's only friend. The story doesn't say what happened to Moulton's soul.

All stories aside, General Moulton was a historical person, and he was rich and influential (the nearby town of Moultonborough was named for him). In addition, his house actually did burn down in the mid-1770s. However, the rest of the story was probably started by envy on the part of his neighbors. Gossip is the great equalizer between the economic classes.

Moulton rebuilt his house, and it still stands to this day as a private residence at 212 Lafayette Road in Hampton, near where Lafayette

intersects with Drakeside Road.

Moulton died in 1787, but his burial location is unknown. I assume, since he cheated on the deal, the devil took both his body and his soul as recompense. However, locals have placed a cenotaph to him in Pine Grove Cemetery on Winnacunnet Road, near his house. The cenotaph is easy to find, as Pine Grove is a small cemetery. In addition, most of its graves are ancient, whereas Moulton's cenotaph is relatively new. It's located to the far left of the entrance, and is often decorated with an American flag, honoring his service in the colonial army.

In the end, Moulton seemed to live an adventurous, well-appointed, duly honored, and famous life that seems to be worth selling your soul for. I probably would (clop, clop, knock, knock).

# Snedeker House
## Southington, CT

FOR SOME REASON, debunked haunted houses still maintain a residue of their original cool for me. I mean, sure, hoaxes, mistaken impressions, and general credulousness suck every which way and should be punished to the full extent of the law, but for some reason it's tempting to be grateful for the few moments of mystery the stories may have yielded before Scooby and the gang unmasked them.

Thus it goes with the Snedeker house in Southington, Connecticut. Actually, the Snedeker house apparently fell under the category of [debunked] possessed house, although I'm not always sure where the line is drawn between possessed and haunted when it comes to domiciles. Classically, experts in the field attribute the former to demons and the latter to ghosts, but also classically, people who style themselves as experts in the field are often pretty batty. And I only stick the word *often* in front of that modifier in case I need to protect myself legally.

The story starts out excellently enough. In 1986, the Snedeker family moved into a simple white duplex rental home that had at one time previously been a different type of home . . . a funeral home.

In the basement of the house, they found various mortuary toys, including (depending on who is telling the story) a hoisting apparatus for coffins, a medical gurney, blood drains, toe tags, and all sorts of things you don't want to dwell too much on . . . or above.

Soon enough, the Snedekers were reporting all kinds of evil, including sexual attacks; apparitions; and abrupt, violent personality changes in the oldest son, who was undergoing treatments for Hodgkin's disease and whose medical care was the reason they had moved to Connecticut.

Of course, if it's the East Coast and it involves demons, then Ed and Lorraine Warren are sure to be on the case. These experts in the field of demonology and hauntings brought their Amityville Horror–tuned publicity machine fresh from the Pennsylvania Smurl haunting to the Snedeker house. After their investigations, they slapped their official stamp of "possessed" on it, and then garnered a book deal, a publicity tour, and various speaking engagements regarding the house.

Well, the thing about public awareness is that it also brings public scrutiny. Eventually, other facts surrounding the case emerged, including the troubled nature of the oldest son, who besides having a drug habit, was diagnosed with schizophrenia and admitted to some of the vileness going on in the Snedeker household. In addition, the entire time the vicious pandemonium was going on, the upstairs neighbor lived blithely . . . as if it was just a house.

Most damning was the testimony of the author hired to write the original nonfiction book for the Warrens and Snedekers, Ray Garton. Garton eventually went on the record to relate that not only was he given obviously conflicting stories from the Snedekers, he was given directions to ignore those conflicts and sensationalize the story by the Warrens.

All in all, it seems that something pretty demonic was definitely going on, just demons of a more earthly sort.

Of course, that didn't stop the story from being popular. In 2002, the Snedeker case resurfaced, when a documentary on the events aired on cable television. Then, in 2009, it was popularized again to a stratospheric degree when a movie called *The Haunting in Connecticut*, which was based on the story, was released to theaters. The movie starred Virginia Madsen and came complete with a Hollywood-backed marketing campaign with "Based on a true story" emblazoned on all the advertising materials.

The Snedekers moved out of the house a long time ago. These days, the occupants of 208 Meriden Avenue in Southington just want people to forget about it. It's just a house on a bustling street, the story that made it infamous was debunked as bunk, and just because you can still see the side morgue doors on the house and can watch a movie about it anytime you want, doesn't mean that the house should be branded as anything more than it is, its occupants hassled, or its story included in books about grim locations. I agree on two out of three of those points.

After all, even though it originally achieved its infamy as a demon-haunted home, it's still got the infamy of being the ex–funeral home location of the Snedeker demon hoax that inspired books, television shows, and a movie. See, that's still kind of cool.

# Lithobolia, the Stone-Throwing Devil
## New Castle, NH

Into everyone's life a few rocks must fall. For George and Alice Walton, it happened in the summer of 1682, and the event birthed an astonishingly specific demon myth.

The Walton family ran a tavern on an island known as Great Island, which is these days called New Castle, in the state of New Hampshire, just a stone's throw from Portsmouth at the mouth of the Piscataqua River. Without any meteorological warning, rocks that ranged in size from pebbles to fists to men's heads suddenly began showering on their home. In addition, everywhere they went they were cruelly pelted with more, always thrown by some unseen attacker. As if those rocks weren't enough, household items began flinging themselves around the house, strange snorting noises pervaded the air, and all kinds of other crazy, silly stuff went on. It all makes you wonder if it's really that boring in other realms of existence.

A rock might feel no pain, and an island might never cry, but the Waltons had to endure much of both before that hazy shade of summer ended. Surprisingly, their attacker had a name, Lithobolia, a stone-throwing devil. That's right. Satan tempted Christ. The Balrog killed Gandalf. Lithobolia threw stones at an obscure colonist. If there's a locker room in hell, he's probably being made fun of to this day.

The story goes that this demon was summoned by a witch who obviously didn't live in a glass house, to torment the Walton family over a land dispute. As it's the sticks and stones that break the bones, Lithobolia was her revenge.

As is normally the case, when the summer finally ended, so did all the fun. The antics of Lithobolia eased, and the Waltons got on with their lives, with a few scars and a newfound terror of cairns that ensured they never forgot the event.

Our entire knowledge of this occurrence, including the name of the demon, comes from a pamphlet printed in 1698 in London by a man named Richard Chamberlain, who was a lodger at the Waltons' tavern during that special summer between rocks and hard places. However, Increase Mather weighed in on the case, as well, who along with his son Cotton, were of course well known for not leaving any supernatural stones unturned.

In contemporary times, the island is hardly noticeable as one, as a main road loops through the island and connects it to the mainland via bridges. A school now stands in the approximate spot on Cranfield Street where the Waltons' tavern stood, and a nearby intersecting road bears their family name

on the usual green, aluminum sign. If the world had any symmetry it would be dented from rock projectiles, but I saw none on my visit.

Honestly, there's not much more blood you can wring from this stone. For a brief period of time a couple of New England colonists were accosted by rocks. Some say it was Lithobolia, the stone-throwing devil; some say it was just a mere prank by local schoolchildren. Others attribute it to disgruntled neighbors. Nobody really knows. The story's set in a dubitable pamphlet, not in stone.

# Zaffis Museum of the Paranormal
## Stratford, CT

So here I was, a skeptic when it comes to the paranormal (at least as it is often presented in our time), visiting a man who not only fully believes in it but had devoted his life to actively engaging it. To make the situation more complicated, he had extended to me the kind invitation to view his personal collection of paranormal artifacts, meaning best behavior on my part was called for. You see, I can be open in certain specific ways to the idea of the paranormal, but will immediately become absolutely close-minded to the point of rudeness the second I see someone acting on it as truth.

In this case, that person was John Zaffis, and the biography on his Web site credits him as a paranormal investigator and a demonologist. I was pretty sure what to expect with the former, due to all the attention that the occupation seems to be getting these days, but was unsure as to the latter. Part of me expected monk's robes.

Instead, I found Zaffis to be a friendly character in his mid-50s, gray-bearded, bespectacled, and dressed casually in jeans and a purple sweatshirt, seemingly completely at ease with whoever I ended up being, with a vocabulary that easily accommodated words like *shit* and *dude*.

Zaffis keeps his Museum of the Paranormal in the bottom floor of a two-story building behind his house, which is in Stratford, Connecticut. The top floor has a meeting space where he holds classes, and his office, a comfortable book-lined room where he studies, schedules lecture tours and investigations, and generally just does his paranormal thing. That's where we started.

We talked about a lot of things prior to viewing his collection. We talked about his past, and how as a teenager he fell under the influence of his uncle and aunt, the famous and controversial Ed and Lorraine Warren, whose

exploits in the world of the demonic and paranormal have inspired books, movies, and more than a little criticism. Zaffis eventually made a name for himself in the trade, as well as becoming a mechanical engineer.

We also talked about the current climate of paranormal acceptance, where decades ago people looked at demonologists as demon worshippers, and how in these days businesses, historical landmarks, and museums are embracing the paranormal as a marketing angle.

We also talked about his ideas of demons, ghosts, and other entities of the invisible, which basically amounted to the concept of intelligent energy . . . which is exactly the kind of idea that I have problems with.

And, of course, we talked about my skepticism, which I was more than prepared to argue red-faced and violently gesticulating, but which he quickly accepted with an understanding nod and the simple statement, "Because you haven't had an experience." Boiled down, I guess it's exactly that.

But I was there for an experience . . . with his collection.

Downstairs, in a large room divided by the stairwell, were artifacts from more than three decades of paranormal and demonic investigations.

According to Zaffis, the collection included actual items from the cases that he worked on, as well as items that were sent or given to him by researchers, clergy, and people who just wanted them out of their house. The collection contained artifacts from all over the world, including Germany,

Greece, and Japan, and ran the gamut from seemingly silly things to be afraid of, such as a china set and a painting of a clown on velvet, to items that one could fully believe could be used as a prop in a horror movie, including tribal masks and a ventriloquist's dummy.

None of the items was labeled, but he had a story for each piece that I pointed to. A black cast-iron human skull was apparently discovered in a secret compartment in the home of a "prominent political family," along with other items of the occult. An Easter decoration that was, strangely, given to a Jewish woman by a Muslim man was thought to have a curse on it. An ominous black idol was supposed to have been used in various black magic ceremonies until things got out of hand. A sword used in satanic rituals that was given to a boy by his father conjured up black-hooded figures until it was removed from the house. A large clock that was inherited from a grandfather seemed to have come complete with his unwelcome presence haunting it. An old-fashioned military jacket purchased at an estate sale and worn by teenage girl for fun began giving her strange and unpleasant soldier-filled dreams until she got rid of it.

Similar back stories enlivened such otherwise sedate artifacts as a bird claw, a Civil War–era cannonball, a pig skull, a wedding dress, and a violin, as well as about 1,000 other objects. Most of the pieces had vague pasts, with their known history starting at estate sales, antique shops, and consignment stores and ending at diabolical encounters with terrors from beyond the nat-

ural world for their owners. "Clairvoyants have a field day in here," Zaffis told me.

One whole section of the room looked like a toy store, with dolls, stuffed animals, and, of course, clowns of every stripe of face paint. I even saw a Winnie the Pooh dressed up as Santa Claus. Demons apparently have no shame.

Also worth specifically mentioning from his collection is a small statue of the Virgin Mary from the famous Connecticut Snedeker case (see page 249), the case that he worked alongside his aunt and uncle, the events of which were turned into a 2009 movie called *The Haunting in Connecticut*. A closer look revealed that the hands of the statue were missing. "They melted off during the exorcism," he explained matter-of-factly.

Currently, the museum is open by appointment only. Zaffis wants to conduct regular tours, but his busy lecture and investigation schedule makes that idea problematic. Still, he plans on taking some of the items on the road at various conventions, publishing an illustrated book about the collection, and eventually just making the items more accessible to the public. If the public dares, I guess.

Zaffis certainly does. In fact, he didn't seem at all perturbed with the nature of his collection, nor their proximity to his house. According to his Web site, the items have all been "cleansed" of any negative energy that might be inherent in them, and those that could not be were destroyed. Although I don't buy that part of it, I am definitely a certain kind of sucker in another way. Tell me something is paranormal, and I'll think it's cool while simultaneously finding it complete rubbish. It's one of about two dozen conflicts always raging inside me. With the Zaffis Museum of the Paranormal, I just found it cool. I mean, strip away the paranormal backstory of each object, and it's still an interesting collection of weirdness. Almost like a flea market or antique store, except it would have to come with a generous return policy if Zaffis let somebody take one of these items home.

# *Ghosts*

I LOVE GHOST STORIES, but these days we've come very close to ruining them what with all the waving about of ill-utilized scientific instruments on the part of people trained by television shows and the touting of every house, graveyard, and historical attraction in the world as haunted by people who need either a marketing angle or a personal sense of importance.

As a result, it would be a futile and silly effort to visit and chronicle every place in New England that someone somewhere claims to be haunted. However, I have carefully chosen a few places to include that are either intrinsically interesting to visit above and beyond the weak fact that someone has shouted "Ghost!" there at some point, or that just have a better ghost story than most. These include a classic New England covered bridge, a gourmet restaurant, an historic rail-road tunnel, a creepy cave, an impressive castle, a colonial-era ghost town, an island fort . . . that kind of stuff. Each place should give its visitors something interesting to do or see when they're not seeing ghosts.

# Emily's Bridge
## Stowe, VT

COVERED BRIDGES SEEM TO BE highly inspirational to three main groups of people: artists, tourists, and suicides. Or at least tales of suicides, which I guess would make that last group storytellers. Still, covered bridges seem to spawn these tales of self-ending as naturally as their roofs keep off the rain. I personally think that it's because these unique structures give these often fictional despondents the convenient choice of either swinging themselves from the rafters or flinging themselves into the rapids.

And, although the causation isn't questioned enough, death stories often birth ghost stories. Of all the many covered bridges in New England, all of which probably have their own legends of deaths and hauntings, Emily's Bridge in Stowe, Vermont, is probably the most infamous.

Built in 1844 to carry what came to be known as Covered Bridge Road over Gold Brook, Emily's Bridge is a single-lane, 50-foot-long bridge . . . barely long enough to cast its own shadow inside. Its wooden frame is dark and weathered, making it just a shade or two under picturesque except under the most ideal turns of season, but elevating its spooky quotient high enough to make one's pace unconsciously quicken in traversing it at night.

Like so many suicides, Emily's story involves unrequited love, and like so many made-up legends, the details vary. In short form, back in the mid-1800s, Emily was supposed to meet her paramour at what was then called Gold Brook Bridge to elope. When he never showed, Emily killed herself in a savage fit of depression. She chose the rafters.

Now, in the inevitable ghost story that follows, you actually get a little more for your money. Instead of just a sad apparition constantly looking for the lover that never arrived, Emily's an angry specter. Tales of clawlike gouges down the sides of cars passing through the bridge and bloody scratches down the backs of pedestrian crossers are bandied about just as much as the sound of loosely dragging feet on the roofs of cars or the noise of a strange voice emanating from inside the short tunnel.

Interestingly enough, it's not just called Emily's Bridge by bored teenagers, camera-waving ghost hunters, and under-contract book writers. The high degree of acceptance of at least the name, if not the myth, is evident by all the quaint little postcards you can pick up in nearby downtown Stowe. Usually, Emily's Bridge is cozily depicted on these pieces of card stock resplendent in a second covering of winter snow or afire in the bright foliage of fall. On the reverse side of these souvenirs are prettily printed the words, "Emily's Bridge." Nothing about claw marks, though.

When I visited, a series of white carnations had been weaved into a metal lattice that lines the inside of the bridge on both sides. Whether they were put there as memorials for Emily or as attempts to accent the picturesqueness of the bridge, it's a good illustration of how this bridge inspires morbid tales of death and after-death while simultaneously representing the beauty of scenic Vermont.

However, if you do ever find yourself crossing Emily's Bridge in the dead of night, and hear a dragging sound over the top of your car, pull over and get the bag of McDonald's that you left there on your last pit stop. But remember Emily. And turn your radio dial to the nearest cynical love song for her.

# Hammond Castle

GLOUCESTER, MA

IN AMERICA, we've gotten into the habit of calling any mansion home of the wealthy a castle. Actually, I guess we've gotten into the habit of calling any house one . . . a man's home, and all that. Every once in a while, though, a rich man in America actually does build himself a castle. And eventually somebody somewhere gets around to calling it haunted.

One such is Hammond Castle, or, as its owner styled it, Abbadia Mare, located on the rocky shores of the Atlantic Ocean in Gloucester, Massachusetts. Built by John Hays Hammond Jr. in the late 1920s, the beautiful and surprising medieval-style castle has a drawbridge, a great hall, turrets, and everything else that makes a castle a castle. It also has a bunch of stuff that makes a castle better than a castle, including a pipe organ with more than 8,000 pipes and an interior pool and courtyard with walls made from the façades of actual medieval buildings to make it seem as if you're outside . . . and in another time period.

Hammond made his fortune through genius. He was a prolific inventor with more than 400 patents to his name, enough of them lucrative to the point that, like most rich people, he had to find ways to spend his enormous bank vaults of cash. Besides castle building and inventing wonders, John Hammond also collected a whole range of antiquities that he displayed in dramatic fashion in his castle.

Now, castles in of themselves aren't macabre, of course, unless they're European, in which case they've been around so long that they take on the ruined aspect of an old tombstone and have accumulated ghost stories like static in a dryer full of wool. For an American-made castle of relatively recent vintage, it takes some doin' to get haunted. And Hammond did that doin.'

For instance, in constructing his castle, he incorporated ancient Roman tombstones right into the walls. Second, in his vast collection of medieval and other historic items, he has what is supposed to be the actual skull of one of Christopher Columbus's crewmen. The crumbling death's head is on display in a glass case in his great hall to this day.

Hammond also had an interest in occultism and spiritualism. I guess when your brain is able to penetrate nature as easily as his was, you have to adventure into more esoteric knowledge. One way that this interest

manifested itself is that Hammond would invite psychics over to experiment with their powers. In fact, a light spot on the floor of the great hall is supposed to be where a Faraday cage once stood, an apparatus designed to shield whatever or whoever is in it from exterior static electric fields. Hammond apparently found it useful during séances when mediums would attempt to speak to the dead.

These days, Hammond Castle is open to the public as a museum. Located at 80 Hesperus Avenue in Gloucester, you can join a guided tour or tour the castle at your own pace, wandering through his bedrooms and turrets and seeing his medieval collection. When I visited, a small psychic fair was going on in the great hall.

Hammond is also buried on the grounds. His grave is unmarked, but the pamphlet you get upon paying the entrance fee shows you where he is interred.

Whatever the real story behind the occultism of Hammond Castle and whatever lingers behind as a result of it, who cares. Jon Hammond invented the remote control. He could've worshipped Satan and still have been bound for heaven.

# Dungeon Rock
LYNN, MA

IN LYNN, MASSACHUSETTS, there is a giant rock with an iron door set in it. Inside that door is a twisting cave that descends into wet blackness before dead-ending in solid rock and dank water. You could imagine a dozen practical purposes for that cave, and you'd be wrong a dozen times. You see, this cave was dug by a man looking for pirate treasure at the behest of a ghost.

Located in Lynn Woods, the rock formation is called Dungeon Rock. The story goes that in the mid-1600s, a pirate named Thomas Veale (or Veal, depending on how you feel about silent *e*'s), lived in a cave in that rock with some of his pirate treasure, the lone survivor of a small band of pirates that had fled to the area. The others had been caught, returned to England, and hanged. Veale lived for a while in his cave until an earthquake ended it, him, and this chapter in the story, earning the rock the name Pirate's Dungeon in the process, which over the years became Dungeon Rock.

From here, the story gets a lot less believable, although, strangely, a lot more verifiable. In 1852, a man named Hiram Marble bought the property on which Dungeon Rock is set. He erected a house and a few outbuildings, moved his wife and son in with him, and then got down to the matter at hand . . . finding the pirate treasure in that rock.

Of course, earthquakes, unlike pirates, do not leave maps with X's drawn on them when they bury treasure. However, Hiram had an ace in the hole, and it came straight from a tarot deck. It turns out, Hiram Marble was a spiritualist, and he believed he was receiving directions to the treasure directly from the ghost of Thomas Veale himself. Apparently, pirate hell has lax security. In a case of skullduggery of one sort fueling skullduggery of another, Hiram would hold regular séances to receive directions from mediums to direct the course of the excavating, which he and his son Edwin undertook double-handedly using dynamite and other mining tools.

It actually wasn't the first time that unearthly communications directed somebody to look for Veale's treasure. A few decades earlier, a man named Brown was directed in his dreams where to find it. He never really got the chance to look, though, instead ending up in an insane asylum in Ipswich, Massachusetts.

Hiram himself escaped that fate, although he did run into other problems. As the years dragged on, pouring money into that hole started having the effects that made that phrase become a cliché in the first place. To help subsidize the dig, he conducted tours of the cave and sold shares in the project. This freed him up to spend the rest of his life in a fruitless search for Veale's treasure. He died in 1868, but Edwin continued to dig until his own death in 1880. No pirate treasure was ever found, but there was probably a lot of father-son bonding.

These days, the cave has an iron door on it that is open for a few hours each day during the warmer seasons or upon request from the local park rangers. To get to Dungeon Rock, just follow the signs in the park. Set on a hill with a path that leads right up to a clearing in front of it, it is either two giant rocks abutting each other or a single rock with a giant crevice splitting it in two. Either way, you enter that crevice to see the door set inside the rock on the right. Inside, the cave is dark, wet, cold and you need a flashlight to see your way around. Thin wooden steps lead to the cavern floor, which then wends an erratic 135 feet into the rock, with every random-seeming turn a specific direction from the spirit world. When I visited, there was inside the cave a small chest with a scroll inside that tells the story of Dungeon Rock. I guess it's there for visitors who want to do their researching in a damp

enclosed space on-site instead of in a recliner with their laptop and a tub of nachos. For the record, I am firmly in that latter category of scholar. Eventually, the shallow cave becomes too small to stand up in and quickly ends in a small disgusting pool of stagnant water.

An empty hole in a rock might be a strange thing to bequeath to the world, but the publicity that the Marbles created helped to keep the story of Dungeon Rock being told. Now, every year in October, the people of Lynn celebrate Dungeon Rock Day in Lynn Woods, where they dress up as pirates and, well, party while dressed up as pirates.

Other traces of the Marble legacy remain in the area. Here and there one can see the remnants of buildings that Hiram Marble built on the property, including a couple of cellar holes and a fragment of wall. Near that fragment of wall, which can be found at the side of Dungeon Rock, is a large pink rock that denotes the grave of Edwin Marble. Hiram is buried at Bay Path Cemetery in Charlton, Massachusetts. In a bit of irony, Edwin's mourners found a large cache of gold coins and jewels while digging his grave. Just kidding.

# Country Tavern Restaurant
Nashua, NH

IF YOU'RE A FRIEND OF MINE, you have to be wary anytime I'm entrusted to make the plans. I have a habit of turning what's supposed to be quality social time for the enjoyment of all involved into a thinly veiled oddity hunt to satiate my own peculiar desires. In addition, if you are the person closest to me, you have to be doubly wary, as for some reason I assume that you are mandated by law to put up with every one of my foibles, no matter how blatantly I indulge them. Thus it happened that on the occasion of a recent birthday of my wife, I took her to a haunted restaurant.

Despite its generic name, the Country Tavern Restaurant and Lounge is a gourmet restaurant located in Nashua, New Hampshire. Much of its appeal is derived from the fact that the restaurant is a converted 1741 farmhouse, giving the place a pleasant, historical ambiance. As a result, the restaurant really is a nice, classy place to take somebody for a birthday dinner. Honestly. It just happens to be haunted, too.

The world has, according to the latest official UN census, hundreds of thousands of buildings that are rumored to be haunted, most of which, suspiciously, are places of business. Naturally, I don't go tramping into every building with a blurry face in its window. So why this one in particular? Well, why do you go to any restaurant? The menu, of course.

Of all the restaurants in the world that claim to be haunted, few are so brazen as to devote an entire page of real estate on their menu to the assertion. The back cover of the Country Tavern's menu is an undated, typo-ridden article reprinted from the local paper about a ghost that purportedly inhabits the restaurant.

The ghost's name, according to the menu, is Elizabeth Ford, and she was a previous tenant of the establishment back when it was a residence. She was murdered by her sea captain husband and thrown down a well after he returned from a yearlong voyage to find that she had recently given birth. That nine-month gestation clause in our biological contracts can really trip us up sometimes. In addition, because all existence is punishable by death, the baby was murdered and buried under a tree. If this had happened today we'd be horrified at the state of society. Because it is supposed to have happened 200 years ago, it's an interesting story worth relishing in polite circles and for some reason doesn't put the damper on an intimate candlelit dinner celebration.

The article on the menu also details some of the instances of ghostliness that have occurred at the restaurant throughout the years. It's nothing you haven't heard before. Common symptoms include archaically dressed apparitions, invisible presences, and flying dinnerware.

Before you start thinking that I'm taking a vinyl-covered, bifolded, oversize piece of wine-stained paper too seriously, keep in mind that the Sirloin au Poivre really was $19.95 and each entrée really did come with a salad, rolls, and my choice of sides. That establishes the necessary pattern of honesty to the appropriate degree for me.

The Country Tavern is located on busy Amherst Street. Its exterior is rustic and humble looking, lit dimly at night, and pretty much looks like the house it once was. The dining area is divided up into separate rooms, which I always like in a restaurant, as it allows for a much more intimate eating experience. If I'm wearing a jacket and trying to pretend an air of culinary cultivation at odds with the truth, I want as few witnesses to the event as possible.

Anyway, you probably won't be surprised to find out that our dinner wasn't once interrupted by any ghostly manifestations. All that happened was that my wife and I ate an enjoyable meal, celebrated her surviving another year of life without being thrown down a well, and departed with the beautiful flush that a bottle of wine shared in comfortable surroundings can give a person. Not exactly a menu-worthy story, unfortunately.

# Haunted Lake
## FRANCESTOWN, NH

IT'S EASY TO BESTOW AN UNUSUAL NAME on something to pretend that the christened thing is unique. Celebrities do it with their babies all the time. And it was with this suspicion that I approached Haunted Lake in Francestown, New Hampshire.

I mean, you'd think that the name Haunted Lake would actually be a nickname for something with a more legitimate appellation or that it would be only recently given as some sort of publicity stunt or that it would be the dubitable product of some random rumor-monger. Turns out, though, that this interesting moniker is actually the long-accepted name of this small body of water, going back more than 150 years.

For instance, most any map detailed enough to show this small spot of New England names it Haunted Lake, and atlases aren't exactly known for their imagination. In addition, an Internet search delightfully reveals more mundane than spectral information about the lake . . . geographical surveys, fishing information, area profiles, that kind of stuff. It's almost as if claiming to see a ghost at a place called Haunted Lake is too easy, even for the seeing-ghosts-in-dust-motes-and-camera-flares crowd. Third, for the past 100 years, the lake has been battling with being redubbed the more pedestrian Scobie (or Scoby) Pond, after some of the area's early settlers, even to the point of having one of the nearby roads named Scobie Pond Road. With gimmicky names, it's usually the other way around. Don't ask me why I know.

Of course, there are spook stories that go along with the name, but whether they spring from the name or vice versa is a game of chickens and eggs that I hate playing because I always lose. The most tendered story involves a man who murders his camping companion and buries him on the shore, the remains of whom are discovered years later when a mill is built on the spot. It's why, these days, architects and engineers are required by OSHA to hire psychics before starting construction. Another tale involves ghostly hands pulling the rowboat of a vacationing family down into the lake. Okay, that last one I just made up, but that's how easy it is.

Upon visiting it, Haunted Lake doesn't look too spooky, I mean, any more than any unplumbed body of water does inherently, at least, and any more than any bit of wilderness can be under the right circumstances. The area's heavily wooded and has its share of private lake houses and even a designated swimming spot or two.

To get there, just take one of the four roads that surround Haunted Lake on three sides (Scoby, Dodge Hill, Scobie Pond, and Journeys End). A few smaller and often unpaved roads shoot off from these and lead closer to its actual shores.

Now, granted, the term *haunted* has other meanings in our language besides "plagued by ghosts," and that could be the actual derivation of the name. I'd be okay with that. Definitely still better than Scobie. Nevertheless, if I were to put together an October camping trip in New England, Haunted Lake would be high on my list. I'd probably have to choose my camping companion carefully, though, I guess.

# Ghost of Charles Dickens
### BRATTLEBORO, VT

IT DELIGHTS ME that in a work devoted to the dark, terrible, and spooky such as you have currently in your hands or on your screen, that I've twice been able to include entries on that old literary guardian of blessed Christmastime, Charles Dickens. Originally, it was for his first American public reading of his famous ghost story, *A Christmas Carol*. And now it's for his ghost.

Charles Dickens died in 1870, the first prerequisite for ghosthood. Unfortunately, he dearly departed the world before finishing his final novel, and, as irony would have it, that final novel was a murder mystery, *The Mystery of Edwin Drood*.

Two years after his death, the rumors began to surface that an itinerant printer with no literary training named Thomas Power James, who was in Brattleboro, Vermont, was channeling the ghost of Charles Dickens to finish *Edwin Drood*. It seemed that the famous writer could not eternally repose without completing the work. It was a testament to how much the world missed Dickens (and how commonplace mediums had become at that time in history) that some of the media took James seriously.

James and his spectral collaborator labored for months, at times releasing sections of the book as proof of his high claims for the work. Apparently, these samples were believable enough to some people that they started inventing theories about the origin of the text other than, "This is a scam." According to a very defensive introduction that James attached to the published work, these theories included its being a publicity stunt by Dickens's heirs to unveil the fully completed *Edwin Drood* that Dickens had, himself, actually finished before his death. Another proposal was that Satan was inspiring James, coming to him in the night with diabolical plot and character development ideas and exiting through the chimney every night. James brushed away these ridiculous theories and stuck to his story that the ghost of a famous dead author was using a random printer guy as a conduit to finish his book from beyond the grave.

James published the new, second part to *Edwin Drood* along with the already completed beginning sometime around Halloween in 1874, with the byline, "By the spirit-pen of Charles Dickens, through a medium." The book ended up being both widely read and widely disparaged, so James (or Dickens, I guess) gave up on the idea that he had previously proposed of future collaborations.

These days, no monuments to the incident stand in Brattleboro. No "Charles Dickens was here" markers acknowledge their possible place in both literary and spiritualistic history. Even the location where James spent those long nights communing with the celebrity afterlife is unknown and unheralded.

But maybe we shouldn't be so hard on James. The situation brings to mind Isaac Asimov's 1954 short story "The Immortal Bard." In it, Shakespeare is brought to the present, anonymously takes a course on his own works, and finds himself flunked by the teacher. Sounds about like us.

I guess we'll never know the truth, though. Actually, we do. James was a fraud involved in a self-promotion scam of rare form and Dickens has only spoken to the world since his death through the works he physically penned himself. *The Mystery of Edwin Drood* was never solved.

# Ghost Town of Monson, NH
## HOLLIS, NH

DUE TO 60-YEAR-OLD RUMORS of a sinister curse that were widespread even before the Internet Age, along with the accompanying random media attention over the course of those decades, Dudleytown, Connecticut, is the most famous ghost town in the Northeast.

This entry is not about that ghost town.

And for good reason. The area of forest that was once Dudleytown is private property highly off limits and guarded by a zealous group of local land owners ominously known as the Dark Entry Forest Association. I know, everything about their efforts to fend off trespassers makes you want to trespass.

Fortunately, most New England ghost towns are all the same . . . a few old cellar holes and some overgrown stone fences. Instead of risking fines, having your car towed, and being hassled by locals and the police just to traipse around some unimpressive-looking foundation stones, I suggest vis-

iting the much more welcoming and better-labeled ghost town of Monson, New Hampshire.

Currently located on the border of the towns of Hollis and Milford, Monson was the first inland colony in the state and was settled sometime in the 1730s. It was finally incorporated in 1746, but tendered its resignation a mere quarter century later, in 1770, due to harsh conditions, lack of planning, and a general spirit of it-wasn't-in-the-cards. Its few hundred inhabitants moved off to greener pastures that wouldn't kill them.

Then, after 230 years of its outlying lands being divvied up into the surrounding modern-day towns and the original town's generally being forgotten about, a developer decided that the center of Monson wasn't that bad a place to settle after all and started in motion plans to build a tract of luxury homes in 1998.

However, thanks to the efforts of locals residing in Hollis and Milford who, despite my phrasing in the last paragraph, hadn't actually forgotten about Monson, and to the efforts of locals Russ and Geri Dickerman in particular, as they donated some of the land and also maintain it, the remnants of Monson were spared, preserved, and made available to the public.

As a result, Monson is now more of an historic park, covering more than 200 acres, with fields, forests, hiking trails, and a small, sometimes-open

museum inside a restored colonial house called the Gould House. The various
Monson ruins are pointed out on a map at the entrance to the ghost town, and
every cellar hole and crumbling wall is labeled with a sign that details the history and genealogy of each homestead's original owners.

Getting to Monson is easy, and takes no hiking, avoiding authority, or
ignoring trespassing signs. It's located on Adams Road, an obscure path of a
road just off Federal Hill Road in Hollis. After parking at the entrance to
Adams, a short walk through a marked gate and some trees soon opens up
into large, stone fence-lined fields where can be seen the Gould House and
from whence the few trails branch off.

Granted, the place isn't intrinsically spooky, but neither is Dudleytown,
really, nor any other historic pile of rubble. I mean, I'm sure alone, at night,
with stories running through ones head, the place can be terrifying. But under
those conditions, so is my upstairs bathroom. Sometimes people just take
the term *ghost town* a bit too literally, I guess. I know I didn't see a single ghost
while I was there. Just garter snakes. And joggers.

# TAPS Headquarters
## WARWICK, RI

WHEN IT COMES TO HUNTING GHOSTS, the cast of the Syfy Channel show
*Ghost Hunters* have it down to, well, a pseudoscience. Originally airing
in 2004, back when it was the Sci-Fi Channel, and with five seasons under
their plumber's tool belts as of the writing of this book, this ongoing paranormal reality show has over the past few years popularized spooks more than
M. R. James, *Casper* cartoons, and both Ghostbusters movies combined.

Basically, *Ghost Hunters* is about a paranormal investigation group called
the Atlantic Paranormal Society, which has the annoying acronym TAPS (you
don't acronym articles, man). The founders of the group, Jason Hawes and
Grant Wilson, started TAPS out of a trailer in one of their backyards while
working as full-time plumbers for Roto-Rooter. In their spare time they and
their originally volunteer teammates tramped through suspected haunted
locations in the middle of the night, waving around fancy tools such as
infrared and night-vision cameras, audio recorders, electromagnetic fre-

quency detectors, and digital thermometers. Ghosts are apparently attracted to technology.

The show quickly gained a large following and soon popularized amateur ghost hunting to a degree of legitimacy that, while still pretty low, is much higher than it should be. As a result of the series, people who have been looking for a calling that takes zero training and expertise other than watching a television show have formed ghost hunting groups all over the country.

Of course, the irony of all this ghost-hunting attention is that not only has it not yielded believable ghosts, but it has yielded large quantities of evidence that belie the existence of ghosts. Thanks to thousands of eager ghost hunters, including TAPS, we have countless hours of audio and video footage of their overreacting to every random dust mote, shadow, mood change, heat source, equipment gauge quiver, and bump in the night, all of which point like Babe Ruth to an overexcited and impressionable imagination that make the more kinder skeptics say, "Yeah, that's kind of what we've been saying all along, guys. You're spooking yourselves out over nothing."

Now, I'm not saying that traipsing through old, historic buildings and dark, spooky cemeteries in the middle of the night is not fun intrinsically. It way is . . . and to the point that it's often just as much fun to watch others do it on television. In fact, *Ghost Hunters* has spawned a slew of copycat shows . . . although it has remained the most popular.

The allure of *Ghost Hunters* that separates it from other paranormal shows is easy to trace. First, it was pretty accessible since it involved a pair of blue-collar plumbers who originally ghost-hunted in their spare time out of a trailer in their backyard. Second, unlike the wide-eyed psychics who melodramatically detect presences in every dim space, as in other shows of this nature, these guys actually brought a tad of skepticism with them. They actually called three out of four dust motes, dust motes.

Of course, as the series continues, both of these aspects seem to be on the wane. These days, it seems as if there's a little too much artifice in the show . . . or at least it's way more evident now. Naturally, no longer are they full-time plumbers (although they still pretend to be); they are now the owners of an official, licensed brand, with all the speaking engagements, classes, publications, radio shows, and television spin-offs that come with that. In addition, the group has upgraded to permanent offices, cavalcades of black Escalades, paid employees, and easy access to popular tourist attractions across the world.

Although the small-group drama of the earlier shows is gone, the biggest drama still remains . . . the question of whether these guys are sincere, fraudulent, or were just lucky enough to find a vein of gold and mine it for all their might. The one definite thing you can say about TAPS is that it's firmly rooted in New England.

Hawes and Wilson founded TAPS in the unheralded town of Warwick, Rhode Island, where they lived. As a result, most of the original episodes occurred in the area, as well. When the team finally moved to an official office (at least for the purposes of the show), they stayed in their hometown of Warwick. This first headquarters was a small, humble, brick building in a strip mall located at 3297 Post Road. The two large windows in the front each bore the signature yellow acronym of the group during filming.

Since that time, they moved to 2362 West Shore Road, just down the street from the original headquarters, but it's still a small, humble, brick building in a strip mall with two large TAPS-emblazoned windows. I doubt they commute there to run their empire, of course, but it's still the address advertised on their official Web site.

At the very least this continued local presence gives one the strange pleasure of being able to drive past the headquarters of an international reality television show about ghosts, and although I could sink fathoms into the irony of that, it's honestly no more ridiculous than anything else that we call reality television.

# Hoosac Tunnel

## NORTH ADAMS AND FLORIDA, MA

ITS NICKNAME IS "THE BLOODY PIT," even though it's a horizontal shaft. But that's no reason to quibble when the first part of the term is dead-on a few times over. About 200 times over, to be closer to exact. Plus canaries.

The Hoosac Tunnel is a railway that burrows almost 5 miles through the Hoosac Mountain Range in western Massachusetts from the towns of North Adams on its west side to Florida on its east. Construction began on this

ambitious project in 1851 and finished in 1875. Over the course of those 24 years, it's reported that around 200 men lost their lives . . . all to shorten the distance from Boston to Albany, New York, by a couple of miles.

The deaths occurred in all the ways that you'd think they would in a situation involving nitroglycerin and black powder being detonated in badly ventilated and underlit conditions under thousands of feet of mountain. Large, ambitious construction projects were always deadly back then, but this one was almost genocidal.

One of the most chilling incidents was the central shaft accident. The tunnel has a 1,000-foot-tall vertical chimney installed in it for exhaust to escape. On October 17, 1867, flammable fumes ignited and caused an explosion that destroyed a hoist that was used to lower equipment, supplies and men. The accident rained equipment, supplies, and flaming hoist parts down onto 13 men who were working at the bottom of the 583-foot-deep unfinished chimney. In addition, the pumps were destroyed, flooding the shaft.

The miners on the surface of the mountain, after various rescue attempts, believed nobody could have survived the accident . . . and they ended up being right, just along a different timeline. Several months to maybe even a year later, when they made it back to finish excavating the shaft, they discovered that some had actually lived for a time and had made a makeshift raft to survive the flooding. They were all dead . . . assumedly of suffocation, but definitely in a horrible way, regardless of the coroner's report.

Despite the death toll and other various setbacks, the tunnel was eventually completed and was used by both passenger and freight trains. To this day, freight trains still use it, although not as many as in the glory days of railroading.

And it has ghosts. Of course, when you have 200 deaths and a dark hole, you have your choice of stories about hauntings. These include phantom sounds of construction, ghostly miner apparitions, strange wails, eerie lights, disappearances. I don't even have to do any research to call all that out. But, after doing the research, the sentence stands. You can make up your own details about each and be pretty much spot on.

Of the two portals of the Hoosac Tunnel, the east is easiest to see. It's located along the Deerfield River. At the intersection of Whitcomb Hill Road and River Road in the town of Florida, take River Road northwest about half a mile until it crosses over a set of tracks. The tunnel entrance can be seen to the left.

The tunnel's west portal is located in North Adams. Off Church Street, which parallels the railroad tracks, close to where it intersects with West Shaft Road, is a path that goes through the woods. The west entrance is about a third of a mile or so down it. The giant hole in the mountain means you're there.

For those of you more into learning about gaping tubes for speeding freight than seeing them firsthand, there's a free museum at 115 State Street in North Adams called Western Gateway Heritage State Park. It's actually a former railroad yard, the buildings of which have been restored and turned into a collective museum showcasing exhibits and implements from the Hoosac Tunnel construction and the railroad industry in general.

Still, there's nothing like staring into one of the maws of the Hoosac Tunnel for yourself and considering all the men it had to swallow before it could clear its throat.

# Lady in Black
## GEORGES ISLAND, MA

FOR REASONS that I'm sure are beyond the ken of mere mortals, female ghosts are often color coded. You've got your ladies in white, ladies in red, ladies in green, ladies in yellow, ladies in blue, and so on. As representative of this trend in ghost storytelling, I chose a lady in black, but only because it meant I could jump on a ferry and visit an island fort. It's always a good idea to have a backup reason to see a haunted place.

Fort Warren is a pentagon-shaped fort that is located on and pretty much takes up the entire 40-odd acres (depending on the tide) of Georges Island in Boston Harbor. To get there, you have to take a 20-minute ferry ride from the Long Wharf in downtown Boston, Massachusetts.

This Civil War–era fort and prison is pretty much like most of the historic forts located up and down both coasts of the country. Large stone walls ratted with various tunnels and rooms surround a flat open area. Also like every old fort, this one has its official ghost story. However, unlike most of the ghost stories of the other forts, which semilogically involve soldiers and prisoners of war, Fort Warren has a lady ghost.

Her name, apparently, is Mrs. Lanier, and she has come to be known locally as the Lady in Black. So what's a girl like that doing in a historically male-dominated place like a fort? Apparently, she was the wife of one Samuel Lanier, a Confederate soldier imprisoned at the fort. To help him escape, she dressed up in men's clothing and snuck in. They were caught and, while trying to get away, she accidentally shot her husband. She was hanged on the island for her crimes, but her last wish before dying was to be executed in women's clothes. The only way to accommodate this request was to make a robe for her from the black drapes of the mess hall. That's the story in a nut-shell, at least. I've averaged out the various versions of the tale.

I visited Fort Warren on a weekday when the tourist level was at low tide. As a result, I often found myself alone in various rooms and corridors. The

fort itself isn't wired for electricity, so there are plenty of dark places to hallucinate a ghostly form and in which I had to use my camera flash to keep from breaking my ankle on steps or smashing my face into a wall.

Behind a red-brick building near the main dock of the island, a gravestone-shaped monument lists the 13 soldiers who died while imprisoned on the island. No women are mentioned (I assume, some of the names only have first initials or are antique enough to not communicate a gender), but one of those soldiers was named Samuel Lanier. Sometimes a single fact is all you need to create an implausible legend.

If you believe the stories, every ghost is technically marooned. The Lady in Black is doubly so, having to inhabit the few acres of Georges Island. This fact also means that as you go mucking about her territory posing with cannons, picnicking, and realizing how bad it must've sucked to be a soldier back then, your fate, if you need to escape from her dark clutches, is dictated by the ferry schedules. But the real lesson in all this is that the clothes you die in are the clothes you'll haunt in for eternity. Always choose your wardrobe carefully, but especially on your most dangerous days.

## *Creepy Plants*

MORE THAN CREEPERS in the plant world are creepy. We are surrounded on this planet by a gigantic mass of vegetable organisms, so it is inevitable that they sometimes intrude into our nightmares. Not being able to see the forest for the trees is more than mere flaw in perception. It's a psychological defense mechanism. Plants deserve a bit of wariness. And not just because we shave the most humble of them with gas-powered blades and turn the most grand among them into fast-food wrappers and advertising circulars, but because with their implacable, faceless, omnipresent existence, they can disturb just as much as the toothiest, hairiest, scaliest monster.

And while New England might be known for its majestic maple, birch, and evergreens, it has its share of macabre plant stories, too. So the next time you try to explain the strange midnight scratching noise that you hear as a tree branch scraping against the windowpane, think . . . is that explanation really that much more comforting?

# Roger Williams Root
### Providence, RI

THE REMAINS OF ROGER WILLIAMS have turned out to be a lot more fun disinterred.

Roger Williams is the legendary founder of Providence, the man who was kicked out of Massachusetts by the Puritans for espousing a freedom of worship a little too free for them, and who then bought land from the natives farther south and started a colony that eventually became the capital of the tiny state of Rhode Island.

Williams died in 1683, was buried, unburied and buried again in 1860, and then unburied and buried a third time in the late 1930s to mark the 300th

anniversary of the founding of the city. Sometimes disinterment is a sign of disrespect, sometimes of utmost respect. Life is drawn in fine lines. In the interim he was eaten by an apple tree and turned into a statue. I wish you could see the straight face I had when I wrote that.

The original burial place of Roger Williams was on his own property in a humble little plot far beneath the status of a city founder. Eventually, the people of Providence felt Williams needed a more deserved final resting place. However, when they dug him up, very little of him remained . . . in his place they found a vaguely anthropomorphic tree root that had filled the coffin, deriving nourishment, it was assumed, from the founder's remains. Apple trees only recognize fertilizer, not preeminence.

However, in doing so, the tree made itself somewhat preeminent . . .

or at least the root with the taste for human flesh. The story goes that as the root traveled through the length of Williams's body, it took his shape, twisting where Williams twisted and splitting where Williams split until it looked roughly like a man-shaped root. You can judge that for yourself, though. The ancient root is now on display in the John Brown House on 52 Power Street, the historical home of one of Providence's past prominent citizens.

The John Brown House offers regular tours, although the root is not something it really pushes. In fact, when I went, the tour guide didn't even bother to mention the root, even though I saw it affixed to a coffin-shaped board on the wall behind him during a whole 10-minute spiel about carriages and statuary. I was too embarrassed of the knowledge I had of it, so neither did I. We went off and learned about period furniture and colonial customs.

It's located in a connecting shed, the entrance to which is in the gift shop where you purchase your tour tickets. The first part of the tour takes place in that shed, where you watch a brief video on the Brown family. Right beside the television is the strange root. I don't remember anything about the video, as a result.

Honestly, though, it's no giant mandrake root. It looks just like a long, twisted bifurcated root (which I guess could be an accurate description of the shape of a human being), but just for the pleasure of touting something as "the root that ate Roger Williams," it's worth stretching one's imagination for.

The little bit of apple tree leftovers that were the remains of Roger Williams's remains eventually wound up, two burials later, interred beneath a giant, disproportioned, 35-foot-tall statue on a cliff in Prospect Terrace Park. The statue's a bit worse for wear, its oversize fingers broken on one hand, graffiti highlights in places, and a weed-grown base, but it's got a superlative view of the city. Prospect Terrace Park itself is a great place for the same reason, and one that was visited regularly by horror legend H. P. Lovecraft, who lived nearby. The statue and park is located on Congdon Street, just a few blocks from the John Brown House.

With remains in stone and remains in wood, Roger Williams seems to have become somewhat of an elemental, and I think Providence should take advantage of that and work at least a pair of gnarled roots into any further effigies it decides to honor its founder with.

# Drowned Forest
RYE, NH

IF YOU CAN'T SEE THE FOREST FOR THE SEA, then you're probably in a drowned forest.

The phrase *drowned forest* yields creepy images of towering underwater oaks submerged in an alien, viscous world where octopi tentacles entangle its boughs, seaweed festoons drip from its branches, sharks encircle its trunks, and small fish peck its bark at heights where only birds could have pecked before.

Of course, the reality is a bit less dramatic. A drowned forest is merely a bunch of slimy stumps . . . although that's still kind of creepy.

Many coastlines have forest remnants off their shores. A melting ice age thousands of years ago raised the ocean level higher than it had been in the past, turning dry land into sea floor and altering coastline signatures. Every once in a while, the heaving ocean tides throw bits and pieces of that stolen world back onto the shore, including pieces of wood, fossilized animal parts, even human implements. Sometimes, a particularly forthcoming low tide reveals a whole forest previously hidden in the ocean's secretive depths, terrifying us with the notion that we could all be underwater at any time nature wishes.

The coastline of New England could possibly have extended some 75 miles prior to the end of the Ice Age, so the area has its share of encroached woodland properties. A few are even sometimes visible. New England's most

well-known are a pair of 4,000-year-old conifer forests off the shoreline of the town of Rye, on the tiny angle of land that is the New Hampshire coast.

One of the drowned forests is off the Jenness Beach area and only surfaces every decade or so. The other, however, located further north off Odiorne Point, occurs with a bit more frequency. You just have to catch it at the right low tide at the right time of year. Oh, and be able tell the difference between the seaweed-covered mound that is the stump of an ancient cedar and the many seaweed-covered mounds that are the rocks that make up the majority of the coast there.

The nearby Odiorne Point Seacoast Science Center might be able to help you out. They handed me a hand-drawn map of the point that included a cluster of humped lines denoting the location of the forest. The best time to see it is during the lengthier days of the spring and summer seasons, as otherwise the lowest tides often occur at night. Also, having incredible luck and/or persistence might help.

Having neither, I have yet to see the sodden lumps with my own eyes. But, as is often the case with my unfulfilled desires, finding a sign denoting them is consolation enough. A historical marker on Route 1A commemorates both the drowned forest and the previous location of a receiving station for the original Atlantic cable. Apparently, the remains of that famous umbilical is currently intertwined among the stumps of the drowned forest.

The sign refers to it as a *sunken forest,* though, which is another term for them, in case you're going to Google the topic at some point. I prefer the violence of the term *drowned forest,* though, as I like to imagine the geographical change as a war between the elements, with the seas trying to erode the shore and the land attempting to maintain its lofty position above the sea. It makes beach vacations more interesting to me.

# Dummerston Vine
## DUMMERSTON, VT

W E OFTEN LIKE TO USE PLANT METAPHORS when describing families. We all have a family tree, with this or that branch of relatives. Apples don't fall far from them, and we have roots in various geographical locations. The

Spaulding family of Dummerston, Vermont, though, might not be so keen to do so.

According to the 200-year-old story, members of the Spaulding family started dying at inexplicably young ages with terrifying regularity due to a strange disease that seemed to gradually suck the life from them. Of course, if this story sounds a lot like the vampire/tuberculosis stories recounted elsewhere in this volume, it's because it is. This time, though, the story comes served with a twist. Or perhaps a leafier garnish.

I'm not sure if it was a commonly held superstition of some sort or if the family had other reasons to believe so, but the general theory that they acted upon to combat this apparent curse was that some kind of evil root or underground vine was burrowing along the family plot in the local cemetery. Each time it touched the coffin of a deceased family member, another Spaulding died.

Because medicine was a lot more do-it-yourself back then, they dug up the last body in the row of Spaulding graves, hacked up the creepy creeper tunneling toward it, burned the body, and ended the curse.

Of course, for the myth to be true there has to at the very least exist a row of 18th-century Spauldings somewhere in a cemetery in Dummerston . . . and there is.

To find it, I merely accessed the research of notable skeptic and paranormal investigator Dr. Joe Nickell. He discovered that the head of the family, Lieutenant Leonard Spaulding, and his wife were buried in separate, unmarked graves, but that six of the children were buried in a row in Dummerston Center Cemetery.

The cemetery's located on an idyllic bit of hill off what's basically a very long, seemingly private driveway off East West Road. The cemetery is visible from the main road, though, and was, in my experience, accessible without awkwardness. The row of six dark, mossy headstones is pretty much centrally located therein, and includes the graves of Josiah and his more weathered-named siblings. Case closed. Vampire vines do exist and prey simultaneously upon both the dead and the living.

Unfortunately for the story, as Dr. Nickell has pointed out, the Spauldings' graves, despite being in a nice row, do not have chronological death dates. In other words, the family members were not buried in the order in which they died and, as a result, no vine could have grown as neatly sequentially as the story states.

That doesn't rule out, of course, that the underground vine or root could have doubled back on occasion or taken roundabout ways to access the corpses and drain the life from their living kinfolk. Common sense does that just fine, though.

We need more plant monster myths, so I'm willing to keep this one around until something better comes along. To paraphrase/rip off my own introduction to this section, why be scared of the unknown thing rustling the branches outside your window when you can be scared of the rustling branches themselves?

# Famous Monsters

SOME MONSTERS, if they jumped out at you in the dark, would make you flee into the night screaming your lungs into your lips at octaves hitherto hit by only the most talented of opera singers and the most shrill of three-year-old girls. Others you'd clap on the back like an old friend. These latter types we know by name, and would even recognize many of their horrible visages quicker than those of our extended family members.

These are the famous monsters of story and cinema, and although many of these often originated centuries ago in the pages of authors worldwide or decades ago in the dank depths of Hollywood and its ilk, you can still find traces of their fame left in New England. Feel free to clap them on the back, but beware. The terror of these monsters is time tested.

# Witch's Dungeon
## BRISTOL, CT

WHEN YOUR GREAT-UNCLE is a movie monster icon, you probably don't need to do much to garner any kind of cachet in horror culture. Any monster fan will buy you a drink for that.

But Cortlandt Hull apparently wants entire meals bought for him because, despite his relation to Henry Hull, the actor immortalized for his portrayal of the titular creature in the 1935 film *Werewolf of London,* Cortlandt has dug out his own unique space in classic cinema monsterhood.

Although many relatives of dead celebrity horror actors spend time making conference appearances, writing books, and doing interviews for film retrospectives and DVD extras, Cortlandt has dedicated his efforts to actively preserving classic monster-movie culture by creating and displaying amazingly detailed, movie-accurate, full-size wax reproductions of classic horror movie icons.

Having started the hobby as a teenager and then falling under the tutelage of such Hollywood effects legends as Dick Smith of *The Exorcist* fame and John Chambers of *Planet of the Apes* fame, he refined his skills while crafting a collection of famous ghouls worth gawking at. He exhibits his creations at various events across the country throughout the year, but the home turf and main attraction of his creature reproductions is his Witch's Dungeon in Bristol, Connecticut.

For only a few hours on select weekend nights in October, a slow-moving queue of visitors wends its way around the Halloween-decorated front lawn of 90 Battle Street, headed toward a small, shedlike building adorned with a glowing witch named Zenobia. For the past four decades, the Witch's Dungeon has faithfully opened every Halloween season on Cortlandt's property, awing visitors with wonders from horror movies from many decades past.

Of course, it all sounds like an extremely homemade venture, and it kind of is, but the skill displayed on the figures themselves makes me think there should be velvet ropes and marble columns surrounding them, complete with benches in front to let you stare at them for hours in peace.

Instead, the Witch's Dungeon is a more rushed, slightly claustrophobic experience, which is a testament to the quality of the exhibits that it has remained so popular. After paying the spare change that is the entry fee (literally . . . I paid a dollar) and waiting your turn in line, groups of no more than three at a time are allowed in, making it seem like you're being given private access to some ancient oracle or wish-granting wizard. A dark-costumed man paces you through what is barely a hallway as the individual exhibits are sequentially lighted on either side of you, while audio from the relevant movie plays. The shed is small enough that you're mere inches from the creatures, which are displayed in full dioramas that incorporate props and costumes from the actual original films.

Vincent Price, himself, recorded the opening narration one hears upon entering specifically for the museum, and numerous other genre legends (and genre legend relatives) have become involved behind the scenes with the tiny museum, lending it a legitimacy that belies its humble surroundings and helping it secure the approval of Universal Studios, which owns the rights to most of the creature licenses.

All the usual ghastlies are represented at the Witch's Dungeon, including Karloff's Frankenstein Monster, Chaney Sr.'s Phantom, the Creature from the Black Lagoon, Lugosi's Dracula, among others, and it also includes a few of the lesser-referenced fiends as well, including one of the Mole People from the movie of the same name and Vincent Price as the awesome Abominable Dr. Phibes. Even Chaney Jr.'s Wolf Man is on hand, despite the fact that it was this werewolf character that shouldered Cortlandt's own great-uncle's role from the Universal monster spotlight. Of course, Hull's Werewolf of London is there, too, complete with Moon Flower in his paw.

However, the experience is over far sooner than you'd like it to be, and you barely have time for your brain to register the wonder and awe before you're back out in the mini-festival of monster fans awaiting their turns.

Hull wants to eventual open a full-fledged year-round monster museum with his creatures, complete with authentic movie props from his collection. And maybe one day he will. But for now, his shed o' monsters will do just fine on a dark October night.

# Count Orlok's Nightmare Gallery
### SALEM, MA

FOR EVERY DEDICATED CREATOR like Cortland Hull, there's a dedicated collector like James Lurgio.

Lurgio is the owner and proprietor of Count Orlok's Nightmare Gallery, a movie monster museum located on 285 Derby Street in Salem, Massachusetts, right in the black heart of all the famous Salem attractions that are often easy to be ambivalent about.

Originally a private collection, Lurgio began displaying his fiends at various Halloween events before finding them more permanent room and board in Salem. The full-size creature cre-

ations that populate Count Orlok's are made of resin, latex, and silicone, much like the actual costumes, appliances, and masks used in the movies that featured the monsters in the first place. In fact, many of the artists he's hired to create the pieces in his collection actually work in the movie industry, some on the actual movie the piece is based on.

The entryway to Count Orlok's is enough to sell one on the rest of the galley. Here, Lurgio showcases free of charge a selection of the more copyright-protected Universal Monsters, including Lon Chaney's Phantom of the Opera, Boris Karloff's Mummy and Frankenstein, Elsa Lanchester's Bride, and Bela Lugosi's Dracula.

As befits its subject matter, the gallery itself is spookily lit with a few dramatic corner turns. The collection is pretty well balanced between classic and modern monster characters and more or less follows chronological order, starting with the gallery's namesake from the 1922 German film *Nosferatu* and extending all the way through other silent-era creations, Universal monsters, Hammer Studios horror characters, '80s slashers, and other less easily classifiable icons of the genre. All told, about 50 different characters were on display when I visited.

Highlights include Vincent Price from *House of Wax*, Alfred Hitchcock alongside the shawled and wigged skeleton-in-a-rocking chair we've all come to know as Mother from *Psycho*, The Darkness from *Legend*, and Linda Blair from *The Exorcist* . . . but if those four hadn't been there, I'd have easily found just as many highlights to replace them. Christopher Lee appears a couple of times, as does his partner-in-horror Peter Cushing. Monsters of a more recent vintage are also uncorked, from *The Shining* and *Fright Night* through to George Romero's one-zombie-movie-too-far *Land of the Dead*.

Besides full-size figures, the collection also boasts a few movie props and movie prop replicas, as well as life casts of famous actors and directors of the macabre.

To keep things interesting, Lurgio changes up and adds to his displays regularly. While I was there, he took us to a back room where buxom horror host Elvira was spread in pieces all over the floor as he prepared her for her debut. She had a spot reserved beside Hannibal Lecter from *The Silence of the Lambs*.

In addition, Lurgio multi-purposes his assets by turning the gallery into a haunted house in October, offering it up for special events, and showing public-domain horror movies during Salem's off-season.

All in all, it's definitely well worth the few bucks to get in. Unlike most of the attractions in Salem that exist only to capitalize on the town's main tourist draw, Count Orlok's is a work of devotion. It's a personal collection that would still exist somewhere even if it didn't have a public space. Besides, you can only tell the story of the Salem witch trials so many times and in so many ways in four square blocks before it becomes uncompelling. With all the zombies, vampires, killer clowns, and classic creeps on display at Count Orlok's, it's a great break from all that witchery.

# Frankenstein Cliff

CRAWFORD NOTCH, NH

FRANKENSTEIN CLIFF is only macabre because of its name, and its name is only macabre because of the storytelling prowess of a 19-year-old authoress from the early 1800s. I don't have to tell you the story of *Franken-stein* nor of its creator Mary Shelley, but I probably do have to tell you why there's a 300-foot granite cliff in the White Mountains region of New Hamp-shire that shares a name with that classic horror title. There is actually a pos-sible connection, although it'll take me a few paragraphs to get there.

Frankenstein Cliff was named after a German immigrant landscape painter in the mid-1800s who at some point became enamored enough with the White Mountains to treat them as subjects for his art. His name was God-frey Frankenstein. That's right. This Frankenstein knew what it was like to be God . . . frey.

I realize that sounds like the opposite of a connection to the almost 200-year-old story that has become one of the most famous in the language. Well, you see, there's this castle in Germany called Frankenstein at which an alchemist named Johann Dipple once lived back at the turn of the 18th cen-tury. Shelley may have visited the ruins of that castle before writing the book (it is at least documented that she passed by there), and many think that she at least drew inspiration from that edifice and its previous tenant.

Back to New England and Godfrey Frankenstein; his original surname was actually Tracht, but his father changed it to Frankenstein when they moved to the United States in 1831 when Godfrey was 11, only 15 years after the publication of *Frankenstein*. Although German immigrants changing their names start happening a lot more frequently about 100 years later, back then there was less reason to . . . and no reason to change it to an even more German-sounding name. Well, maybe one. Some speculate that Godfrey's father changed the surname to remind his family of home . . . which was near that same Castle Frankenstein already mentioned. That's a connection. Possibly.

Frankenstein Cliff is located a few miles outside the town of Bartlett in Crawford Notch and is part of a 5-mile trail loop that passes by 200-foot Arethusa Falls and under a railroad trestle also named for Godfrey Frankenstein and over which the tourist-laden Conway Scenic Railway passes.

Incidentally, Arethusa is the name of a nymph in Greek mythology, and is the title of a Percy Bysshe Shelley poem about her. Percy was the husband of Mary Shelley, who (not finished yet) subtitled her *Frankenstein* story *Prometheus Unbound,* after another character in Greek mythology. See? Connections everywhere.

At its highest, Frankenstein Cliff is just over 1400 feet above sea level and is popular for most reasons that giant looming rocks are popular, hiking, rock climbing, and even ice climbing. Like the end of *Frankenstein* itself.

Still, even though the explanation of this cliff's name is more mundane than macabre, a part of me still takes solace in the hope that Godfrey Frankenstein at least went around correcting everybody's pronunciation of his name, like Gene Wilder in *Young Frankenstein:* FrankenSTEEN.

# Flying Monkeys
## BURLINGTON, VT

MOST PEOPLE VISIT THE CITY OF BURLINGTON, VERMONT, for the pleasant waterfront of Lake Champlain, the quirky shops and restaurants on Church Street, and the various cultural benefits that come with being a university town. Those are all the right reasons; however, you can also visit

Burlington, Vermont, for its flying monkeys. For some reason these horribly comical and hilariously terrifying fantastical creatures adorn the roofs of two of the signature buildings of Burlington's harbor.

If you drive down the hill of Main Street toward Lake Champlain, you'll see at its terminus the old Union Station, now called the One Main building because of its address. One Main is a tall, dignified stone building beautifully framed by the blue Adirondack Mountains across the lake. It's quite the screensaver of a sight . . . that's completely saved from beauty-to-the-point-of-blandness by a pair of black, jagged-furred flying monkeys made of steel that are perched atop the building's roof.

Vermont's state bird is the Hermit Thrush, in case you were wondering. It has no state primate. So why is a pair of flying monkeys playing king-of-the-mountain in the most visible place in town? Spending their retirement years, is the answer. And not just from doing the bidding of a green-skinned witch in the land of Oz (see page 28 "Horror Legends and Personalities" to read about the actress who played the Wicked Witch of the West in the famous movie version of the tale). But that's not completely unrelated to the truth.

You see, this pair of creatures was originally created in the 1970s by a man named Steve Larrabee, to expand upon the *Wizard of Oz* theme of a (now defunct) local waterbed store called Emerald City. Yup, they were in the advertising business. When that store went the way of, well, waterbeds in general, these flying monkeys needed a new home. Eventually, after a couple of decades of perching at other locations around the area, they finally settled on One Main and have been absolutely unshooable since. They just stuck around long enough that people started digging them. Digging them enough, in fact, that more flying monkeys were called for. You can never have enough flying monkeys, it seems.

The most prominent of them adorns the central gable of One Main and acts in the auspicious position of standard bearer, its steel claws wrapped protectively around a pole on which hangs, flutters, and whips (depending on weather and mood of the simiavian) the official flag of Vermont, which depicts a deer and a cow, but, sadly, no flying monkeys.

You have to step around to the backside of One Main to see the second flying monkey better, and once you do, you'll see not just it, but two more, making a total of four so far in our Burlington safari. These latter two are diminutive enough that they're obviously intended to be baby flying monkeys. The closer vantage behind the building allows you to see much more clearly how kind of scary these creations are, with their serrated black outlines and general flying-monkeyness. They also make a person think that, if evolution had gone in this slightly different direction, we'd be a much cooler species now.

Keeping up with the Joneses is the unofficially named Lake and College building located almost next door to One Main. It has flying primates roosting atop its roof, as well, although this pair is newer, smoother, and made of undarkened copper so that they're shiny, at least until time and the elements decide otherwise. They also look a little more like winged sloths than winged monkeys to me, for some reason. One of these newer flying monkeys howls oddly wolflike above the Waterfront Theatre, one of the tenants of the building. The theater has even adopted this particular monkey as its symbol and includes a silhouette of the creature on its signage. And why wouldn't you? It's not every day that you get to legitimately include a flying monkey in your branding campaign.

Anyway, if you lost count or if my writing ability has lived up to its reputation of muddling the most simple of descriptive tasks, Burlington has a total of six flying monkey sculptures on the roofs of its harbor buildings. Enough, I think, to merit their own day of Christmas.

# ACKnOWLEDGMEnTS

As I mentioned in the introduction, this book took a lot of road trips to put together. My wife, Lindsey, was in the passenger seat for most of them, and she should be acknowledged both for that and for taking most of the pictures in this book. I would also like to extend my thanks to every family member and friend who got dragged into one of these road trips under various auspices so that I could find this or that gravestone or this or that random bit of obscure grisliness.

In addition, finding many of the items in this book (and a few that didn't make it in) necessitated the attention of at least one curator, historian, researcher, public relations associate, or random Internet presence (and once even a park ranger), to each of whom I owe gratitude for providing valuable information and resources for me in the writing of this book. There are too many to name, of course, but a few I would like to specifically thank for their direct interest in the project and for taking time out of their schedules to personally show me around and ensure that I had everything that I needed.

These include Michelle Marcella from Massachusetts General Hospital in Boston, for guiding me through that city of a place and of whom I'm jealous of her for having the opportunity to hold a decapitated mummy's head; Betsy Stacey from the Nature Museum at Grafton, Vermont, for showing me my first museum basement; John Zaffis of Stratford, Connecticut, for opening his home to a stranger, although he's seen stranger; and Gary Lind-Sinanian at the Armenian Library and Museum of America in Watertown, Massachusetts, who I'm sure has more legitimately important things to do than indulge an author's morbid curiosity and yet was still kind enough to do so.

I'd also like to thank Kermit Hummel and the editorial staff at The Countryman Press for digging the *Grimpendium* concept and believing this dark little jaunt of a book was worth publishing.

Finally, I would like to thank Brian Weaver, the talented artist responsible for the design and creation of the cover of *The New England Grimpendium*. My words are honored to wear his art.

# Index